Party Organization and Activism
in the American South

Party Organization and Activism in the American South

Edited by
Robert P. Steed
John A. Clark
Lewis Bowman
Charles D. Hadley

The University of Alabama Press
Tuscaloosa and London

∞

The paper on which this book is printed meets the minimum requirements of
American National Standard for Information Science-Permanence of Paper for
Printed Library Materials, ANSI Z39.48-1984.

Library of Congress Cataloging-in-Publication Data

Party organization and activism in the American South / edited by Robert P.
Steed, John A. Clark, Lewis Bowman, Charles D. Hadley
    p. cm.
    Includes bibliographical references.
    ISBN 0-8173-0894-6 (alk. paper)
    1. Political parties—Southern States. 2. Southern States—Politics and
government—1951–   I. Steed, Robert P.
JK2295.A13P35 1997
324.275—dc21   96-52004

British Library Cataloguing-in-Publication data available

Contents

Illustrations

Figures

Tables

Acknowledgments

We appreciate the support, encouragement, and assistance of many people who contributed in various ways to the successful completion of the project. The funding for the Southern Grassroots Party Activists Project, the study on which this book is based, was provided by a grant from the National Science Foundation (Grant SES-9009846), and the funding for expenses related directly to the production of this volume was provided by a grant from The Citadel Development Foundation. We are grateful to both for the monetary support essential to the success of the research. The University of New Orleans administered the National Science Foundation grant and, in the process, provided necessary administrative support during the data collection and data preparation phases of the project. Samuel J. Eldersveld, emeritus professor of political science at the University of Michigan, gave early encouragement for the project. Professor James Gibson of the University of Houston also gave early encouragement and shared, as well, some useful materials from the Party Transformation Project. Diane D. Blair, professor of political science at the University of Arkansas, and Anne E. Kelley, emeritus professor of political science at the University of South Florida, were part of the research team that collected the data utilized here. Melissa English and Jennifer Sherrock of the University of Georgia assisted in the preparation of the bibliography and helped ready the final manuscript for submission to the University of Alabama Press. We are also indebted to the two anonymous reviewers whose numerous suggestions helped us to improve the final version of the volume. Finally, we are grateful to Malcolm MacDonald, the former director of the University of Alabama Press, and to Nicole Mitchell, the current director of the University of Alabama Press, for their assistance throughout the production process. They and their staff, particularly Kathy Swain, eased the burdens of publication for us and helped make this volume a reality.

Party Organization and Activism
in the American South

Introduction

Local Political Parties and Party Scholarship

John A. Clark
Lewis Bowman
Robert P. Steed
Charles D. Hadley

Much of the recent scholarship about American political parties has attempted to assess the condition of the party system. Are parties becoming increasingly obsolete? Have they forfeited the functions they traditionally performed? Or have they adopted a different role in the political system such that their achievements have gone unrecognized? In short, are American parties in decline, in resurgence, or undergoing some other transformation? We assume that the question of decline in parties at the local level is at best misdirected and possibly wrong. Nevertheless, because of its prominence in current assessments of political party organizations, we deal with the question at length here. In this book we report findings on this and related questions about grassroots party organization and activism in the American South.

The South, with its traditions of one-partyism and demagogic candidates (Key, [1949] 1984), might seem to some an unlikely study site to find evidence about vital party organizations. The resurgence of party competition in the region, however, argues just the opposite. The development of two-party competition likely spurred organizational growth at the grass roots. If so, this suggests the South currently is one of the best political laboratories in the nation for examining the possibility of revitalization of grassroots party activism.

To look into this proposition and its corollaries, in 1990–91 a research team composed in toto of faculty located at colleges or universities in each of the eleven southern states conducted a regionwide study of local party organization and activism, known as the Southern Grassroots Party Activists Project. The major effort of this study was a survey of local party activists occupying positions at the precinct and county levels of political party organizations at the time of the study. Not only in the American South as a whole but also to varying degrees in each of the eleven states, the survey revealed that large numbers of grassroots party officials were giving an increasing degree of time and energy to further the work of their local party organizations.

These data provide an opportunity to explore the contemporary condition of party organization and activism in the South in a more comprehensive manner than previous studies.[1] Also, the data give insight into the conditions of local parties more generally in an era of rapid political change. Overall, our approach is to establish a comparative baseline description of party organization and activism in the eleven states. Then we analyze the characteristics, attitudes, and activities of party activists in their local party organizations. Finally we extrapolate, as seems reasonable, from these findings to considerations of political party organization and theories of political party.

Viewing Local Political Parties and Activists

Contributors to this volume utilize a variety of diverse research techniques and approaches, but all share a common outlook about the study of political parties. Following Eldersveld (1964: 1), we conceptualize a political party as "a social group, a system of meaningful and patterned activity within the larger society. It consists of a set of individuals populating specific roles and behaving as member-actors of a boundaried and identifiable social unit." This book, therefore, is organized around three related propositions:

(1) The party is composed of individuals who bring attitudes and predispositions to their organizational participation.

(2) The party is an organization conducting a variety of activities to accomplish a set of goals, chief among them the winning of elections.

(3) The party is located within a broader political system, and it both affects and is affected by changes in that system.

These propositions are not at all new; in fact, nearly all research on political parties follows them in whole or in part. We continue to utilize them because we believe that any effort to address the condition of local party organizations must understand the importance of exploring the party at all levels of analysis, while simultaneously recognizing the difficulty of understanding the party at any one level of analysis. Hence, this book is organized into an introduction and three sections, structured according to these three propositions.

The first section of the book describes the individual activists in their party organizational context. The second section examines what the local party organizations do and how they conduct their business. The third section explores the relationship between the party organizations and the political environment in which they operate.

In the remainder of this introductory chapter we discuss the various approaches, assumptions, and findings of related studies in order to assess recent findings of other researchers about the condition of local parties. In particular we deal with the party-in-decline school. While this approach recently has been subjected to revisionist criticism, we agree that the jury is still out about the condition of political parties at the grass roots. Then we introduce the useful context of the South as a region in which to study local political parties. Our interest is in political parties rather than southern politics per se, however, and we discuss the possibility of using findings from these data to examine what is occurring in local party organizations on a wider basis, rather than focusing on their meaning only in the context of the American South.

Parties in Decline?

A quarter century ago, journalist David Broder looked at the condition of American politics and concluded that the era of party politics had ended. His book *The Party's Over* (1972) captured the despair of that moment in history before Watergate. In its wake, political scientists responded with equally pessimistic appraisals of the state of the parties. Textbooks on the subject were given titles like *Parties in Crisis* (Scott and Hrebenar, 1979) and *American Parties in Decline* (Crotty and Jacobson, 1980). Among the symptoms identified were increased independence among voters (Ladd, 1978; Wattenberg, 1984), a loss of control over the nominating process (Pomper, 1977; Polsby, 1983; Kirkpatrick, 1978), and reduced levels of party voting in Congress (Brady, Cooper, and Hurley, 1979; Collie and Brady, 1985). Advocates of this thesis of party decline (e.g., Burnham, 1970) noted that changes in society and technology, as well as the rise of other political organizations such as political action committees (PACs) and personal candidate organizations, had sapped political parties' ability to fulfill those political activities often expected of them.[2] The result was said to be the inability of the parties to govern effectively (Broder, 1972; Sundquist, 1982), leading to increased dissatisfaction on the part of voters.

The empirical evidence gathered by these and other researchers has been debated in the literature about parties, with that literature questioning the researchers' interpretations of some findings. Recent scholarship has been more positive with regard to the condition of the parties. After a period of attempted scholarly resuscitation (Pomper, 1980; Price, 1984), the parties seem to have staged a recovery on their own. The optimism for their success can be found in such works as *The Party's Just Begun* (Sabato, 1988) and *The Parties Respond* (Maisel, 1990).

Parties in Change?

Is the transformation real, or is it only an artifact of the research enterprise? Some have argued that the confusion exists primarily in the minds of political scientists. For example, Denise Baer and David Bositis (1988: 3) claim that "the crisis is not in the party system, but in the party scholarship." They note that researchers have focused on either the party-in-the-electorate, the party-in-government, or the party organizations (Key, 1964; Beck and Sorauf, 1992) to the exclusion of broader considerations in evaluating the evolution of American political parties. This emphasis on specialized "party-related research," they argue, has eclipsed our understanding of "the dynamic interaction of party variables" (Baer and Bositis, 1988: 21).

The assessment becomes increasingly confusing when conclusions drawn from one branch of the party system are generalized to other branches. A decline in the partisan affiliations of voters does not necessarily signify a corresponding decline in the party organizations, for example. An alternative result might be compensatory change by party organizations in response to a more independent electorate (Cotter et al., 1984; Schlesinger, 1985). For example, the threat of decreasing electoral support might encourage the party organizations to increase their activities in an effort to ensure organizational maintenance, a phenomenon often occurring when organizations face threats to their survival. Similarly, a change in the activities of the national committees in response to the increased role of PACs and personal campaign organizations does not necessarily mean a resulting change in the activities of state and local party organizations. In fact, the increased funneling of "soft money" through state and local party organizations seems to support expectations of growth rather than decline in the party organizations.

The Development of Local Party Scholarship

If we are to do more than speculate on the condition of local party organization, it is necessary to collect and analyze data about local party organization. Merely drawing inferences from other avenues of research, or providing flippant responses based on book titles, is inadequate.

Although there is a great deal of research on local parties, a closer look at the literature reveals that only a small portion of it focuses on local parties from a national or even a regional perspective. Most studies have varied considerably in methodology, and the great majority are reports of grassroots activism in a specific locale. Their findings continue to be used extensively, but many are too casebound, too lacking in rigor, and without comparative research design. They do not support the summative and comparative utilizations often made of them.

Generally the efforts to produce data capable of broader generalization about grassroots activism were limited either because of difficulties in operationalizing organizational functions and in making longitudinal analysis and comparison (Edwards, 1984) or because of the practical difficulties of conducting research in an area of little funding during a period of inflation in survey research costs. Samuel Eldersveld (1984: 4) summarized these difficulties: "We have had a great series of community studies, but no national study. . . . In the U.S. we have ignored this area of inquiry in allocating funds for behavioral research. And, as we all know, as a consequence our research has been of the 'post-hole digging' variety. . . . The objectives of these studies often vary considerably, as do their research designs, and the methods of interviewing respondents. The theoretical questions . . . also vary greatly. . . . It has been difficult, therefore, to compare findings across communities and to generalize about the phenomenon of 'party activism' in the U.S."

This lack of data presents problems for making direct longitudinal comparisons. Still, past research provides a useful guide for new studies of local party organization. From the earliest days of political science, the scholarship on political parties has had an organizational focus. The best early work on local parties in the United States analyzed the patronage-driven machines in urban areas. For example, Gosnell (1937) provided a thorough description of the Chicago machines between 1928 and 1936. Using some rather sophisticated analyses, he was able to separate the impacts of party organizational activity and the news media on aggregate voting patterns. Unfortunately, such case studies were not always generalizable across contemporaneous cities, let alone to nonurban settings or other time periods (see also Kent, 1930; Mosher, 1935; Forthal, 1946).

Addressing this situation in an essay written in the early 1960s, Frank Sorauf outlined an agenda for the study of political parties, noting "the absence of materials on the organization and operations of the American parties as political organizations. As a rough index to the problem, one might say that the voids will not be filled until we know at least as much about the parties as we know of their electorates, as much about rural and small-town parties as about their metropolitan counterparts, as much about other party functions as about their campaigning for election, and as much about their leaders and workers as about their more casual voters" (Sorauf, 1964: 176).

As scholars responded to this concern in the 1960s, party organizations became the focus of the new ideas developed in organizational theory. Clark and Wilson (1961) created a typology of motivations for activism in organizations. Wilson (1962) applied the typology to contrast the traditional patronage organizations with "amateur" Democratic clubs that were springing up in some states and communities. Eldersveld's (1964) exhaustive study of the grassroots party activists in Detroit provided a rich theoretical and empirical profile of local parties in that locale and time period. Schlesinger (1965) developed a theory of party organization that focused on candidates rather than on the formal party apparatus.

The urban metropolitan areas often were sites for grassroots party research, and their political party organizations were not representative of most local organizations in the 1960s or at any other time. As the behavioral era took hold, scholars began to look at state or regional cross sections of local party organizations and at local parties in a variety of areas, not just metropolitan centers. Beck (1974) interviewed a national sample of county chairs in 1965. Crotty (1968a) and Wright (1971) edited volumes that focused on the organizational aspects of political parties. Indeed, the 1960s and early 1970s witnessed a wide-ranging variety of research that formed the basis of the scholarly discussion of local parties for the next two decades.[3]

Interest in local political parties gradually dwindled during the 1970s as increasing attention was given to reforming the political parties at the national level. In this process the national parties established a presence that preempted some functions of the local party apparatus and tended to reduce the power of the grassroots party organizations. The trends noted by the "parties-in-decline" school began to be observed. The American National Election Studies and other major surveys of the mass public made party identification an important research topic.

Other sources of data on party elites, particularly national convention delegates (e.g., Soule and Clarke, 1970; Soule and McGrath, 1975; Kirkpatrick, 1976; Jackson, Brown, and Brown, 1978; Roback, 1980a, 1980b), replaced the local organizations as the focus of scholarship. The Democratic reforms of the 1970s made local party actors appear less important, and their dwindling power at the national nominating conventions seemed to bear this out (e.g., Kirkpatrick, 1976). The only nationwide survey of county chairs in this period was not reported until 1980 (Montjoy, Shaffer, and Weber, 1980; see also Maggiotto and Weber, 1986).

Scholars of political parties returned their focus to local and state party organizations in the 1980s, a decade that also saw a great deal of attention to delegates to national party conventions (e.g., Miller and Jennings, 1986) and state-level activists (Rapoport, Abramowitz, and McGlennon, 1986; Gibson et al., 1983; Cotter et al., 1984; Moreland, Baker, and Steed, 1982; Steed, Moreland, and Baker, 1986, 1990b; Baker et al., 1990). A primary impetus was provided by the work of Cornelius P. Cotter, James L. Gibson, John F. Bibby, and Robert J. Huckshorn in surveying the universe of local party chairs in 1979 and 1980. Approximately four thousand chairs responded to the mail questionnaire. Their research (Cotter et al., 1984; Gibson et al., 1983), along with that of others building from their data (Norrander, 1986; Gibson, Frendreis, and Vertz, 1989), created a baseline for future researchers and stirred debate about the condition of party organizations (e.g., Edwards, 1984; Margolis and Owen, 1985; Pomper, 1990).

Another group of scholars conducted a comparative study of urban parties in the early 1980s (Crotty, 1986a). Precinct committeepersons were surveyed in Los Angeles, Chicago, Detroit, Houston, and Nashville (with the Los Angeles and Detroit surveys being part of ongoing studies conducted by Dwaine Marvick and Samuel Eldersveld, respectively). Similar survey instruments were used in each locale. Although differences in the political cultures of the five cities made direct comparisons difficult (Eldersveld, 1986), according to Crotty (1986b: 30), these cases provided evidence "that the local parties are active in critical areas of campaigning, that they appear to be principal actors in the electoral process, and that there is no evidence of an atrophying of party activity or organization."

More recently, Mildred Schwartz (1990) utilized network analysis to study local party organizations. Her focus was the Republican Party in a single state, Illinois. This study focused on grassroots actors in the local party networks—that is, county chairs and precinct committee members—but it is the relationships between these and other actors that give the analysis its depth. Schwartz (1990: 284) concluded that the Republican Party in Illinois was a robust organization, saying that "in its robustness, the party displays an overall vigor, separate from the situation of particular actors or segments, that enables it to continue despite recurring defeats." This network approach ties the most recent developments in organizational theory to the study of party organizations.

Obtaining adequate data to estimate the possible decline in local party organizations has proven to be a daunting task. A rough empirical indicator of the decline and resurgence in local party *scholarship* can be constructed, however. Crotty (1986a: 235–244) provides an extensive, though only partial, bibliography of the literature on political parties. The entries that it contains can be broken down by date of publication, type of publication, and topic. Entries were classified as either (1) books, or (2) journal articles, book chapters, or unpublished papers. Topics were categorized as local politics, state or national politics, historical studies, or more general topics. References that dealt exclusively with politics in foreign countries were excluded, but cross-national comparisons were included if the United States was one of the countries. Of the 195 entries in the bibliography, 187 were coded. While we must be careful not to generalize too broadly from these limited data, the resulting pattern suggests a dip in the frequency of local party scholarship in the 1970s and a rise in scholarly interest in local parties in the 1980s.[4]

The focus on party organizations in the 1960s and the 1980s has helped to rectify the situation observed by Sorauf in the 1960s, but Frendreis and Gitelson (1993) point out that there is still a void in longitudinal and comparative research on local parties. Only a few studies provide longitudinal analyses of local party organizations (e.g., Marvick, 1980, 1986; Eldersveld, 1986; Margolis and Owen, 1985; Gibson et al., 1983; Gibson, Frendreis, and Vertz, 1989). A lack of comparable data also has imposed severe limitations on researchers. While our data do not allow us to track changes in local parties across time, a portion of our survey instrument elicited estimations of change over time. Additionally, we do have information about a large number of party organizations and activists at a single important point in time. This enables us to make comparisons with the findings of research done over the past three decades. It also enables us to make systematic comparisons among grassroots party organizations at various stages of development across the American South.

The Southern Political Context

This book focuses on local party organizations and activists, not on southern politics. Still, almost every chapter here acknowledges in some way the impact of southern party history and recent southern political developments on the particular points of concern being addressed in the chapter. One might ask, then, Why use the South as a research site to address questions of general interest to parties scholars? Some might argue that the South is too similar intraregionally to offer adequate differentiated comparisons among grassroots politicians. Others might take the viewpoint that southern politics has become so nationalized as to diminish its distinctive political and social characteristics, thereby making it less attractive as a political laboratory. Those taking either point of view simply have not taken into account the political variations in local politics in the South, both historical and current. The South has had political and social diversity at the grass roots throughout the twentieth century (Key, [1949] 1984; Heard, 1952; Bowman and Boynton, 1964; Matthews and Prothro, 1966). Recently it has been one of the regions in the United States having the greatest change in political organization and activity (Ladd and Hadley, 1975: 129–177; Bass and DeVries, 1976; Hadley and Howell, 1980; Black and Black, 1987). The recent switch from being distinctively, even overwhelmingly, Democratic to being more Republican in presidential politics illustrates the sweep of political change in the region (Black and Black, 1987: chap. 12; Black and Black, 1992; Steed, Moreland, and Baker, 1994).

Similarly broad changes in southern state and local party politics are evident (Hadley and Bowman, 1995). The dramatic political change has accompanied similarly dramatic economic and social changes spurred by such factors as population shifts (in-migration and rural-to-urban movements) and the civil rights movement. However, it is clear that these changes are mixed, varying by state, by subregion within the South, by party voter groups, and within selected party cadres (Baker et al., 1990; Steed, More-land, and Baker, 1990b; Hadley and Bowman, 1995).

As the southern party system has changed, it has increasingly taken on the broader characteristics of the national party system (for a general summary, see Steed, 1990). Data illustrate, for example, that parties in the South have higher levels of formal organization than was previously the case (Hadley and Bowman, 1995). The data also show that the parties have undergone a sorting process that contributes to their respective abilities to structure electoral conflict for the electorate in ways resembling nonsouthern parties (Bowman, Hulbary, and Kelley, 1990; Steed, Moreland, and Baker, 1995). Focusing on the South, then, provides an opportunity to examine political parties and to draw generalizations about the larger party system in ways that would not have been possible even two decades ago. It has the added benefit of allowing analyses of data gathered in a time of significant political change in the region. While peculiarities of the South remain (as they do in every region), they no longer seem so great as to negate the value of these analyses for a general understanding of local party activists and organizations.

The Southern Grassroots Party Activists Project

In an effort to provide systematic, comparative data by which to examine contemporary local parties, a research team of seventeen political scientists in eleven southern states collaborated in the Southern Grassroots Political Activists Project. The National Science Foundation funded this project under Grant SES–9009846 to the University of New Orleans, which in turn awarded subcontracts to participating universities or colleges in the individual states. Charles D. Hadley of the University of New Orleans and Lewis Bowman, then of the University of South Florida, served as codirectors of the project. Professor Hadley administered the project on a day-to-day basis; his research assistants, Annie Johnson Benifield, Jennifer E. Horan, and Brad Gomez, provided assistance at various stages of the project.

The researcher or research team members for each state were as follows: Alabama: Patrick R. Cotter, University of Alabama; Arkansas: Diane D. Blair, University of Arkansas; Florida: William E. Hulbary, Anne E. Kelley, and Lewis Bowman, University of South Florida; Georgia: Brad Lockerbie and John A. Clark, University of Georgia; Mississippi: Stephen D. Shaffer and David A. Breaux, Mississippi State University; Louisiana: Charles D. Hadley, University of New Orleans; North Carolina: Charles L. Prysby, University of North Carolina at Greensboro; South Carolina: Robert P. Steed, Laurence W. Moreland, and Tod A. Baker, The Citadel; Tennessee: David M. Brodsky, University of Tennessee at Chattanooga; Texas: Frank B. Feigert, University of North Texas; and Virginia: John J. McGlennon, College of William and Mary.

A three-wave mailing was sent to members of county-level political party organizations and their respective chairs during the spring and summer of 1991.[5] Each mailing included a questionnaire, self-addressed postage-paid return envelope, and appropriate variations of a common cover letter. The individual state party return rates ranged from 40 percent for Louisiana Democrats to 67 percent for North Carolina Republicans. A total of 10,458 usable questionnaires were returned, for an average return rate of 53 percent for members of both county-level political parties in the eleven southern states.[6]

Outline of This Book

In Part I we describe the individual party officials and their patterns of involvement in the local party. The analyses address how and why activists become involved in local party organizational politics and examine such topics as these activists' purist/pragmatist orientations and ambition as factors in understanding party activism. Beyond description of the current state of affairs, we hope this section provides a baseline for future studies in a step-by-step approach to longitudinal analysis.

Part II emphasizes activities within the local party organizations. How do the parties structure political conflict? How do they deal with organizational maintenance? How does the organization work at campaign activities, and what are the organizational communication patterns, especially in terms of their tendency toward hierarchy or "stratarchy" (to use Eldersveld's term)?

In Part III we are concerned with external context and local political parties. What is the impact of outside forces on the party activists and the party organizations? Does factionalism in the party generally influence the grassroots party operations? How is linkage effected between the activists, their organizations, and the public? Are party attachments significant measures of external control? What possibilities exist at the grassroots level for agents of change to make a difference in the organizations and in politics?

In sum, then, this book addresses what we believe to be an important element of the American political system. It is designed to build on a substantial body of previous research to enhance our understanding of contemporary local party organizations. A large regional database provides the opportunity to extend the analyses here beyond what is normally possible in research on local party organizations and activists, thus addressing some of the significant gaps in previous research. We count ourselves among those who feel that a clearer understanding of local parties is important for understanding American politics. This volume is designed to contribute to such an understanding.

Part One
Individuals in Organizations

In order to survive, political party organizations must be able to perpetuate themselves by recruiting and socializing new activists. There must be some reasonable fit between the potential activists' motivations and the parties' respective incentive structures in both the recruitment and the retention of party officials. Therefore, how the parties recruit activists and the types of activists they recruit (and retain) are highly important to the future directions and potential success of the parties. Ultimately, these are matters that go to the heart of the issue of party organizational vitality, and, as Paul A. Beck and Frank J. Sorauf note (1992: 134), "the organization's effectiveness in the political marketplace . . . depends crucially on its vitality."

The chapters in Part I focus on these questions. In chapter 1, William E. Hulbary and Lewis Bowman examine the recruitment patterns of our grass-roots party activists. They are particularly concerned with identifying similarities and differences in parties and with examining the party organization's involvement with the recruitment process. Hulbary and Bowman also describe the end results of the recruitment function as they offer summaries of the major background characteristics of the precinct officials and county chairs in each party.

In chapter 2, Stephen D. Shaffer and David A. Breaux shift the analytical focus to the various motivations of activists in becoming involved in local party work. They use Clark and Wilson's (1961) conceptualization of material, solidary, and purposive incentives to examine both initial and sustaining motivations for activism among grassroots officials. Like Hulbary and Bowman, they are interested in identifying interparty differences and similarities and in exploring the role of the party itself as a factor in attracting and retaining activists.

Wilson (1962) tied incentives for activism to the stylistic orientations of party activists. He classified activists as either "amateurs" or "professionals" based on their concern for either maintaining issue purity or winning elections. In chapter 3, Charles Prysby develops a purism/pragmatism index for our grassroots activists. Comparing Republicans with Democrats and county chairs with precinct officials, he attempts to map patterns of amateurism and professionalism among local party activists to assist in our understanding of local party organizations.

As one element of activists' motivational patterns, some of them see their activity as but a step on the path to a larger political career. Indeed, some scholars (e.g., Schlesinger, 1966, 1985, and 1993) see political ambition as being inextricably linked with the organization and operation of political parties. In chapter 4, Robert P. Steed, Laurence W. Moreland, and Tod A. Baker examine the relationship between ambition and political activity. They are especially interested in ascertaining the extent to which ambition theory still has relevance in understanding local party organizations and activists.

Collectively, the chapters in Part I address the critical questions of how parties attract activists, why activists choose to be involved in party work, both initially and over the long term, and who these activists are. In addition, these chapters provide a foundation for the later analyses of what these activists do and how they relate to the party organization and to the larger environment.

1

Recruiting Activists

William E. Hulbary
Lewis Bowman

Recruiting party activists seems simple at first glance; it is the process of obtaining personnel for political parties. Recruitment efforts seek to ensure a requisite supply of organizational skills, political values, and social values for political party development and maintenance. The overall goal is "to maintain the small but active cadre of citizens who assume primary responsibility for the operation of the [political party] system" (Bowman and Boynton, 1966b: 667). But in reality recruiting local grassroots party activists is a complex process. Sometimes recruitment involves enlisting, inducting, gathering, even cajoling and drafting; at other times it involves simply accepting those who put themselves forward for political party positions. Replenishing the political party's activists, recruitment is a continuing process with varying degrees of activity, often depending upon the ebb and flow of the electoral cycle.

Interest in political elites and their recruitment patterns—who they are, how they are constituted—is usually high, for good reason in view of the role they are perceived to play in helping organize and structure societal conflict.[1] Studies of party elites and elite recruitment, like the study of party activism generally, often have floundered in attempts to go beyond the level of case description. Too many studies stumbled from description to description, with little attention to the refinement of concepts and the building of theory. In recent years, however, this pattern has changed.[2] Summarizing efforts to bring more systematic approaches to the study of political activists and organizations, Crotty (1986a) illustrated that much of the research about political party activism has focused on recruitment as the integrating conceptual approach: "Such research has investigated the means or institutions through which categories of political actors have entered political life and such actors' identifications, demographic characteristics, socialization, backgrounds, professionalization and career advancement patterns, policy views and ideological commitments, introductory and sustaining motivational drives, and activity styles" (Crotty, 1986b: 15).[3]

We follow several of Crotty's suggestions, melding these with a model that

viewed recruitment to local party activism as part of the more general phenomenon of political participation (Bowman and Boynton, 1966b: 668). We
assume the selectivity inherent in recruitment will be manifest in the kinds
of characteristics and variables mentioned by Crotty. Consequently, we focus
our analysis on several general, though not mutually exclusive, paths of
party activist recruitment: self-selection, insider selection, social background, political experience, party identification and commitment, and
partisan ideological and issues orientations.

The Context of Southern Party Activist Recruitment

By the end of the 1980s southern party politics had evolved into a competitive two-party system similar to the national party system in many respects.
Though accelerated and most visible during the Reagan era, the growth of
southern Republicanism began two decades earlier and capitalized on two
important trends (Black and Black, 1987, 1992; Flanigan and Zingale, 1994;
Lamis, 1990). The first was a substantial influx of northern migrants, most
of whom were affluent retirees or middle-class, working-age families seeking
new jobs in the rapid economic development and expansion of the "New
South" Sunbelt states. Many of these migrants were lifelong Republicans
naturally disposed to support the party when they moved south. The second
trend involved native southerners who were conservative Democrats—a sizable group composed mostly of affluent, middle- and upper-middle-class
whites who were active participants in southern economic expansion. They
also were social and/or fiscal conservatives increasingly disillusioned with
what they perceived as the growing liberalism of the national Democratic
Party. Thus they constituted a growing number of likely converts, ready to
switch to the Republican Party as it became more and more competitive.
These two groups formed the core supporters of the growing southern Republican Party.

The emergence of a competitive Republican Party in the South was
based in large part on issues and ideology. Southern Republicans targeted
conservatives and recruited activists by stressing cohesiveness and commitment to a conservative ideology and issue agenda (Black and Black, 1987).
The Democrats, with their long record as the dominant party, were a
broader-based, more diverse "umbrella" party—harboring more supporters
having more divergent perspectives on issues and ideologies and less ideological cohesion. The success of the civil rights movement brought substantial numbers of African Americans into the Democratic fold, adding even
more diversity to the southern Democratic Party but increasing white defections to the Republicans. Nevertheless the Democrats tried to maintain
party strength by stressing party solidarity, long-time commitment, and loyalty to the party itself. Many activists had family and long-time friends and

neighbors who were also party members, and these primary group relationships reinforced party solidarity and psychological commitment to the Democratic organization.

We expected these changes in party competitiveness and loyalties to have important effects on the recruitment of southern party activists. Our general hypothesis was that the parties would recruit activists more heavily from among their core constituencies and supporters as these have changed and evolved over the past few decades. Consistent with their greater diversity, we expected the Democrats to recruit more native southerners and more African Americans and Hispanic Americans. We expected Republicans to attract a higher percentage of whites and those who grew up outside the South. Also we expected Republican activists to be more affluent than Democrats and more likely to have middle-class, white-collar jobs in the private sector.

Because the two parties are at different stages in their organizational development, we expected partisan differences in political experience and background. As the dominant party in the region for so long, the Democratic Party until recently offered more numerous and varied opportunities for party work and officeholding. Thus Democratic activists should have more political experience, and experience of a more varied nature. Republicans should have less varied careers and less experience, as a greater percentage began their activism only in the 1980s.

Also we expected Republicans to display strong attachment and commitment to their national and state party and to be more ideologically cohesive and conservative. Democrats should have weaker ties to their party, especially at the national level, and display more ideological and issue diversity. Further reflecting the divergence of party organizational development and recruitment, we expected more Republicans to be party switchers (former Democrats) and to have parents who were either independents or members of the other major party when they were growing up.

Despite differences in organizational development and differing reactions to growth in party competition, southern Democrats and Republicans have become increasingly competitive electorally. If one party were dominant, then ambitious self-starters might naturally be attracted to the dominant party, while the minority party might have to devote substantial resources and effort to recruiting new activists. But in the more competitive context of contemporary southern politics, there should be less difference between the parties in the methods they employ to recruit new activists. Specifically, both should be equally attractive to highly motivated self-starters, prompted by their own internal political drives; and both should be equally active in their efforts to "draft" new activists who, though willing recruits, are less self-motivated than are self-starters.

Although partisan differences in method of recruitment should be small, we expected self-starters to differ from those selected and recruited by others, regardless of party. We hypothesized that self-starters possessed a stronger, more "inner-directed," motivation to party activism. Also we expected them to be more committed to realizing issue and policy goals through long-term party activity. Consistent with these basic differences, we expected self-starters to be more numerous among those who were younger and at an earlier stage in their occupational careers; better-educated, more affluent, and higher-status professionals; more experienced politically, with more of a lifelong commitment to political activism; more issue-oriented and more ideologically extreme; and more strongly motivated by personal political ambition broadly defined.[4]

The Party Activists Recruited

Social Backgrounds

Our analysis rests on the general hypothesis that social background differences between Republican and Democratic activists are consistent with differences in the core social groupings that provide the base of support for the two parties.

Race and gender. The data yielded no evidence of a "gender gap" favoring the Democrats in recruiting women activists. A little more than 35 percent of the grassroots activists in both parties were women (table 1.1). Both parties were more likely to attract men than women activists (almost 2 to 1), but both attracted men and women activists in roughly equal proportions. Some degree of gender diversity was evident in both parties, but the goal of complete gender equality (equal percentages of men and women) remained elusive.

Compared with rank-and-file activists, the top leadership position (county chair) in local party organizations showed even less diversity. Only 22 percent of Democratic chairs and 26 percent of Republican chairs were women. The absence of women county chairs is especially notable among Democratic organizations in Deep South states; only 16 percent of Democratic county chairs in these states were women.

The racial and ethnic composition of the two parties was consistent with expectations (table 1.1). Nearly all Republican activists (96 percent) were white, emphasizing the strong and growing appeal of the party for white southerners. Nonwhites (African American, Hispanic American, or others) found the Democratic Party a more appealing affiliation. Among Democratic activists, the percentage of nonwhites was beginning to approximate that of the region's general population and voting electorate.[5]

Migration and region of origin. A majority of activists in both parties were native southerners, and region-to-region migration *within the South* was

Table 1.1. Demographics, Socioeconomic Background, and Party Recruitment (in percentage)

Variable	Democrat	Republican
Gender		
Men	63	64
Women	37	36
(N)	(5456)	(4802)
Race/ethnicity		
White	83	96
African American	14	2
Hispanic American	2	1
Other	2	1
(N)	(5390)	(4769)
U.S. region of origin (where grew up)		
Deep South	37	38
Rim South	50	36
Non-South	13	26
(N)	(5513)	(4772)
Age (years)		
39 or younger	15	19
40–49	23	22
50–59	21	23
60–69	25	24
70 or older	16	13
(N)	(5384)	(4756)
Education		
High school or less	25	13
Some college	28	31
4-Year college degree	18	30
Advanced college degree	29	25
(N)	(5509)	(4821)
Family income		
Less than $30,000	31	21
$30,000–$59,000	43	44
$60,000 or more	26	35
(N)	(5331)	(4648)

Table 1.1. continued

Variable	Democrat	Republican
Occupational status (excluding retirees)		
Executive, managerial	25	31
Professional specialties	32	27
Technical, sales, admin. support	15	20
Blue-collar (skilled and unskilled)	21	14
Not in labor force (mainly homemakers)	6	10
(N)	(3407)	(3203)
Religious affiliation		
Mainline Protestant	41	47
Conservative Protestant		
Evangelical	9	15
Baptist	23	14
Southern Baptist	13	12
Catholic	9	9
Jewish	2	1
Other	1	—
Nonbeliever	2	1
(N)	(5489)	(4797)

quite small. Fewer than 10 percent of Republicans and fewer than 5 percent of Democrats indicated they had migrated to a region of the South different from where they grew up.

Of course, migration *into the South* has been an important element in the growth of southern Republicanism (Black and Black, 1987; Lamis, 1990). Mainly retirees and middle-class workers seeking new jobs in rapidly expanding Sunbelt economies, these migrants were more Republican than Democrat and provided a sizable reservoir of potential new Republican activists. Among southern activists, the region of origin (where they grew up in the United States) suggests that Republicans benefitted more than Democrats from this migration (table 1.1). More than 25 percent of Republicans grew up outside the South, a figure that is twice the comparable percentage for Democrats.[6]

Age. Both parties were predominantly middle-aged or older, although the Republican activists tended to be somewhat younger than Democrats (table 1.1). These age differences, while not large, were consistent with prevailing trends in the southern electorate. Since the 1960s the growing strength of the Republican Party in the South has been based partly on its greater appeal for young voters just entering the electorate. During the Reagan-Bush era the Republican Party was especially successful in attracting the support of young first-time voters. Less successful in attracting new young supporters, the Democrats were forced to rely increasingly on their dwindling and aging electoral majority.

Socioeconomic status. Like other political elites, the activists in our survey possessed relatively high socioeconomic status (SES). They were better educated and more affluent than the general electorate, and they worked in higher-status occupations (executive-managerial occupations and professional specialties).

Party differences in SES reflected documented differences in the core electoral support (Black and Black, 1987; Flanigan and Zingale, 1994: 91–109). For example, Republican activists tended to be more affluent and better educated than Democrats. Compared to Democratic activists, about 10 percent more Republicans had family incomes above $60,000, and 10 percent fewer Republicans had incomes below $30,000. Similarly, 87 percent of Republicans had education beyond high school, and 55 percent had four-year college degrees; corresponding figures for Democrats were lower by 12 and 8 percentage points, respectively.

Consistent with these education and income data, the Republicans attracted a greater percentage of activists from higher-status white-collar occupations in executive-managerial or technical, sales, and administrative support groupings. In contrast, Democrats were more likely to have blue-collar occupations. The only white-collar occupations where Democrats were more numerous were those in the professional specialties category. In addition, Democrats and Republicans tended to be drawn from different occupations within the same higher-status, white-collar occupational categories. Thus, Republicans were more likely to be self-employed businessmen; CEOs or private-sector managers in finance, marketing, advertising, and real estate; and medical doctors, architects, engineers, or clergy. Democrats were more likely to be educational administrators; appointed or elected public officials; and teachers or lawyers.[7]

Socioeconomic status was linked to racial and ethnic differences among Democratic activists but not in the manner one might expect.[8] By nearly 10 percentage points, nonwhites (mainly African Americans and Hispanic Americans) had lower family incomes, but by the same 10 percentage point margin they also were better educated than white Democrats. Nonwhite Democrats were more likely than their white counterparts to have blue-collar jobs but also more likely to have jobs falling into the higher-status, professional specialty category.

Religion. Looking only at broad religious categories (such as Protestants, Catholics, and Jews), the religious affiliations of Democrats and Republicans differed little. Slightly more Republicans than Democrats were Protestant, but both parties were 86–88 percent Protestant and differed by only 1–2 percentage points in the proportion of Catholics, Jews, others, and nonbelievers (table 1.1).

There was clear evidence, however, of the growing appeal of Republicanism to the socially conservative religious right. This appeal was most apparent among evangelicals, who are among the core supporters of the religious right and who tend to be among its most avid and dogmatically inflexible adherents. Not surprisingly, Evangelicals were nearly twice as numerous among Republicans as Democrats and, among Republicans, constituted the largest conservative Protestant group (slightly larger than Baptists or Southern Baptists).

The growing appeal of Republicanism was clear as well among other conservative Protestants linked with the religious right. Although these groups traditionally have been more Democratic than Republican in the South, they now appear to be equally numerous among both Democratic and Republican activists. In table 1.1, among conservative Protestants, only Baptists (as distinct from Southern Baptists) were more numerous among Democrats than Republicans. This difference, however, was due mainly to the large percentage of African Americans who were Baptist.[9] Among whites, who are much more likely than African Americans to be sympathetic to the religious right, the percentage of Baptists in the two parties is quite similar.

Religious self-descriptions provided further evidence of the growing link between southern Republicans and the religious right. One survey item asked whether respondents would describe their religious views as "charismatic," "fundamentalist," "born again," and/or "evangelical"—all terms commonly associated with the theological beliefs of the religious right. Those who felt most comfortable describing their beliefs in these terms would be most sympathetic to the political beliefs of the religious right. Furthermore, the extent of their sympathy with the religious right should be reflected in how many of the terms they selected to describe themselves; those who chose two, three, or four terms should be more sympathetic than those who chose only one. Consistent with the devout Protestantism characteristic of the South, nearly half of the activists in both parties (D—46 percent; R—48 percent) selected at least one term. Moreover, nearly four times as many Republicans as Democrats (15 percent and 4 percent, respectively) selected two or more of these terms to describe their religious views. Clearly these results are entirely consistent with, and reinforce, the results derived from religious affiliations. The Republican Party in the South has a strong and growing appeal to those most supportive of religious conservatism and the religious right.

Political Experience and Recruitment

Turnover among local party activists traditionally has been quite rapid. Southern grassroots activists in the early 1990s continued to fit the traditional pattern. More than 85 percent of the Republicans in our survey first occupied their current positions as recently as the Reagan-Bush era (1980–91), with more than half (55 percent) during the Bush years (1988–91) alone. Democratic turnover was not as rapid, but even among Democrats more than three-quarters (76 percent) occupied their positions during the Reagan-Bush era, with 40 percent during the Bush era alone.

Such high turnover among local party activists did not signify a lack of political experience. On the contrary, both Democrats and Republicans had substantial and varied political experience. Nearly half had held at least one other position in the party or an elective or appointive office outside the party. For example, one-quarter of the Democrats and nearly one-third of the Republicans had held at least one other party position in addition to their current one (table 1.2). Furthermore, about one in five had held an external elective office, and more than one in five had held an appointive office. The Republicans were somewhat less likely than Democrats to have held elective or appointive offices outside the party and more likely to have held other positions inside the party. This reflects the greater ease of electing Democrats in an area where the party was so dominant until recently. It also suggests more elite circulation within the Republican Party.

The number of years during which southern activists were active in state politics, and politics generally, also suggests extensive political experience. Well over half the Republicans and two-thirds of the Democrats had been active in state politics for more than ten years. Furthermore, 60 percent of Republicans and 70 percent of Democrats had been politically active (beyond merely voting) for more than ten years.

The political experience of southern party activists also provides evidence of the decline of Democratic dominance in the late 1970s and 1980s. By a considerable margin, more Republicans than Democrats became politically active and active in state politics during the Reagan era, a trend that continued into the early 1990s. Conversely, more Democrats than Republicans became politically active and active in state politics before the 1980s, a period when the Democrats, though beginning their decline, were still dominant in the South.

Party Identification and Commitment

To build a viable organization able to compete effectively against the Democrats, southern Republicans recruited activists of two types—traditional Republicans and conservative southern Democrats. Traditional Republicans had been Republicans all their lives and usually had been raised in Republican families where both parents were Republicans. They were naturally attracted to Republican activism.

Conservative southern Democrats, on the other hand, were usually disaffected Democrats who felt increasingly alienated from the national party.

Table 1.2. Political Experience, Party Identification, and Recruitment (in percentage)

Experience	Democrat	Republican
Other positions held[a]		
Another party position	25	32
Elective office	21	16
Appointive office	22	20
Year first became active in state politics		
Before 1960	18	10
1960–69	21	22
1970–79	29	24
1980–87	23	29
1988–91	9	15
(N)	(5396)	(4738)
Year first became politically active beyond merely voting		
Before 1960	19	12
1960–69	22	23
1970–79	29	25
1980–87	23	29
1988–91	6	11
(N)	(5393)	(4745)
National party identification		
Strong	72	87
Weak	12	4
Disaffected	16	9
(N)	(5397)	(4809)
State party identification		
Strong	83	82
Weak	7	6
Disaffected	9	12
(N)	(5507)	(4811)
Switched parties?		
Yes, issues most important	5	27
Yes, issues not most important	2	2
No, never switched	93	71
(N)	(5411)	(4739)

Table 1.2. continued

Experience	Democrat	Republican
Year switched parties		
Before 1960	10	12
1960–69	22	21
1970–79	27	24
1980 or after	41	42
(N)	(321)	(1322)
Parents' party identification		
Both parents Democrats	81	44
Mixed	13	24
Both parents Republicans	6	32
(N)	(5196)	(4534)

[a]For each type of office, N = 5601 Democrats and 4857 Republicans. Respondents could have held one or more of each of the three kinds of offices.

Although reared as Democrats and inclined to identify with the Democratic Party, they were conservative on many national issues—civil rights and affirmative action, taxes and spending for social programs, and issues dealing with moral and social values. Their issue and ideological conservatism led them to become increasingly disenchanted with the liberal leanings of the national Democratic Party, and their disaffection manifested itself in either party switching or split party identification. Party switchers represent the most alienated conservative southern Democrats. They rejected the Democratic Party at all levels, becoming Republicans and "former" Democrats and providing new party activists for the rapidly growing southern Republican Party (Bowman, Hulbary, and Kelley, 1990; Prysby, 1990; Steed, Moreland, and Baker, 1995). Split party identifiers were those whose disaffection was confined to the national Democratic Party; they considered themselves independents (or even Republicans) in national politics and often voted Republican in presidential elections. In state and local politics, however, they still were closely identified with the Democratic Party (Hadley, 1985; Wekkin, 1991).

Among the activists in our survey, evidence of split party identification was quite consistent with these trends (see table 1.2). Both Democrats and Republicans closely identified with their own state party, with more than 80 percent reporting "strong" identifications. Republican identification with the national party was equally strong, but Democratic identification was considerably weaker. The level of split party identification among Democrats was twice as high as among Republicans. Nearly 30 percent of Democrats lacked "strong" identification with the national party, and 16 percent considered themselves "disaffected" (either independents or Republicans) in national politics. Thus disenchantment with the national party clearly was greater among Democrats than Republicans. This in turn implies that disenchanted southern Democrats will continue to be a potential source of new Republican activists.

Evidence of party switching among southern grassroots activists reinforces this conclusion. Much party switching occurred during the Reagan-Bush era of the 1980s; more than 40 percent of those Republicans and Democrats who had switched had done so since 1980 (table 1.2). The reported level of party switching during the Reagan-Bush period was 15–20 percentage points higher than in either of the previous two decades. In this respect the politics of the Reagan-Bush era accelerated a defining moment in southern party politics.

Republicans were much more likely than Democrats to report having switched parties. Overwhelmingly those Republicans who had switched were former Democrats moving to the Republican Party, and most of these switched because of their views about public issues. In contrast, nearly all Democrats (more than 90 percent) had been Democrats all their lives, and a substantial percentage (81 percent) came from families where both parents were also Democrats. A much smaller percentage of Republicans came from families where both parents were also Republican. In fact more than two out of five Republicans came from families where *both parents were Democrats* and nearly a quarter from families where parental partisanship was mixed. Clearly, Democrats experienced weakened ties to the party, especially the national party, providing fertile ground for the recruitment of southern Republican activists.

Recruitment Paths

Self-Starters or Selected?

Democrats and Republicans were equally likely to be self-starters (48 percent in both parties). Activists in both parties also were equally likely to be recruited by party workers (41 to 43 percent) and by others such as candidates and elected officials (10 to 11 percent). By a slight margin, Republicans were more likely to be recruited by county chairs, but this difference was barely 5 percentage points. What stands out are the similarities in methods of recruitment by both parties, similarities that attest to the resurgence of Republicans and the decline of Democratic dominance. The absence of differences in method of recruitment supports the view that southern party competition has become a struggle between equals.

Regional differences in method of recruitment suggest that party competition may be more fully developed in the Rim South than in the Deep South. In the Rim South, Democrats (45 percent) and Republicans (47 percent) were equally likely to be self-starters, consistent with the equal competition model. But in the Deep South, self-starters were somewhat more numerous among Democrats (54 percent) than Republicans (48 percent). By a small margin, Deep South Republicans appeared to devote more efforts to recruiting new activists and had more activists recruited by other party workers. This result is more consistent with the dominant/minority party model and with the general view of the Deep South as a region where the residual effects of Democratic dominance are still lingering.

Background and Recruitment Method

Were members of different social, economic, and demographic groups more likely to be recruited by different methods? We expected self-starters to be more ambitious and politically aware and more motivated to political activism in general. They also should possess background characteristics that generally differentiate political elites from the mass public. Self-starters should be more numerous, for example, among the more educated and affluent and among younger activists and those earlier in career. Because men are still more likely to be politically ambitious than women, we also expected more men than women to be self-starters.

These hypotheses were generally correct (table 1.3). Younger activists in both parties were more likely to be self-starters, while those later in career or already retired were more likely to be recruited by other party workers. Similarly, regardless of party, those with more education were more likely to be self-starters. Occupational differences were smaller but consistent with those for education. Democrats and Republicans with higher SES occupations, particularly those with professional and technical specialties usually requiring more education, were somewhat more likely to be self-starters. Those with lower-status occupations were more likely to be recruited by other party activists. Family income was linked to differences in recruitment method among Democrats only. More affluent Democrats were also more likely to be self-starters. However, among Republicans, the affluent and the not-so-affluent were equally likely to be self-starters.

Gender differences did not quite fit the anticipated pattern. As expected, women Republicans were less likely to be self-starters and more likely to be recruited by other party workers (table 1.3). Among Democrats, however, women were almost as likely as men to be self-starters. Elsewhere we have noted that Democratic women differ from Republican women in social background (Kelley, Hulbary, and Bowman, 1990). Democratic women tend to be younger, better educated, more economically independent, and more likely to work outside the home in relatively high-status jobs. Their relative youth and more career-oriented social and economic background may account for the lack of gender differences in method of recruitment among Democrats.

Minority group activists, whether African American, Hispanic American,

Table 1.3. Background, Political Experience, and Recruitment Method (in percentage)

Background/ experience	Democrats				Republicans			
	Recruitment method				Recruitment method			
	Self	Party	Other	(N)	Self	Party	Other	(N)
Age (years)								
39 or younger	53	37	10	(688)	55	36	9	(801)
40–59	51	37	12	(1947)	45	45	10	(1734)
60 or older	44	44	12	(1698)	48	44	8	(1391)
Education								
High school or less	44	43	13	(1014)	45	44	11	(492)
Some college	48	39	13	(1259)	47	43	10	(1226)
4-Year college degree	49	41	10	(787)	49	43	9	(1218)
Advanced college degree	52	38	10	(1347)	50	42	8	(1028)
Occupational status								
Executive, managerial	49	38	13	(700)	48	41	10	(814)
Professional specialties	52	38	9	(911)	51	40	9	(713)
Technical, sales, admin. support	51	36	12	(434)	45	43	12	(519)
Blue-collar	48	39	13	(607)	47	43	10	(367)
Not in labor force	49	42	9	(169)	48	42	9	(265)
Family income								
Less than $30,000	46	42	42	(1256)	47	44	9	(788)
$30,000–$59,000	49	40	11	(1888)	49	42	9	(1702)
$60,000 or more	51	38	12	(1136)	47	44	9	(1354)
Gender								
Men	49	39	12	(2824)	50	41	9	(2563)
Women	47	42	11	(1564)	44	46	10	(1389)
Race/ethnicity								
White	47	42	12	(3624)	48	43	9	(3779)
African American	61	30	9	(573)	59	36	5	(75)
Hispanic American	52	21	27	(71)	61	30	9	(23)
Other	56	35	9	(71)	56	31	13	(52)

Table 1.3. continued

Background/ experience	Democrats				Republicans			
	Recruitment method				Recruitment method			
	Self	Party	Other	(N)	Self	Party	Other	(N)
No. of other positions held (party, elected, or appointed)								
None	46	42	12	(2234)	45	45	10	(2059)
1	49	41	10	(895)	48	43	8	(653)
2	51	38	10	(603)	48	42	10	(482)
3 or more	53	33	14	(741)	55	37	8	(796)
Year first became active in state politics								
Before 1960	48	40	12	(736)	53	39	8	(363)
1960–69	51	38	11	(894)	50	41	9	(847)
1970–79	50	38	12	(1314)	49	42	9	(944)
1980–87	47	42	11	(1054)	48	43	10	(1172)
1988–91	42	46	12	(384)	41	48	11	(613)
Year first became politically active beyond merely voting								
Before 1960	48	40	12	(798)	52	40	9	(424)
1960–69	52	37	11	(960)	51	41	9	(891)
1970–79	50	38	12	(1313)	48	43	9	(1004)
1980–87	46	43	11	(1039)	47	43	9	(1171)
1988–91	41	47	12	(271)	41	47	12	(456)

or members of other minority groups, were more likely than whites to be self-starters (table 1.3). Compared to whites, relatively few minority group members attracted to party activism indicated that party workers were important agents in their recruitment. In part this is a consequence of traditional barriers to minority activists in southern parties. We expected minority activists, if they were recruited by other party activists, to be recruited primarily by activists who were also members of their own minority group. But even as recently as the early 1990s, most southern party activists were whites; few nonwhite activists were available to recruit more members of their group. Thus most minority group members attracted to party activism were highly motivated, politically aware self-starters rather than potential activists recruited by other party workers.

Political Experience and Recruitment Method

Activists recruited by party workers and others may have a limited commitment to partisan activity. But self-starters, drawn by their internal drive for political involvement and higher political awareness, should be more highly motivated and strongly attracted to partisan politics. Consequently, those with more political experience and a deeper, longer-lasting commitment to party politics would be more likely to be self-starters than those recruited by party workers and others.

Consistent with this hypothesis, the link between political experience and recruitment method was quite similar in both parties (table 1.3). Regardless of how we measured political experience, those with more experience were more likely to be self-starters than those recruited by other agents. Those who had held other party offices and those who had held elective or appointive offices outside the party were all more likely to be self-starters. Regardless of the kind of position held, those who had held more positions were also more likely to be self-starters. For length and duration of political activism, the same relationship emerged. Those who had been active longer in state politics, and those who had been generally active (beyond merely voting) for a longer period, were more likely to be self-starters.

During the 1980s, particularly the late 1980s, the parties apparently made concerted efforts to recruit new activists. More recently recruited activists and those with less experience—particularly those recruited in the late 1980s—were more likely to stress the importance of other party workers as the prime agents in their recruitment. Prompted by heightened party competition, the recruitment of activists in the 1980s seems to have shifted away from self-starters and toward more vigorous recruiting efforts by the parties themselves. Alternatively, the commitment of new activists who are not self-starting may be short-lived, waning over time as more of them abandon party activism.

Ideologies, Issues, and Purposive Incentives

Issue salience and ideology should be a distinctive mark of well-motivated self-starters, differentiating them from activists recruited by party workers and others. The dominant issue positions and ideology of a party serve as a powerful magnet attracting self-motivated activists. Those with more extreme ideological orientations consistent with their party and those who stress issues and purposive incentives for party activism should include a greater percentage of self-starters and fewer activists recruited by others in the party.

These interpretations clearly apply to southern party activists in the early 1990s. The connection between ideological issue positions and method of recruitment was as anticipated; those most strongly committed to the dominant ideology in their party were more likely to be self-starters. To assess this link, we constructed a composite ideological issues scale, a general measure

Table 1.4. Ideology, Incentives, and Recruitment Method (in percentage)

	Democrats				Republicans			
	Recruitment method				Recruitment method			
	Self	Party	Other	(N)	Self	Party	Other	(N)
Political ideology scale								
Liberal	54	38	8	(687)	44	48	7	(27)
Somewhat liberal	53	37	11	(1355)	45	45	9	(165)
Moderate	44	43	13	(1894)	45	46	9	(1597)
Somewhat conservative	48	37	15	(286)	50	41	10	(1450)
Conservative	39	50	11	(38)	53	39	8	(633)
Recruitment incentives when first became active								
Material	64	29	7	(140)	60	33	7	(82)
Purposive	56	35	10	(1449)	52	40	9	(1900)
Solidary								
Party commitment	48	40	12	(1624)	47	44	10	(1210)
Social interaction	39	47	14	(1192)	39	50	11	(759)
Recruitment incentives for seeking current position								
Material	73	21	6	(154)	57	34	9	(112)
Purposive	55	35	10	(1370)	51	40	9	(1961)
Solidary								
Party commitment	49	40	11	(1975)	50	41	9	(1350)
Social interaction	33	52	16	(850)	25	61	14	(485)

of issue liberalism and conservatism as displayed in attitudes on sixteen separate issues in four categories—social issues, civil rights, the proper role of government, and foreign policy.[10] On this scale, self-starters were relatively more numerous among those most committed to the dominant ideology of their party—liberal Democrats and conservative Republicans (table 1.4). Moderates, conservative Democrats, and liberal Republicans, of course, were more ambivalent about, or opposed to, the dominant ideology of their party. The more opposed they were, the more likely they were to be non-self-starters recruited by other party activists.

Incentives for becoming involved in party activism also were linked to method of recruitment. Only 3–4 percent in both parties mentioned material incentives as most important for first becoming active or for seeking their current positions. Such a small percentage suggests that parties are no longer seen as primary vehicles for material rewards or personal ambition—for upward economic mobility (jobs and patronage) or as a necessary tool of business success in the private sector. Instead of material considerations, the primary incentives for party activism have shifted toward solidary and purposive incentives.

Nonetheless, among the small group for whom material incentives were important, such incentives reflected desires for personal ambition and socioeconomic well-being more than any of the other incentives we examined. Consequently, we were not surprised to find a large proportion of highly motivated self-starters in this group (table 1.4). Whether we focused on incentives for first becoming active or those for seeking current party positions, the result was the same. More than any other motivation, an emphasis on material incentives was characteristic of those who were more likely to be self-starters and less likely to be recruited by party workers and others.

But purposive and solidary incentives, rather than material incentives, were the most widespread motivations for activism. Those who stressed purposive incentives were expressing more concern with issues and more interest in moving government and politics in a direction consistent with the parties' goals and policy agenda. Also they were more likely to be self-starters, motivated by their own issue and policy concerns, and less likely to be recruited by others.

Alternatively, those who stressed solidary incentives were more attracted to activism by party loyalty and commitment or by social solidarity with friends, family, community, and tradition. As expected, they were less likely to be self-starters and more likely to stress the role of others in their recruitment. By a wide margin, those who emphasized solidary incentives denoting social interaction were least likely to be self-starters and most likely to be recruited by others. Those stressing "party loyalty" kinds of solidary incentives, especially among Republicans, were somewhat more likely to be self-starters and more resembled those who stressed purposive incentives.

Summary

The contemporary context of recruitment to grassroots party positions in the South is being restructured by the influences that impact southern political participation generally. These include migration from outside the South, party conversion (or sorting) of persons within the South, and generational realignment. In turn, these influences have produced differential recruitment between the two major political parties. As the long-term majority party, the Democrats have emphasized regional and state solidarity and commitment to the state party, as well as primary group relationships (particularly family and immediate peers), to maintain adequate cadres of party activists. On the other hand, the Republicans have emphasized ideology, issues, and loyalty to the national party. These concerns have enabled the Republicans to draw upon in-migration, the conversion of disaffected southerners, and a new, younger generation of southern conservatives in recruiting party activists.

Southern grassroots party activists tended to be disproportionately white, male, and middle-aged or older. They also tended to be native southerners with higher socioeconomic status and more education than the general population. Compared with Democrats, however, the Republicans tended to be somewhat younger and to have even higher socioeconomic backgrounds. Many Republican activists also had less political experience than the Democrats because they had become politically active more recently, during the Reagan and Bush eras.

As political party parity evolved, both parties drew upon similar proportions of self-starters. The self-starters tended to be younger, better educated, and more upper-middle class. They also tended to have more political experience. As parity neared, the proportion of self-starters dropped, and more party activists were selected by others, particularly other party officials. Illustrating their drive to get ahead and pursue their preferred policy agenda, the self-starters of both parties tended to be driven more by purposive and material incentives. They also were more issue oriented and policy oriented and more committed to their party's dominant ideology—liberalism for the Democrats and conservatism for the Republicans.

Although the model of equal party competition fit the contemporary recruitment patterns of the Rim South better than the Deep South in this study, we expect these regional recruitment differences to ameliorate or disappear throughout the South as the parties approach competitive parity. In turn, the accelerating nationalization of politics in the southern region of the United States argues that this model may fit recruitment context and paths in the United States generally.

2

Activists' Incentives

Stephen D. Shaffer
David A. Breaux

A time-honored concern of scholars of political parties has been what motivates people to become involved in local party organizations and to stay involved over the years. The reasons proposed for local organizational activity include people's expectations of acquiring material benefits, enjoyment of social and interpersonal relations, and desires to shape public policy. Researchers have also been intrigued about whether party workers' motivations for activism change over time in response to their environment or to maturation. A less-examined question is whether the types of motivations for activists influence how dedicated they are to the party or what types of activities they engage in. This chapter examines the incentives that motivate southern grassroots party activists to become and remain involved in their local party organizations.

It is particularly intriguing to focus on incentives motivating party activists in the South, given the significant partisan realignment that has been transforming the region from a one-party Democratic bastion into a competitive two-party system (Swansbrough and Brodsky, 1988; Lamis, 1990). Especially in presidential elections, voters in recent decades have clearly responded to the events, issues, and candidates specific to the races, rather than relying solely on a partisan tradition grounded in the institutions of civil war and racial segregation. While such developments may suggest an especially prominent role for activism motivated by public policy concerns, others have pointed out that such political transformations as ideological realignment in the Congress and party sorting at the grassroots levels have resulted in southern political orientations that resemble national patterns (Steed, Moreland, and Baker, 1990c).

The Literature on Motivational Incentives for Activism

For three decades, researchers have generally classified party workers' motivations for becoming and remaining active in party organizations into material, solidary, and purposive incentives. Material incentives are tangible rewards that can be translated into monetary values. Solidary incentives are intangible, derive from the act rather than the ends of associating, and include such factors as socializing, group identification, and enjoyment. Purposive incentives are intangible and are grounded in the overall goals of the organization, such as its demands for enactment of various public policies. Incentives in a political party organization can change because of changes in the environment or in the membership's motivations. For example, limited access to material rewards and limited success with purposive goals may influence the organization's leaders to stress the solidary benefits of group membership (Clark and Wilson, 1961).

Conway and Feigert (1968) and Bowman, Ippolito, and Donaldson (1969) pioneered the quantitative empirical study of motivations for activism among grassroots party officials. The former found "impersonal" motivations, such as civic duty and a desire to influence public policy, to be the most frequently cited reasons for becoming politically active and seeking precinct chairmanships in two northern counties. In the latter study, precinct and ward chairs in five communities in North Carolina and Massachusetts cited purposive incentives as the most important reasons for being involved in politics, followed by solidary reasons, with material incentives rated as least important. Party officials most liked the personal satisfactions and rewards of their jobs and most disliked any conflicts within the organization.

More recent studies have examined motivations among new groups of activists—1972 presidential campaign contributors (Hedges, 1984), delegates at twenty-two state party conventions in 1980 backing presidential hopefuls (Abramowitz, McGlennon, and Rapoport, 1983), and campaign workers in two Kentucky Democratic gubernatorial primaries (Miller, Jewell, and Sigelman, 1987). Campaign contributors, especially McGovern supporters, rated purposive motivations—influencing public policy, a sense of obligation to the community, and a wish to affect election outcomes—as most important incentives, while material incentives such as business contacts were of little importance. Purposive incentives were rated most important reasons for becoming involved in each party's 1980 presidential campaign, though party loyalty was a close second. The overriding incentive for activism in the gubernatorial primary campaigns was a newer, candidate-centered motivation—"to support a particular candidate I believe in." Of the three motivational types, purposive incentives were most important to campaigners in the primaries, while material incentives were least important.

Early studies suggested that motivations changed over the years, with purposive motivations becoming less important. Conway and Feigert (1968) found that precinct leaders were most likely to say that they would miss social contacts and "other personal satisfactions" such as material goals if they resigned their positions. Environmental factors were evident, as majority rather than minority party activists showed greater current satisfaction with purposive incentives, while the "evolution away from purposive motivations" was most evident in the more affluent county, where such motivations for initial activity were especially strong. Bowman, Ippolito, and Donaldson (1969) suggested that shifts toward solidary incentives occurred as organization members found material incentives largely unavailable and purposive goals difficult to achieve. The personal importance of their party position as well as a strong sense of party loyalty appeared to motivate party members to remain politically active. Candidate friendships appeared to encourage sporadic activity, as some inspired by a favorite candidate to seek party positions dropped out of the organization after the candidate had left the political scene.

Other studies of grassroots party officials suggested that motivations for political activism could remain stable over time. Ippolito (1969a) found that county executive committee members in Nassau County, New York, were primarily motivated by impersonal incentives and that their motivations tended to stay the same. He speculated that the organizational level may have contributed to such motivational stability, as high-level county officials may have been better able to shape the incentives that the organization provided than were lower-level activists. At the national level—national convention delegates to the 1972 and 1976 conventions—Roback (1980a) found that purposive incentives were rated most important for remaining active in the party organization, especially among Reagan supporters, while material incentives were regarded as least important. Different ways of phrasing questions about incentives made examining motivational changes over time problematic, though Reagan delegates did appear to exhibit greater purposive continuity than other delegates. Moving beyond specific conditions for motivational stability, Hedges (1984) found considerable stability of motivations for initial and current political activity among presidential campaign contributors, while Miller, Jewell, and Sigelman (1987) also found considerable continuity in the three motivational scales between the two primary election years for campaign workers.

Compared with the extensive literature that focuses on stability of motivational incentives for activism, fewer studies have examined the relationships between motivational incentives and recruiters of activists, intensity and type of political involvement, and ideological orientations. Conway and Feigert's (1974) study of precinct chairs in two northern counties found that the environment affected how purposive motivations were translated into specific party tasks. In areas of higher socioeconomic status characterized by higher turnouts, those motivated by purposive incentives stressed communicating principles as their most important party task, while in areas of lower socioeconomic status such activists stressed the primacy of increasing voter turnout. Roback's (1980a) study of Republican national convention delegates also found a conditional effect: incentives affected candidate support depending on the agent of recruitment. Among those who first became active in the party because of someone else's encouragement, solidary and material incentives tended to predict support for Gerald Ford, while among self-recruited partisans purposive incentives correlated with support for Ronald Reagan. Abramowitz, McGlennon, and Rapoport (1983) argue that state convention delegates are motivated by partisanship as well as purposive goals and that purposive incentives are correlated with such organizational loyalty measures as years of activity in the party, regularity of campaign involvement, and organizational and electoral experience. Though ideological self-identification was a more important predictor of candidate support than partisan intensity, intensely partisan motivations reduced support for Edward Kennedy among very liberal delegates as well as among those most motivated by purposive incentives.

Methodological Issues Involving Incentives

When examining motivational incentives for activism, previous studies have sometimes neglected to think carefully through their theoretical concepts or to examine whether indicators were valid measures of their concepts, leading to inconsistent treatment of various indicators. Clark and Wilson (1961) conceptually define party attachment as a solidary motive, while Ippolito (1969a) classifies it as an impersonal or purposive incentive. As in many other studies, Roback (1975) did not perform any validity test when assigning specific incentive items to each material, solidary, and purposive scale. Hedges (1984) employs a factor analysis that subdivides the solidary dimension into a "specific solidary" subgroup that includes politics as a way of life as one item and party attachment as another. And Roback (1980a) was unable to measure precisely the motivational continuity over time because of using different lists of items in determining initial incentives and sustaining incentives.

When forming simple additive scales of solidary, material, and purposive incentives to simplify our in-depth examination of the correlates of motivations and behavior (and to reduce random measurement error), we tested the validity of the items by performing factor analyses as well as examining the correlation matrices. A factor analysis (varimax rotation) of the incentives for activism produced five factors, three of which were clearly the solidary, material, and purposive incentives (table 2.1). The solidary dimension incorporates the diverse topics that Clark and Wilson mention, such as party, friendship, and fun, as well as one's family history of political activism. The material dimension incorporates business contacts and building a personal position in politics, as well as recognition in the community, which party workers apparently perceive as helping attainment of the other two

Table 2.1. Rotated Factor Matrix (Varimax) for Incentive Items

Items	Factor 1 (Solidary)	Factor 2 (Material)	Factor 3 (Purposive)
Solidary			
V17 (party)	.70	-.05	.23
V18 (friendship)	.55	.26	-.05
V19 (family)	.64	.09	-.07
V20 (fun)	.61	.36	.15
Material			
V21 (position)	.17	.75	.24
V25 (business)	.05	.75	0
V27 (recognition)	.14	.71	0
Purposive			
V22 (influence/campaign)	.17	.13	.85
V23 (influence/party)	.11	.09	.86
V28 (issues)	.09	-.04	.58

Note: Respondents were asked to "rate each of the following in terms of its importance in your personal decision to seek your current party position." Response categories were "very important," "somewhat important," "not very important," and "not important at all." Complete wordings of each variable follow; variables were combined into three scales for each incentive group.

Solidary
V17: I am strongly attached to my political party
V18: I enjoy the friendship and social contacts I have with other party workers
V19: My family's involvement in party politics
V20: I like the fun and excitement of campaigns
Material
V21: I am trying to build a personal position in politics
V25: Party work helps me make business contacts
V27: Party work gives me a feeling of recognition in the community
Purposive
V22: I see campaign work as a way to influence politics and government
V23: I see working in the political party generally as a way to influence politics and government
V28: My concern with public issues

material goals. The purposive dimension is fairly standard, including issues and two items on influencing government. A fourth factor measures a candidate–civic duty dimension, while a fifth factor is a personal friendship dimension.[1] The following analyses concentrate on the first three dimensions, which are of greater relevance to previous studies of motivations for activism.

Table 2.2. Correlation Matrix among Incentives for Activism (Pearson _R_ values)

	V17	V18	V19	V20	V21	V25	V27	V22	V23	V28
V17	—									
V18	.39	—								
V19	.28	.32	—							
V20	.36	.49	.33	—						
V21	.13	.20	.14	.34	—					
V25	.10	.27	.19	.27	.43	—				
V27	.19	.38	.21	.37	.40	.47	—			
V22	.29	.19	.13	.31	.23	.10	.16	—		
V23	.28	.15	.11	.23	.19	.09	.15	.73	—	
V28	.26	.17	.09	.19	.10	.04	.12	.41	.41	—

Note: See Table 2.1 for details on questions asked (V numbers).

Average intracluster item correlations	Average intercluster correlations
Solidary items = .36	Solidary–material items = .23
Material items = .43	Solidary–purposive items = .20
Purposive items = .52	Material–purposive items = .13

We confirm the validity of simple additive scales of each of these three incentives by examining a correlation matrix of the items. The average Pearson correlations among items tapping the same dimensions ranged from .36 to .52, reasonably high correlations given such attitudinal data and the demanding statistic employed (table 2.2). Additional confirming evidence is provided by the average correlations between items from different dimensions, which in all cases were lower than the average intracluster correlations.[2] The existence of correlations between the dimensions suggests that the three incentives for activism are not mutually exclusive and that party workers may be motivated by more than one type of incentive, a subject to which we shall soon turn. A further test of the generalizability of these three dimensions involved repeating the analyses for each party separately. The same patterns of factor loadings for the items in table 2.1 existed for each party, confirming the existence of solidary, material, and purposive dimensions for both Democrats and Republicans. The only deviant item was issues for Democrats, which loaded equally on the purposive and candidate–civic duty dimension, though it was slightly more related to the purposive items than to the other two items and is classified as such in subsequent analyses.[3]

**Table 2.3. Incentives for Seeking Current Party Position
(percentage rating as very important)**

Incentive	Democrats	Republicans	All
Solidary			
Strongly attached to party	57	53	55
Friendship/social contacts	31	21	26
Family involved in party	21	14	18
Campaign fun/excitement	29	22	26
Material			
Build personal positions in politics	10	8	9
Business contacts	6	3	5
Community recognition	14	7	11
Purposive			
Campaigns influence politics/gov.	45	55	49
Party work influences politics/gov.	47	61	54
Concern with public issues	63	70	66
Other			
Candidate friendship	18	14	16
Party official friendship	22	20	21
Politics is way of life	43	37	40
Close to people doing important things	26	16	21
Fulfill community obligation	42	34	38
Support candidate I believe in	62	65	63

Note: Question asked was: "Rate each of the following in terms of its importance in your personal decision to seek your current party position." Complete wordings of many of these incentives are provided in Table 2.1. The survey did not include comparable detailed questions rating the importance of each motivation in initiating the respondent's interest in politics.

Findings and Interpretations

Importance of Motivations for Activism

Purposive incentives appeared most important in motivating southern grassroots activists to accept their current positions as county committee members or chairs. The motivation cited most frequently by both Democrats and Republicans as *very* important in their personal decisions to seek their current positions was a concern with public issues (table 2.3). Two other motivations that appeared in the top five were also purposive in nature—perceiving campaigns and party work as ways of influencing politics and government. Yet we should recognize that nonpurposive incentives also played an important role in motivating party workers to seek their current positions. The second most frequently cited incentive (out of a list of sixteen items) was a desire to support a candidate in whom one believed, illustrating the importance of the modern candidate-centered style of campaigning and governing that has displaced the primacy of the party bosses as parties have declined in influence throughout this century. Yet while partisanship may be a less central force than in previous decades, it remains an important motivator inasmuch as being strongly attached to a party psychologically is one of the top five incentives of each party's activists. Our study also confirms the relative unimportance of material motivations; business contacts, building a personal political position, and gaining community recognition were the three items cited least frequently by both parties.

More direct comparisons between the two parties provide some interesting insights into the nature of the party organizations in the contemporary South. Democrats appear to be more motivated than Republicans by a diverse range of factors—solidary motives such as friendships and social contacts, the excitement of the campaign, family party involvement, as well as other motives such as community obligation and recognition and being close to important people (table 2.3). Republicans were more motivated than Democrats by purposive incentives—public issues and a desire to influence government. These party differences may be related to the historical position of the Democrats as the majority party in the South, with the most competitive primaries, thereby providing more opportunities for activists to make friends and serve their community. The more ideologically cohesive, minority Republican Party often gained adherents by capitalizing on popular discontent with the increasingly liberal nature of the majority party.

When asked their single *most* important reason for occupying their current party positions, activists in both parties cited a concern over issues (table 2.4). Using party work to influence government, party attachment, and candidate support also remained among the most important goals. When activists were required to prioritize the incentives, other factors emerged as important motivations—a feeling of obligation to the community and seeing politics as a way of life. Apparently, contemporary southern activists are motivated by a diversity of concerns, not simply by purposive goals. However, such material incentives as business contacts and recognition by the community remain among the lowest priorities of both parties. Regarding interparty differences, once again Republicans are more motivated by a concern over public issues and a desire to influence government, while Democrats place a higher priority on their partisan attachments and a perceived obligation to serve the community.

Turning to what first motivated party members to become active in politics, we find the operation of a similar diversity of incentives. A concern with issues was the top priority in both parties, while candidate support, influ-

Table 2.4. Sustaining Incentives by Party
(percentage rating as most important)

Incentive	Democrats	Republicans	All
Solidary			
Strongly attached to party	14	9	12
Friendship/social contacts	3	1	2
Family involved in party	3	2	3
Campaign fun/excitement	1	1	1
Material			
Build personal positions in politics	2	2	2
Business contacts	1	0	0
Community recognition	1	0	1
Purposive			
Campaigns influence politics/gov.	5	7	6
Party work influences politics/gov.	10	20	15
Concern with public issues	16	23	19
Other			
Candidate friendship	5	3	5
Party official friendship	6	5	5
Politics is way of life	10	8	9
Close to people doing important things	1	1	1
Fulfill community obligation	13	8	10
Support candidate I believe in	9	10	9

Note: Sustaining incentives were measured by asking, "Which consideration listed above was the most important in your personal decision to occupy your current party position?"

encing government, party attachment, and a sense of community obligation were other high priorities of both Democrats and Republicans (table 2.5). As with sustaining motivations, Republicans were significantly more motivated than Democrats to start becoming active in politics by purposive incentives such as public issues and a desire to influence government, while Democrats were somewhat more motivated by party attachments and a sense of obligation to the community.

A direct comparison between what motivated party workers first to become active in politics and then to occupy a position in the party organization sheds some light on whether motivations tend to shift from purposive to solidary orientations or whether they tend to remain stable over time. While some individual reasons become more or less important over the years, the broader motivational types remain remarkably unchanged in the

**Table 2.5. Initiating Incentives by Party
(percentage rating as most important)**

Incentive	Democrats	Republicans	All
Solidary			
Strongly attached to party	10	7	9
Friendship/social contacts	3	2	3
Family involved in party	7	5	6
Campaign fun/excitement	3	3	3
Material			
Build personal positions in politics	2	1	2
Business contacts	1	0	0
Community recognition	1	0	1
Purposive			
Campaigns influence politics/gov.	6	7	6
Party work influences politics/gov.	8	16	11
Concern with public issues	19	25	22
Other			
Candidate friendship	6	5	5
Party official friendship	5	4	5
Politics is way of life	5	3	4
Close to people doing important things	2	1	2
Fulfill community obligation	10	7	8
Support candidate I believe in	12	14	13

Note: Initiating incentives were measured by asking, "When you first became active in politics (beyond merely voting), which consideration listed above was the most important?"

aggregate.[4] Regarding purposive incentives, activists of both parties over the years became slightly less motivated by a concern over public issues but somewhat more motivated to use party work as a way to influence government (table 2.6). In terms of solidary goals, reflecting the natural maturation effect of aging and growing apart from one's parents, workers in both parties became somewhat less motivated by their family's partisan involvement as well as the fun and excitement of campaigns. On the other hand, their strong attachments to the parties, as well as their coming to view politics as a way of life (an item correlated with the solidary dimension), became increasingly important motivators.[5] Material incentives were quite stable in every respect, being equally unimportant as motivators for either becoming or remaining active in politics. One factor that did change in priority was candidate support, which became a weaker motivation for both parties' ac-

**Table 2.6. Change in Importance of Incentives for Each Party
(difference in percentage rating as most important)**

Incentive	Democrats	Republicans	All
Solidary			
Strongly attached to party	+4	+2	+3
Friendship/social contacts	0	−1	−1
Family involved in party	−4	−3	−3
Campaign fun/excitement	−2	−2	−2
Material			
Build personal positions in politics	0	+1	0
Business contacts	0	0	0
Community recognition	0	0	0
Purposive			
Campaigns influence politics/gov.	−1	0	0
Party work influences politics/gov.	+2	+4	+4
Concern with public issues	−3	−2	−3
Other			
Candidate friendship	−1	−2	0
Party official friendship	+1	+1	0
Politics is way of life	+5	+5	+5
Close to people doing important things	−1	0	−1
Fulfill community obligation	+3	+1	+2
Support candidate I believe in	−3	−4	−4

Note: Each number reflects the difference between the percentage of activists who ranked that incentive as the most important consideration for first becoming active in politics and the percentage who ranked it the most important consideration for occupying their current party position. A positive sign indicates that the incentive became more important over time, and a negative sign indicates that it became less important.

tivists over time, reflecting the departure from the political scene of an inspiring candidate who first motivated people to become highly active in politics, as well as the absence of equally inspiring successors.

Our study provides some evidential support for both of the conflicting traditions regarding whether motivations shift over time. In response to a changing political environment, the opportunities that it provides in actuality, and changing personal needs, Democratic and Republican activists' specific motivations will indeed tend to shift. However, their more general motivations toward political activity tend to remain the same. Both parties are motivated primarily by purposive incentives and secondarily by solidary concerns (see tables 2.4, 2.5). However, Republicans are especially motivated by purposive incentives, while Democrats appear more motivated

Table 2.7. Incentives and Agents of Recruitment

Incentive	Factor	Factor's categories
Solidary		
Party comm. member	Not consideration (7.3)	Major consideration (8.3)*
County chair	Not consideration (7.6)	Major consideration (8.5)*
Elected official	Not consideration (7.6)	Major consideration (8.8)*
Candidate for office	Not consideration (7.7)	Major consideration (8.8)*
Own decision	Not consideration (7.2)	Major consideration (8.2)*
Most important consideration	Other people (8.0)	Own decision (8.0)
Material		
Party comm. member	Not consideration (3.4)	Major consideration (3.8)*
County chair	Not consideration (3.6)	Major consideration (3.8)*
Elected official	Not consideration (3.4)	Major consideration (4.4)*
Candidate for office	Not consideration (3.5)	Major consideration (4.5)*
Own decision	Not consideration (3.2)	Major consideration (3.9)*
Most important consideration	Other people (3.6)	Own decision (3.8)*
Purposive		
Party comm. member	Not consideration (8.0)	Major consideration (8.3)*
County chair	Not consideration (8.1)	Major consideration (8.3)*
Elected official	Not consideration (8.1)	Major consideration (8.3)*
Candidate for office	Not consideration (8.1)	Major consideration (8.6)*
Own decision	Not consideration (7.6)	Major consideration (8.5)*
Most important consideration	Other people (8.1)	Own decision (8.3)*

Note: Cell entries are means of the solidary, material, and purposive scales for subgroups listed. Means range from low scores for unimportant considerations to high scores for very important considerations. The solidary scale ranges from 1 to 13, and the material and purposive scales range from 1 to 10.
*Indicates t test result for difference between means is statistically significant at .05 level.

than Republicans by solidary concerns as well as an obligation to serve the community.

The Correlates of Motivational Incentives

Very few studies have examined the correlates of incentives for activism, focusing instead on the relative importance of these incentives and whether they tend to change over time. Surprisingly, agent of recruitment to party office is related to all three types of incentives, rather than to only one type, such as solidary goals. Those saying that party committee members, county chairs, elected officials, and candidates for office were major considerations in their decision to seek their current party office rated solidary, material, and purposive incentives as more important than did those claiming that such political figures were not considerations (table 2.7). However, solidary incentives were most highly related, and purposive motivations least related, to socialization agents. Furthermore, when asked the *most* important consideration for seeking their party positions, additional differentiation of motives emerged: those saying that they had decided to run pretty much on their own rated purposive and material incentives somewhat more highly than did those citing any of the four types of political activists, while solidary incentives were not differentiating factors.

Motivational incentives are significantly related to level of political activity. Furthermore, amount and variety of motivation appear more important in inducing activism than does any one type of motivation. Those reporting high activity in local, state, and national campaigns rated solidary, material, and purposive incentives as very important in their decisions to seek the party office they were currently holding (table 2.8). However, solidary incentives did exert a greater impact than other incentives on level of party position and personal importance of the party position. County chairs and those considering their party positions as being personally important rated solidary incentives as a substantially more important motivation than did county committee members and those devaluing their party position.

Partisan intensity is also related to all three types of incentives, as strong partisans rated solidary, material, and purposive incentives as more important than did weak partisans and independents (tables 2.9, 2.10). However, within both parties differences in magnitudes are evident for each type of incentive: solidary incentives appear most highly related to partisan intensity, while material incentives are least important. Among Democrats the same patterns emerge for the 1988 presidential vote, where Dukakis voters rated each incentive as more important than did Bush defectors, with solidary incentives most important and material incentives least important. No significant relations between the vote and incentives emerge among Republicans.

While solidary incentives appear to play a special role in promoting partisanship, purposive incentives exert a special impact on ideological considerations, especially among Republicans. Republicans who are conservative or very conservative rate purposive incentives as more important than do liberals and moderates (table 2.9). On the other hand, there is some tendency for less conservative Republicans to rate solidary and especially material incentives as more important than do conservatives. Hence, ideological dissidents from the conservative nature of the contemporary southern Republican Party are able to derive some satisfaction from nonpolicy reasons for party activism. Liberal Democrats are more likely than conserva-

Table 2.8. Incentives and Party Involvement

Incentive	Factor	Factor's categories
Solidary		
Party position	County comm. member (8.0)	County chair (8.5)*
Personal importance of being county comm.		
member	Not Important (5.9)	Very Important (9.4)*
Local elect. activity	Not Active (6.5)	Very Active (8.7)*
State elect. activity	Not Active (6.0)	Very Active (8.9)*
Nat. elect. activity	Not Active (6.8)	Very Active (8.8)*
Material		
Party Position	County comm. member (3.7)	County chair (3.8)*
Personal importance of being county comm.		
member	Not important (2.7)	Very important (4.3)*
Local elect. activity	Not active (2.9)	Very active (4.0)*
State elect. activity	Not active (2.9)	Very active (3.9)*
Nat. elect. activity	Not active (3.5)	Very active (3.7)*
Purposive		
Party position	County comm. member (8.2)	County chair (8.4)*
Personal importance of being county comm.		
member	Not important (7.2)	Very important (8.8)*
Local elect. activity	Not active (7.4)	Very active (8.5)*
State elect. activity	Not active (6.7)	Very active (8.7)*
Nat. elect. activity	Not active (7.2)	Very active (8.8)*

Note: Cell entries are means of the solidary, material, and purposive scales for subgroups listed. Means range from low scores for unimportant considerations to high scores for very important considerations. The solidary scale ranges from 1 to 13, and the material and purposive scales range from 1 to 10.

*Indicates t test result for difference between means is statistically significant at .05 level.

tives to rate all three types of incentives as very important, though material incentives are least related to ideological concerns (table 2.10).

The next chapter thoroughly examines activists' styles, such as their amateur/professional orientations. As a transition to that topic, we find that a diverse range of incentives appears to be related to a more professional orientation, suggesting that professionals may be more psychologically involved in politics than amateurs.[6] The two most important sources of a professional orientation are solidary incentives and a strong attachment to the party (table 2.11). Interpersonal relations are highly related to a professional orientation in other ways as well, as those rating friendships with a

Table 2.9. Incentives and Partisan-Ideological Orientations of Republicans

Incentive	Factor	Factor's categories
Solidary		
1988 Pres. vote[a]	Dukakis (7.2)	Bush (7.7)
State party identif.	Not strong Rep. (6.1)	Strong Rep. (8.0)*
Nat. party identif.	Not strong Rep. (6.0)	Strong Rep. (7.9)*
Ideology	Conservative (7.7)	Liberal, moderate (7.7)
Issues scale	Conservative (7.4)	Liberal, moderate (8.1)*
Ideology	Not very conservative (7.6)	Very conservative (7.7)
Issue scale	Very conservative (7.2)	Not very conservative (7.9)*
Material		
1988 Pres. vote[a]	Bush (3.4)	Dukakis (3.8)
State party identif.	Not strong Rep. (3.2)	Strong Rep. (3.4)*
Nat. party identif.	Not strong Rep. (3.2)	Strong Rep. (3.4)*
Ideology	Conservative (3.3)	Liberal, moderate (3.6)*
Issues scale	Conservative (3.2)	Liberal, moderate (3.7)*
Ideology	Very conservative (3.2)	Not very conservative (3.5)*
Issue scale	Very conservative (3.1)	Not very conservative (3.5)*
Purposive		
1988 Pres. vote[a]	Dukakis (8.3)	Bush (8.5)
State party identif.	Not strong Rep. (8.1)	Strong Rep. (8.6)*
Nat. party identif.	Not strong Rep. (8.1)	Strong Rep. (8.6)*
Ideology	Liberal, moderate (8.2)	Conservative (8.6)*
Issues scale	Liberal, moderate (8.3)	Conservative (8.6)*
Ideology	Not very conservative (8.3)	Very conservative (8.8)*
Issue scale	Not very conservative (8.4)	Very conservative (8.7)*

Note: Cell entries are means of the solidary, material, and purposive scales for subgroups listed. Means range from low scores for unimportant considerations to high scores for very important considerations. The solidary scale ranges from 1 to 13, and the material and purposive scales range from 1 to 10.

[a]Only thirty-three Republicans voted for Dukakis.

*Indicates t test result for difference between means is statistically significant at .05 level.

candidate or with a political party official as very important in their decision to seek their current party position were significantly more likely to be professionals than were those rating friendships as unimportant. A sense of community obligation, material incentives, and believing in a candidate were other incentives that were somewhat related to a professional orientation. Amateurs appear to possess a far narrower range of motivations, as the only incentive related to an amateuristic style was a purposive one, and that was the case solely for Republicans.

Table 2.10. Incentives and Partisan-Ideological Orientations of Democrats

Incentive	Factor	Factor's categories
Solidary		
1988 Pres. vote	Bush (6.6)	Dukakis (8.8)*
State party identif.	Not strong Dem. (6.1)	Strong Dem. (8.9)*
Nat. party identif.	Not strong Dem. (6.9)	Strong Dem. (9.0)*
Ideology	Conservative (8.0)	Liberal (8.8)*
Issues scale	Conservative (7.2)	Liberal (8.8)*
Ideology	Not very liberal (8.4)	Very liberal (8.8)*
Issue scale	Not very liberal (8.1)	Very liberal (9.0)*
Material		
1988 Pres. vote	Bush (3.7)	Dukakis (4.0)*
State party identif.	Not strong Dem. (3.4)	Strong Dem. (4.1)*
Nat. party identif.	Not strong Dem. (3.8)	Strong Dem. (4.0)*
Ideology	Conservative (3.8)	Liberal (4.0)*
Issues scale	Conservative (3.6)	Liberal (4.1)*
Ideology	Not very liberal (3.9)	Very liberal (4.1)
Issue scale	Not very liberal (3.8)	Very liberal (4.3)*
Purposive		
1988 Pres. vote	Bush (7.0)	Dukakis (8.2)*
State party identif.	Not strong Dem. (6.9)	Strong Dem. (8.1)*
Nat. party identif.	Not strong Dem. (7.3)	Strong Dem. (8.2)*
Ideology	Conservative (7.5)	Liberal (8.4)*
Issues scale	Conservative (7.3)	Liberal (8.2)*
Ideology	Not very liberal (7.9)	Very liberal (8.6)*
Issue scale	Not very liberal (7.6)	Very liberal (8.6)*

Note: Cell entries are means of the solidary, material, and purposive scales for subgroups listed. Means range from low scores for unimportant considerations to high scores for very important considerations. The solidary scale ranges from 1 to 13, and the material and purposive scales range from 1 to 10.
*Indicates t test result for difference between means is statistically significant at .05 level.

Conclusions

The decline of party machines and the rise of voter independence has led some scholars and journalists to focus on the weaknesses of contemporary American parties, producing books such as Crotty's *American Parties in Decline* (1984) and Broder's *The Party's Over* (1972). More recent studies have suggested a surprising resilience of the party organizations themselves, as local and county party organizations in the late 1970s and early 1980s appeared to be stronger and more active than in previous years, prompting one scholar to conclude that organizations had shown qualities of "adap-

Table 2.11. Incentives for Party Activism among Amateurs and Professionals

Incentive for seeking current party position	Factor	Factor's categories
Solidary incentives	Not important (5.8)	Very important (7.8)*
Strong party attachment	Not important (5.6)	Very important (7.5)*
Friends with party official	Not important (6.2)	Very important (7.4)*
Candidate friendship	Not important (6.4)	Very important (7.6)*
Community obligation	Not important (6.4)	Very important (7.3)*
Material incentives	Not important (6.4)	Very important (7.2)*
Belief in candidate	Not important (6.4)	Very important (7.1)*
Purposive incentives (Rep. only)	Very important (6.2)	Not important (6.4)*
Purposive incentives (Dem. only)	Not important (7.1)	Very important (7.4)*

Note: Cell entries are means of the amateur/professional scale for the subgroups listed. Means range from 1 for most amateuristic to 13 for most professional.
*Indicates t test result for difference between means is statistically significant at .05 level.

tiveness and durability in a changing and frequently hostile political environment" (Bibby, 1992: 118; see also Gibson et al., 1985). Our study of grassroots party members' incentives for activism also highlights the strengths of the parties in adapting to a rapidly changing environment in a region that has been experiencing dramatic partisan change for decades.

Southern party organization members in our study exhibit significant durability and stability in their attachments to general purposive, solidary, or material incentives as the years go by, consistent with other recent studies that have examined campaign workers, contributors, and convention delegates (Roback, 1980a; Hedges, 1984; Miller, Jewell, and Sigelman, 1987). Southern party activists mirror the organizations nationally in being primarily motivated by purposive incentives, secondarily shaped by solidary motives, and least affected by material incentives, which are largely unavailable (Conway and Feigert, 1968; Bowman, Ippolito, and Donaldson, 1969). And while contemporary southern party activists do not exhibit the movement away from purposive incentives found in these early landmark studies, some do demonstrate an adaptiveness to their political environment that provides lessons in party building.

Attractive candidates and exciting campaigns provide an important opportunity to recruit for long-term party organizational work those backing a specific candidate. Intergenerational transmission of partisanship also plays some role, as the motivation for some people to become active is their family's involvement in a party. As time passes and these initial solidary incentives and candidate stimuli fade away, some remain active in the party for other solidary-related reasons, coming to see politics as a way of life and becoming more motivated by strong party attachments. Contrary to early studies in other parts of the country, party organizations in the contemporary South may actually enhance and channel purposive motivations over the years. In both parties, activists exhibit a slight decline in motivation by a general concern over public issues, as they come to view party work specifically as a way of influencing government.

The differing emphases of incentives between the two parties also show an impressive ability of the contemporary southern party organizations to adapt to their political environment. Republican activists are motivated more by purposive incentives, as the GOP organization capitalizes on the popularity of its party's more conservative candidates (as in presidential elections) in the most conservative region of the nation. Southern Democrats cope with an ideologically divided party organization in their region and a less popular national party of a more liberal bent by relying on nonpurposive incentives. They are motivated somewhat more by friendships and social contacts, such as relationships with candidates and party officials, and by family and community ties. Democrats are also affected more by strong partisan attachments and views of politics as a way of life, and some even find material rewards for activism.

Party differences among contemporary southern grassroots activists are not consistent with Conway and Feigert's (1968) hypothesis that majority party members may exhibit greater satisfaction with purposive incentives due to their greater ability to influence public policy, but they are consistent with Roback's (1980a) discovery of the greater importance of purposive motivations to convention delegates backing more ideological candidates such as Ronald Reagan. The more ideologically extreme members of each southern party organization today are especially motivated by purposive incentives. Compared to more moderate party members, liberal and very liberal Democrats and conservative and very conservative Republicans regard purposive incentives as very important motivations.

Our study also sheds light on the little-researched areas of what motivational types are recruited for party activity by the political establishment and the implications of motivational incentives for electoral activity and amateur/professional stylistic orientations. Party and elected officials appear to seek the most highly motivated people to join the southern party organizations, as those encouraged by these establishment figures rate all three types of incentives—solidary, material, and purposive—as important considerations in their decision to seek their current party position. One payoff of recruiting such highly motivated people is that their party positions become very important personally to them, and they tend to work hard in their positions, becoming highly active in election campaigns at local, state, and national levels. We confirm Abramowitz, McGlennon, and Rapoport's (1983) conclusion that purposive motivations are not necessarily destructive to a party's goal of seeking winnable candidates, since purposive motives are correlated to campaign involvement and organizational loyalty. We also point out that such activism is not confined to those having purposive incentives and that attachment to solidary or material incentives also serves to motivate one to be intensely partisan and highly involved in political campaigns.

While party leaders may wish to continue to seek out highly motivated people attracted by a diverse range of incentives, there is a special advantage to targeting those possessing solidary and related motivations. Those most highly valuing solidary incentives, party attachments, and party and candidate friendships are especially likely to possess professional rather than amateuristic stylistic orientations. Such professionals avoid association with intraparty factions and help to keep the party organization unified behind the party's nominee and an inclusive platform in order to win the general election. The most central members of the local party organizations—county chairs—are especially likely to be motivated by solidary incentives. Such pragmatic professionals motivated by solidary goals help to counteract the more ideologically extreme views of their party colleagues motivated more by purposive incentives.

In short, the party isn't over for grassroots party activists in the New South, as both parties show significant durability and adaptability. While Republicans are more motivated by purposive incentives and Democrats by solidary incentives and other factors, neither party is monolithic in its motivations. And the differences in tendencies between the southern parties appear rational adaptations to their political environment, rather than dysfunctional to their organizational goals. As the South is a more conservative region, the candidates nominated by Republicans promoting a conservative philosophy will not necessarily be too extreme for voters (though as chapter 10 suggests, this possibility is nevertheless present). Southern Democrats can compensate for the relative unpopularity of their national party's liberalism by shying away from an issue-oriented style and by emphasizing historical party loyalty and the importance of friendships and interpersonal ties forged in party work.

3
Purist versus Pragmatic Orientations

Charles Prysby

What kinds of people choose to be active in political party organizations? This simple question has been the focus of a great deal of research. The question has attracted considerable attention because many political analysts believe that the nature of the party organization is affected by the characteristics of the active members. In particular, both commentators and scholars have voiced concerns that party activists increasingly are uncompromising ideologues who worry more about ideological purity than electoral victory. The result is a new style of partisan politics, one that is more issue oriented, less amenable to compromise, and less likely to produce a broad consensus in the body politic.

Examining party organizations is worthwhile even though political parties have been in protracted decay according to many accounts (Broder, 1972; Burnham, 1982; Crotty, 1984). Evidence of such decay would include the erosion of voter loyalty to the party (Wattenberg, 1984). Others suggest, however, that the argument for party decline is debatable. National and state political party organizations are in many ways stronger than ever (Cotter et al., 1984; Gibson et al., 1983; Kayden and Mahe, 1985). Even at the local level, activity persists. In some areas, local political party organizations may be even stronger than in the past (Gibson et al., 1985). Recent research has established that political party organizations remain worthy of study even in an antiparty age (Maisel, 1990; Miller and Jennings, 1986; Sabato, 1988). This study begins from that premise. It assumes that political parties are critical institutions for the functioning of American democracy and that understanding these organizations is essential for a complete understanding of the American political system.

Political party organizations in the South are especially fascinating. The growth of Republican electoral success has encouraged the development of Republican Party organization at the state level, although local level developments are more questionable (Gibson et al., 1985; Bullock, 1988, 1991). The Democrats, faced with increased competition, have in many cases responded with greater emphasis on party organization, something that in the past frequently received little attention. The development of party organizations is an important aspect of political change in the South (Baker et al., 1990; Hadley and Bowman, 1995).

The Orientations of Party Activists

Political party organizations are made up of individuals who have chosen to devote time to political activity. Most of these individuals are active at the local level, in their county party organizations. These grassroots activists are an important component of the party organizations. Their significance may have been diminished by new campaign technology and an increase in candidate-centered campaigns. They may be less important than the party's officeholders, or the party's top state officials, or potential contributors to the party. But grassroots activists are still valued, and their attitudes and behavior affect the parties. They can influence the recruitment of candidates at the local level, impose constraints on issues that are stressed by party candidates in campaigns, and help shape the party's public image.

Wilson's (1962) study of Democratic activists introduced a new concept that has had a profound impact on research on political parties: amateur versus professional activists. Wilson differentiated amateurs from professionals along several dimensions. For our purposes, the most important difference is that amateurs are more concerned with their party taking the correct position on issues, even if it might impede electoral success, whereas professionals are primarily concerned with winning office and see issues as a means to that end. We can conceptualize this dimension as a purist/pragmatist continuum. At one end of the continuum are extreme purists, who emphasize ideological correctness regardless of its electoral consequences. At the other end are extreme pragmatists, who are concerned solely with victory and care nothing about issues. Viewed this way, few if any activists are complete purists or pragmatists; almost all fall between these two extremes. But activists can be distinguished by the degree of their purism; some are relatively more purist or relatively more pragmatic.

Wilson also distinguished amateurs from professionals by their motives for being involved in party politics. These motives can be divided into three types: purposive, solidary, and material (Clark and Wilson, 1961). The distinction between these three types is discussed in the previous chapter. Compared to professionals, amateurs are driven much more by purposive motives. Amateurs further differ from professionals in their concern for intraparty democracy, something that professionals place little value on. But while amateurs favor strong internal democracy, they want their party to be programmatic and cohesive. Amateurs believe that a party should stand for clear policy goals.

The multidimensional nature of Wilson's amateur/professional concept creates problems in utilizing it in empirical research (Hofstetter, 1971).

While the terms *amateur* and *professional* are frequently used in the research literature, quite often the authors use the terms to refer to only one of the dimensions outlined by Wilson, such as motives for participation in political parties. In the situation where the researcher is interested in one aspect of the amateur/professional difference and is not willing to assume that the other aspects of the difference are necessarily present, a preferable approach would be to use terminology that explicitly identifies the dimension being studied.

This study is concerned with the relative emphasis that activists place on issues versus winning office. To make that clear, the terms *purist* and *pragmatist* are used (Polsby and Wildavsky, 1996). Although we may call individuals purists or pragmatists, it should be understood that these are relative terms. As indicated previously, pristine purists or pragmatists are not to be found. No one is solely focused on ideology, without any worry about winning office, nor is any activist completely devoid of concern for issues. But activists do differ greatly in the relative emphasis that they place on these matters.

One of the themes in the literature on American politics over the past twenty-five years is the growth of issue-oriented party activism. This phenomenon has been examined especially as it relates to presidential nominations. Studies of delegates to presidential nominating conventions in the 1960s and 1970s pointed out the growth in issue-oriented delegates (Clarke, Elliott, and Roback, 1991; Roback, 1980a, 1980b; Soule and McGrath, 1975). In some cases, authors identified the dire consequences of this development (Kirkpatrick, 1976; Soule and McGrath, 1975). Other researchers argued that the dangers of increased purism were greatly exaggerated (Abramowitz, McGlennon, and Rapoport, 1983; Hauss and Maisel, 1986; Stone and Abramowitz, 1983). Activists might be more concerned with issues than in the past, but they still might have a healthy concern with winning elections and a substantial degree of party loyalty (see, for example, Maggiotto and Weber, 1986).

While disagreement exists over the ideal mix of purism and pragmatism, consensus exists on many of the sources of purism. One obvious expectation is that purist orientations are linked to purposive motives for participating in political parties. As discussed, both dimensions were seen by Wilson (1962) as part of a broader amateur/professional difference. Moreover, it seems logical that individuals who participate in party politics because they want to have an effect on public policies (a purposive motivation for involvement) should be more purist in their party orientations than individuals who participate because they like the excitement of campaigns or enjoy the organizational involvement.

Another common hypothesis is that purist activists will be more ideologically extreme, a hypothesis based on the assumption that individuals with more moderate views are more willing to compromise. Among Democrats, extreme liberals should be more purist than moderates; among Republicans, extreme conservatives should be more purist than moderates. Thus, in both parties more moderate and more pragmatic activists conflict with more extreme and more purist activists. The presidential nominations of Barry Goldwater by the Republicans in 1964 and George McGovern by the Democrats in 1972 are held up as examples of purist victories in the nomination process, followed by—as the moderates in the party would be quick to emphasize—a predictable defeat in the general election. Most of the empirical research in this area does find that purism and ideology are linked in the expected direction (Abramowitz and Stone, 1984; Clarke, Elliott, and Roback, 1991; Hitlin and Jackson, 1977; Soule and McGrath, 1975). However, at least one study fails to find the predicted relationship (Soule and Clarke, 1970).

Demographic factors also should affect party orientations. Younger activists are expected to be more purist than older ones (Hitlin and Jackson, 1977; Shaffer, 1990; Soule and Clarke, 1970). The difference could be the result of aging (i.e., growing older mellows one politically) or of generational differences (i.e., younger activists grew up and were socialized in a more ideologically charged era). Moreover, older activists are more likely to have been involved in party politics longer, which may promote pragmatism, and they are more likely to hold party office, which may increase pragmatic orientations (Abramowitz and Stone, 1984; Hitlin and Jackson, 1977; Soule and Clarke, 1970). Education also may play a role, as more educated activists have a greater comprehension of and affinity for the ideological questions that underlie specific public policy issues (Hitlin and Jackson, 1977; Soule and Clarke, 1970). Gender and race also could be relevant. Having been relatively excluded from politics, especially in the South, women and blacks might be more purist in their orientations.

The consequences of purist orientations are as important as the sources of these attitudes. Purists have been portrayed as individuals who will not work for the party if they disapprove of the party's nominee (Abramowitz, McGlennon, and Rapoport, 1983). They display candidate, not party, loyalty. Pragmatists are frequently seen as the loyal soldiers of the party, faithfully working to elect the party's candidates regardless of their personal affinity for the individuals. If this is so, the implications for the party organization of including many purists are obvious. An increase in purist activists in the party also may affect the nomination process. The strong candidate loyalty and commitment to issues of the purists may lead to more conflict over the nomination of party candidates. More divisive primaries (or conventions, in the few states where this method of nominating candidates is employed) may harm the chances of the party nominees in the general election.

Analyzing Party Orientations

The 1991 Southern Grassroots Party Activists survey provides an excellent data set for analyzing the research questions and hypotheses discussed here. While much of the research on the orientations of party activists has examined delegates to state or national party conventions in a presidential election year, this study focuses on grassroots party activists, such as county and precinct chairs, in a nonelection year (although two of the eleven states in the study, Louisiana and Mississippi, conducted state elections in 1991). While presidential-year convention delegates overlap with grassroots party activists, there are important differences between the two, making it desirable to study both groups.

The central concept of this study is the degree of purism or pragmatism among party activists. This variable is measured by a "purist index" that combines the responses to three position statements: (1) good party workers support any candidate nominated by the party even if they basically disagree with the candidate; (2) party organization and unity are more important than free and total discussion of issues that may divide the party; (3) controversial positions should be avoided in a party platform to ensure party unity.[1] The resulting purist index has a ten-point scale, with a 10 being the most purist position and 1 the least purist, or most pragmatic, position.

The distribution of Democratic and Republican grassroots party activists on the purist index is displayed in table 3.1. Relatively few activists in either party are extreme pragmatists or extreme purists; about 8 percent of all activists fall in the top two categories of the scale, and a similar percentage falls in the bottom two categories. The index indicates significant differences between the parties, however. Strong purists are more prevalent among Republicans; nearly 20 percent of the Republican activists are in the top three categories, compared to about 11 percent of the Democrats. The mean score on the purist index for Republicans (6.14) is nearly a full point higher than the mean score for Democrats (5.23), a very substantial difference.

Why should southern Republican grassroots activists be significantly more purist than their Democratic counterparts? One possibility is that this difference simply reflects the demographic differences between the two parties. As noted here, the literature indicates that age, education, gender, and race are all potentially related to purism. Southern Republican activists are more likely than Democrats to be white and are better educated and younger—differences that reflect in large part the types of voters each party appeals to in the South (Prysby, 1990; Wattenberg, 1991). However, the gender composition of both sets of activists does not differ—men were about 63 percent of both the Democratic and Republican activists—even though in recent years Democrats have appealed somewhat more to women in the electorate.

Table 3.1. Purist Orientations by Party (in percentage)

Purist index	Democrats	Republicans	All activists
1. Most pragmatic	4.6	1.6	3.2
2	6.1	2.2	4.3
3	9.3	4.7	7.1
4	15.2	10.5	13.0
5	17.4	15.2	16.3
6	19.4	21.5	20.4
7	16.7	23.5	19.9
8	6.1	9.9	7.9
9	2.7	6.0	4.3
10. Most purist	2.4	5.0	3.6
Mean index score	5.23	6.14	5.66
(N)	(5098)	(4607)	(9705)

Note: See text for details on purist index.

How much of the difference in purism between Democratic and Republican southern grassroots party activists is the result of simple demographic differences? The answer can be determined through a multiple regression analysis in which demographic characteristics and party are used to predict purism.[2] Table 3.2 presents the results of such an analysis. Among the demographic characteristics, age has the greatest effect. Education has a modest effect in the predicted direction. Gender has only a very slight effect, and the impact of race is the opposite of what was expected, as we find black activists to be less purist. But the most important finding in table 3.2 is that the party differences remain even when all four demographic variables are controlled. In fact, holding these characteristics constant only marginally diminishes the party differences. The overall difference between the mean scores for the two parties (see table 3.1) is about .9, whereas the partisan difference with demographic factors controlled is about .8 (see the regression coefficient for party in table 3.2). Thus, demographic differences between Democratic and Republican activists account for only a very small amount of the difference in purist orientations.

The greater degree of purism among Republican activists could well be due to the motivations that are behind involvement in the party organization. The previous chapter focuses on the incentives for activism and finds that Republicans are more likely to be motivated by purposive goals. This difference in the motivational basis for involvement probably is a result of the newly emerging status of the Republican Party in the South. We should

Table 3.2. Regression Analysis of Purist Orientations

Independent variable	b (SE)	Beta	t Score (p <)
Age	-.029 (.001)	-.20	-19.59 (.01)
Gender	.094 (.042)	.02	2.24 (.03)
Race	-.608 (.068)	-.09	-8.95 (.01)
Education	.169 (.019)	.09	9.05 (.01)
Party	.769 (.041)	.19	18.80 (.01)
Constant	6.035 (.169)		

$R^2 = .11$
$N = 9254$

Note: These data are the results of a multiple regression analysis with the purist index as the dependent variable. The regression coefficient (with standard error), beta coefficient, and t score (with significance level) are listed for each independent variable.

expect that involvement in the minority party in an area will be more heavily based on purposive incentives (Bowman and Boynton, 1966b; Conway and Feigert, 1968). Even as that party moves toward a competitive position, purposive incentives should still predominate for some period of time, especially when the growth of the party is fueled by a strong emphasis on issues and ideology.

Activists were asked why they first became involved in party politics and why they sought their current party position. In both cases, they were asked to identify the most important reason from a list of sixteen possibilities, ranging from concern with public issues to a desire to make business contacts. These possible reasons have been dichotomized into purposive and other motives.[3] Table 3.3 presents the mean scores on the purist index by participation motives and by party. Within each party, it is clear that those who identified purposive motivations, for either first or current involvement, are more purist than those identifying other reasons for participating. The average difference between the purposive and the other category is about .65 on the purist index. However, even when we examine activists with similar motives, substantial party differences (about .8 on the purist index) remain. In fact, Democrats who claim to have been motivated primarily by purposive goals have lower levels of purism than Republicans who identify other motives for involvement. Although clear differences exist between Democratic and Republican activists in terms of motivational base, these differences account for very little of the party differences in purism.

Ideological differences between Democrats and Republicans could account for the differences in party orientations. The Democratic Party in the

Table 3.3. Purist Orientations by Participation Motives and Party

	Democrats		Republicans	
Participation motives	Mean (SD)	N	Mean (SD)	N
Motive for current participation				
Purposive	5.65 (1.98)	1974	6.44 (1.83)	2639
Other	4.95 (2.04)	2906	5.72 (1.94)	1786
Motive for first participation				
Purposive	5.58 (2.04)	2237	6.36 (1.89)	2793
Other	4.95 (2.01)	2708	5.80 (1.91)	1700

Note: Entries are mean scores on the purist index, with standard deviations in parentheses. The reasons that party activists gave for first becoming involved and for seeking their current party positions have been classified as purposive or other in nature. See text for discussion of this classification.

contemporary South encompasses a wide span of individuals, from strong liberals to moderate conservatives, whereas most Republicans are clearly conservative, many of them strongly so (Moreland, 1990a). The discussion of ideology in chapter 5 of this volume elaborates on this point. As discussed previously, much of the literature argues that purism and ideological extremism are linked. Therefore, the southern Democratic grassroots party activists may be more pragmatic than their Republican counterparts because they are ideologically more moderate.

This hypothesis is easily tested. Table 3.4 presents mean scores on the purist index broken down by party and ideology. A look at the Ns in each category confirms that Republican activists are a fairly cohesive conservative group; very few call themselves liberals of any kind, and only about one in eight even identifies as a moderate. Democratic activists are a more heterogenous group, including not only many moderates but even a sizable number who call themselves somewhat conservative. But these clear differences in ideology are largely unrelated to the differences in purism. There is very little difference in purism among the Democratic activists as we go from strong liberals down to those who are somewhat conservative (there are too few in the most conservative category to analyze). Among Republican activists, those who are very conservative are more purist than those who are somewhat conservative, but the moderates rank a close second in their level of purism. Overall, the relationship between ideology and purism within each party is fairly weak, contrary to what was expected.

The view of southern Republicans as having an extremely conservative wing that is highly purist can be examined from another perspective. A number of observers have argued that the Republican Party in the South is

Table 3.4. Purist Orientations by Ideology and Party

	Democrats		Republicans	
Ideological placement	Mean (SD)	N	Mean (SD)	N
Very liberal	5.23 (2.04)	499	4.92 (2.75)	13
Somewhat liberal	5.14 (1.94)	136	6.02 (2.18)	90
Moderate	5.19 (1.93)	1743	6.20 (1.90)	573
Somewhat conservative	5.36 (2.06)	1114	6.03 (1.80)	2141
Very conservative	5.57 (2.55)	26	6.29 (2.04)	1747

Note: Entries are mean scores on the purist index, with standard deviations in parentheses.

becoming a home for an increasingly active religious right (Baker, 1990; Green and Guth, 1988). These activists may be particularly purist in orientation, as they are concerned especially with moral and social issues, which are less amenable to compromise. Perhaps it is this set of party activists from the Christian right who account for the more purist character of the Republican Party.

Unfortunately, the survey data do not contain direct measures of involvement in or support for the Christian or religious right. The best we can do is to examine the relationship of religiosity to purist orientations. Two measures of religiosity are available: (1) church attendance and (2) identifying oneself as fundamentalist, evangelical, charismatic, or "born again" Christian. These are admittedly imperfect measures, as some individuals who attend church regularly and describe themselves as fundamentalist or evangelical are nevertheless not supporters of the religious right, much less participants in the movement (Baker, 1990).

Table 3.5 presents mean scores on the purist index broken down by party and religiosity for white Protestant activists. African Americans and non-Protestants are not included because we would not expect greater religiosity among these individuals to translate into support for the Christian right. We do find that among Republicans the more religious tend to be more purist, but the differences are only modest in nature. It is possible that within the set of Republicans who are regular church attenders there is a core of extremely purist adherents of the Christian right, but this would have to be a very small group. Furthermore, even the Republican activists who attend church infrequently score fairly high on the purist index, and the same is true for those who do not describe themselves in terms such as *fundamentalist* or *evangelical*. Among Democrats, the less religious tend to be somewhat more purist in their party orientations, a pattern that is both unexpected and difficult to explain.

At the grassroots level, county party chairs are the most important indi-

Table 3.5. Purist Orientations by Religiosity and Party

	Democrats		Republicans	
Religiosity	Mean (SD)	N	Mean (SD)	N
Church attendance				
Once a week	5.16 (2.05)	1490	6.33 (1.95)	1909
Almost every week	5.24 (2.03)	639	6.04 (1.77)	628
Once a month	5.36 (1.94)	362	6.02 (1.86)	371
Few times a year	5.27 (1.99)	649	6.00 (1.86)	599
Never	5.43 (2.07)	111	6.38 (1.93)	109
Self-identification				
Fundamentalist, evangelical, Charismatic, and/or "Born Again"	5.02 (2.05)	1767	6.30 (1.95)	2044
None of the above	5.47 (1.96)	1508	6.05 (1.83)	1595

Note: Data are for white Protestants only. Entries are mean scores on the purist index, with standard deviations in parentheses. See text for details on measures of religiosity.

viduals in the party organization, making them an especially interesting group to analyze. Table 3.6 shows the scores on the purist index for county party chairs and other members, broken down by party. We see that in each party, county party chairs are significantly more pragmatic than the rank and file. Two explanations exist for this relationship. First, individuals who are more pragmatic may be more likely to be chosen county chairs. Second, the role of being a county chair may alter the individual's orientations (Maggiotto and Weber, 1986). But the party difference in purist orientations clearly remains, even when we focus on this strategically important group. This finding suggests that the differences in party orientations among grassroots activists have a real impact on the nature of the party organizations.

Table 3.6. Purist Orientations by Position and Party

	Democrats		Republicans	
Position	Mean (SD)	N	Mean (SD)	N
County chair	4.83 (1.92)	588	5.85 (1.82)	584
Member	5.28 (2.06)	4509	6.19 (1.93)	4023

Note: Entries are mean scores on the purist index, with standard deviations in parentheses.

Consequences of Party Orientations

It might be tempting to infer from the preceding analysis that the stronger purist orientations in the Republican Party will hamper its ability to sustain electoral growth. But while Republicans are more purist than Democrats, it does not follow that purist orientations among Republicans are so strong as to make the party ideologically rigid. The mean score on the purist index for Republicans is 6.14; a score of 6.0 would be achieved by disagreeing (but not strongly so) with two of the three position statements and agreeing with one of them. While there are some highly purist Republican activists, the center of gravity for the party does not seem extreme.

One supposed consequence of having more purist activists in a party is that organizational and campaign work will suffer, a point discussed earlier. Purists, it is argued, will be less likely to work consistently for the party. When they become ideologically disaffected, as can easily happen, they respond by being less involved. The extent to which purist orientations are related to campaign involvement among grassroots activists is examined in two ways in this study. First of all, an index of campaign activity was constructed. This index measures the range of campaign activities that grassroots activists reported engaging in during recent elections; the more activities reported, the higher the individual's score on the index.[4] Second, an index of election work was constructed. This index measures the degree of involvement in local, state, and national election campaigns reported by activists; a higher score indicates greater overall involvement.[5]

In addition to party orientation, a number of other variables should affect the party activity and election work of activists. County chairs should be more active than others in the county party organization. Those who have been involved in the party organization for a longer time should display more activity. Also, demographic variables may play a role. In order to distinguish the effects of purist orientations on activity and work from the confounding effects of other factors, a number of relevant variables were used to predict party activity and election work. The results of multiple regression analyses of these two dimensions of behavior are found in tables 3.7 and 3.8.

Similar patterns exist in both tables. Purist orientations do lead to less campaign involvement, but the impact is small, at least when other variables are held constant. County chairs, as one would expect, engage in more work than others in the party. Those who have been involved in the party for a longer period of time also are more likely to work. Demographic variables have less impact overall, although some significant effects exist. Finally, there are definite party differences. Republican activists report more activity and more work. This is a very interesting finding. Even though the Republicans are more purist, the party does not appear to have a problem in

Table 3.7. Regression Analysis of Party Activity

Independent variable	b (SE)	Beta	t Score (p <)
Purist index	-.119 (.015)	-.08	-7.85 (.01)
Party position	-1.862 (.091)	-.21	-20.56 (.01)
Years active in politics	.011 (.002)	.05	4.57 (.01)
Gender	.536 (.062)	.09	8.60 (.01)
Race	-.005 (.015)	-.01	-.37 (.71)
Education	.336 (.002)	.05	4.57 (.01)
Party	.828 (.061)	.14	13.64 (.01)
Constant	5.280 (.252)		

$R^2 = .09$
N = 9165

Note: These data are the results of a multiple regression analysis with the party activity index as the dependent variable. See text for details on this index. The regression coefficient (with standard error), beta coefficient, and t score (with significance level) are listed for each independent variable.

its activists' willingness to work in election campaigns. Quite possibly, their commitment to issues makes them more willing to participate, or perhaps their minority status stimulates them to try harder. Of course, in many areas in the South the Democratic Party has a greater number of activists, which could more than compensate for the lesser amount of work done per indi-

Table 3.8. Regression Analysis of Election Work

Independent variable	b (SE)	Beta	t Score (p <)
Purist index	-.177 (.010)	-.18	-17.43 (.01)
Party position	-.648 (.060)	-.11	-10.77 (.01)
Years active in politics	.027 (.002)	.17	16.51 (.01)
Gender	.209 (.042)	.05	5.03 (.01)
Race	-.002 (.009)	-.01	-.17 (.87)
Education	.033 (.018)	.02	1.79 (.07)
Party	.471 (.041)	.12	11.62 (.01)
Constant	2.478 (.168)		

$R^2 = .09$
N = 8989

Note: These data are the results of a multiple regression analysis with the election work index as the dependent variable. See text for details on this index. The regression coefficient (with standard error), beta coefficient, and t score (with significance level) are listed for each independent variable.

vidual, so we should not infer overall party differences from the above individual-level data.

Conclusion

The preceding analysis may be summarized very briefly. Southern Republican grassroots party activists are more purist in their party orientations than are their Democratic counterparts. Very little of this partisan difference in orientations can be explained by such variables as demographic factors, ideology, or religiosity, even though there are clear differences between the parties on these dimensions. Rather, this higher degree of purism is spread across most subgroups in the party, including county party chairs. Put simply, the Republican activists are more purist in general. The difference appears to represent a true party difference.

These differences in purist orientations may be rooted in the different status or situation of each party. The Republican Party has achieved competitive status only fairly recently. Despite significant growth, southern Republicans are rarely the governing party in the state. Even where they have been successful in capturing the governorship, control of the state legislature has been more elusive. And southern Republican members of Congress, especially those in the House of Representatives, have found themselves in a situation comparable to that of their party colleagues in the state legislature. In an effort to improve their electoral fortunes, southern Republicans have emphasized policy issues, especially during the decade prior to this survey. Indeed, some of the congressional Republicans who have pushed the hardest for their party to take a clearly issue-oriented, conservative offensive against the Democrats have been southern Republicans, such as Newt Gingrich in the House and Phil Gramm in the Senate. This strategic orientation of the party, both regionally and nationally, is reflected in the party orientations of its activists.

Southern Democrats, by contrast, are a diverse biracial coalition (Lamis, 1990; Scher, 1992). They have relied much more on long-standing party loyalties among the electorate for support, although this base of support is eroding. As members of what is usually the majority party in the state government, many incumbent Democratic officeholders are able to stress their experience, power, and influence, factors on which few Republicans in the region can genuinely campaign. Within their own national party, southern Democrats tend to form the more conservative wing. Given this political context, it is not surprising that Democratic activists display a greater degree of pragmatism than do Republicans.

While the Republicans in this study are more purist than the Democrats, these data do not indicate that the Republican Party is filled with ideologically rigid activists. It is especially worth noting that purist orientations are not particularly related to ideological extremism in either party. Thus, Republican purists are about as likely to be in the ideological middle of their party as on the right wing. This fact tempers the impact of purism. Also, significant numbers of a militant religious right do not seem to be present among southern grassroots activists at the time of this study. Still, the potential for purism to be a barrier to electoral success is greater among Republicans than among Democrats. Whether that potential becomes a reality will depend on a variety of forces that are difficult to predict at this time.

4
Ambition and Local Party Activists

Robert P. Steed
Laurence W. Moreland
Tod A. Baker

Students of American politics and democratic theory have long assumed that ambition is a key ingredient in understanding the behavior of political activists, especially those holding public office. The fundamental notions of accountability and responsiveness to the public are rooted in the idea that public officials will act, at least in part, out of concern for their political futures; it is further assumed that this concern will affect a range of considerations, such as those related to electoral strategy, to party organizational nomination efforts, and to positions on issues.

Over the past three decades a number of systematic, empirical efforts have been undertaken to examine and develop this notion. The seminal work in this area is widely considered to be that of Joseph Schlesinger (1966), which approached ambition as an independent variable with behavioral consequences. It thereby departed from earlier research, which had been mainly concerned with explaining *why* people have political ambitions (e.g., Lasswell, 1948; George and George, 1956). Schlesinger contended that the "central assumption" of ambition theory is that "the politician as officeseeker engages in political acts and makes decisions appropriate to gaining office" (Schlesinger, 1966: 6).

More recent studies have extended ambition research to examinations of various public officials. In the late 1960s and 1970s, studies of city council members (Black, 1970, 1972; Prewitt and Nowlin, 1969; Prewitt, 1970a, 1970b), state legislators (Soule, 1969), state prosecutors (Engstrom, 1971), congressional challengers (Fishel, 1971, 1973), members of the U.S. Congress (Mezey, 1970), and even members of the Soviet Politburo (Ciboski, 1974) all explored the behavioral and attitudinal consequences of political ambition. More recent research, much of it related to members of Congress, has further extended the concept and relevance of the ambition approach (e.g., Rohde, 1979; Hibbing, 1982, 1986; Loomis, 1984, 1988; Ehrenhalt, 1991; Kazee, 1994). While these efforts have not answered all questions about the role of ambition in individual political careers and in the operation of the political system, they have established its value as a political variable of importance.

Logically, ambition theory should be useful in the study of political party organizations and activists. Indeed, Schlesinger has argued that the ambition of those seeking public office is the main factor in the development and maintenance of political parties: "For reasons I have stated elsewhere most goals are inadequate to lead individuals to pay the costs of creating and maintaining political parties. Of all the goals, only ambition for political office is sufficient to warrant the effort" (Schlesinger, 1993: 482–483). Schlesinger further argued that, given this importance of ambition theory in understanding political parties, its relation to the performance of key tasks by the party is a major factor in understanding changes in the parties, particularly those associated with changes in the external environment (e.g., election rules, term limits). In short, ambition theory should be useful in attempting to understand the role of contemporary parties in the American political system in a period of great change.

The attempt to extend ambition theory to understanding political parties, however, has been limited and only partially successful. Schlesinger, for example, suggested that categorizing party activists as office seekers and as benefit seekers is useful in developing a theory of political parties (Schlesinger, 1975), and James Carlson (1986) successfully employed such a categorization in an analysis of data on delegates to state party conventions in 1984. Efforts to extend these lines of analysis to other groups of party activists have not, however, been very successful. For example, research on other party convention delegates in the 1980s revealed little utility in the application of ambition theory inasmuch as there was little evidence that ambition made much difference for state party activists' orientations toward selected party activities, issue positions, or electoral considerations (Steed, 1986; Moreland, 1990c).

These mixed findings for data on party activists may well be related to the methods of analysis used and/or the types of party activists examined, and they point toward the need for further research to clarify the link—if there is one—between ambition and party activism. The analysis in this chapter is designed to build on previous work that applied ambition theory to the study of political parties. Utilizing the data on local party officials in the South (from the Grassroots Party Activists Project), it will describe who the ambitious activists are and will then explore the relationship between ambition and local party activists' orientations toward a wide range of economic and social issues, party organizational activities, and electoral strategies. If aspiration for further political positions on the part of party activists does have consequences for the political party, it should emerge in at least some of these topical areas. Inasmuch as our database focuses on the local level, we expect our examination of ambition and party activists to be more revealing than an analysis of state party convention delegates, assuming that local leaders represent a more continuing and fully involved core of activists.

Most previous research on ambition has examined those persons who actually ran for office. Our approach is somewhat broader inasmuch as we focus on the motivation for seeking the currently held party position as the basis for our operationalization of ambition. Specifically, from a lengthy list of incentives for involvement (see chapter 1), we selected as ambitious those who said that "trying to build a personal position in politics" was "very important" to them in deciding to become politically active. Since relatively few people seemed willing to admit that such a blatantly political reason had led them into politics (only 9 percent of the Democrats and 7 percent of the Republicans), we thought that this approach was sufficiently discriminating to identify those with political ambitions.[1] Within each party, then, we differentiate the ambitious from the nonambitious and examine the two groups within each party on a variety of variables where patterns of difference might be expected.

Background Characteristics

A brief description of the demographic characteristics of the precinct officials will help identify more clearly the two groups of party activists under analysis.

With regard to a number of standard socioeconomic and demographic characteristics, the ambitious and the nonambitious are strikingly similar. (See table 4.1.) With the exception of age in both parties and gender in the Republican Party, there are only small aggregate variations. The ambitious activists are younger in both parties, and among Republican officials men are more highly represented among the ambitious than among the nonambitious (76 percent to 63 percent). There are no significant differences with regard to race, education, income, region of childhood (although among Republicans the ambitious are slightly more likely than the nonambitious to have grown up in the South), religious affiliation, and levels of church attendance. Additional data, not reported in table 4.1, reveal no ambition-based differences with regard to either occupation or self-identification with religious categories such as fundamentalist, evangelical, and born-again.

While the similarities in these personal background characteristics are not necessarily surprising, we would expect to find that the ambitious and the nonambitious differ in some important respects in their political backgrounds. For example, it would be reasonable to expect that party activists with ambitions for developing a personal political career would be more likely to come from politically active families, exhibit different recruitment

Table 4.1. Personal Background Characteristics of Local Party Activists, by Ambition (in percentage)

	Democrats		Republicans	
Characteristic	Ambitious	Nonambitious	Ambitious	Nonambitious
Age (years)				
39 or younger	37	16	46	19
40–49	26	21	23	21
50–59	17	21	17	22
60 and older	20	42	14	38
(N)	(500)	(5101)	(334)	(4523)
Gender				
Male	68	63	76	63
Female	32	37	24	37
(N)	(494)	(4962)	(329)	(4473)
Race				
White	73	80	90	92
African American	18	13	5	2
Other	9	7	5	6
(N)	(488)	(4902)	(325)	(4444)
Education				
High school or less	18	26	11	13
Some college	26	28	24	32
College degree	22	17	32	30
Graduate degree	34	29	33	25
(N)	(493)	(5016)	(333)	(4488)
Family Income				
Less than $20,000	14	16	9	8
$20–29,000	13	16	11	12
$30–39,000	15	17	18	16
$40–49,000	16	14	13	15
$50–59,000	12	12	12	13
$60,000 or more	30	26	38	35
(N)	(480)	(4851)	(325)	(4323)
State of Childhood				
South	88	85	82	72
Non-South	12	15	18	28
(N)	(500)	(5101)	(334)	(4523)

Table 4.1. continued

	Democrats		Republicans	
Characteristic	Ambitious	Nonambitious	Ambitious	Nonambitious
Religious Affiliation				
Protestant	83	86	83	89
Roman Catholic	11	9	13	9
Jewish	2	2	1	1
Nonbeliever	2	2	2	1
Other	2	1	1	1
(N)	(488)	(5024)	(330)	(4484)
Church attendance				
Once a week	38	48	46	52
Almost every week	21	17	17	17
Once a month	15	10	11	10
Few times a year	21	19	21	17
Never	5	5	4	4
(N)	(491)	(5006)	(332)	(4460)

patterns, and have a more extensive record of involvement in a variety of political positions than those party activists with no professed aspirations for developing a political career.

The data in table 4.2 give only partial support to these expectations. For example, the expectation concerning family political activity receives very little support from these data inasmuch as ambitious Democrats are only slightly more likely to come from active families, and ambitious Republicans are no more likely at all to have such family involvement. Similarly, in both parties the ambitious and the nonambitious are essentially undifferentiated with regard to party switching and split-ticket voting (at least in 1988).

In spite of these similarities, however, there are other elements of the activists' political backgrounds that show some variations by ambition. In keeping with the age differences noted above, the ambitious in both parties tend to have fewer years of past political activity. This is more evident among Republicans, where three-fourths of the ambitious have been active in politics fewer than 20 years, as compared with slightly under two-thirds of the nonambitious. Also, in each party—but again somewhat more pronounced among Republicans—the ambitious are indeed more likely to have held other party, elective, and appointive political positions.

In these data, the most revealing differences relate to recruitment patterns, the personal importance attached to being on the local party com-

Table 4.2. Political Background Characteristics of Local Party Activists, by Ambition (in percentage)

Characteristic	Democrats		Republicans	
	Ambitious	Nonambitious	Ambitious	Nonambitious
Years politically active				
10 or fewer	28	28	42	36
11–20	36	29	33	28
21–30	22	21	18	21
More than 30	14	22	7	15
(N)	(500)	(5101)	(334)	(4523)
Other political positions held				
Party position	34	28	41	35
Elective position	32	24	28	18
Appointive position	34	26	35	22
(N)	(429)[a]	(4183)[a]	(292)[a]	(3863)[a]
Importance of county committee membership				
Very important	58	40	53	34
Somewhat important	33	43	37	46
Not very important	7	12	8	15
Not important at all	2	5	2	5
(N)	(486)	(4901)	(324)	(4351)
Party switcher?				
Yes	10	6	28	29
No	90	94	72	71
(N)	(485)	(4926)	(323)	(4416)
1988 Presidential vote				
Bush	16	18	98	98
Dukakis	79	78	1	1
Other	2	1	1	1
Did not vote	2	3	1	1
(N)	(491)	(4978)	(331)	(5012)
Parents or relatives active?				
Yes	56	51	47	45
No	44	49	53	55
(N)	(476)	(4796)	(327)	(4333)

Table 4.2. continued

Characteristic	Democrats		Republicans	
	Ambitious	Nonambitious	Ambitious	Nonambitious
Recruitment by[b]				
Party comm. member	42	46	48	45
County chair	27	27	30	32
Elected official	31	23	24	14
Cand. for office	18	10	16	9
Decided on own	77	57	70	56
(N)	(402)[a]	(3480)[a]	(282)[a]	(3406)[a]
Most important recruitment factor				
Comm. member	17	28	20	25
County chair	8	14	12	18
Elected official	9	9	8	6
Candidate	2	2	2	4
On my own	64	47	58	47
(N)	(415)	(4058)	(290)	(3700)
Plan to run for public office?				
Yes	60	14	64	11
No	14	61	10	63
Undecided	26	25	26	26
(N)	(495)	(5011)	(331)	(4470)

[a]Minimum N for these separate questions.
[b]Entry indicates the percentage of each group saying that this was a "very important" consideration in their decision to become active in party committee work.

mittee, and plans to run for public office in the future. The ambitious activists are somewhat more likely to say that recruitment efforts by elected officials and candidates for public office were very important in their becoming members of the party committee, and they are much more likely than the nonambitious to say that deciding to run for committee membership on their own was very important (77 percent to 57 percent among Democrats and 70 percent to 56 percent among Republicans). This is further confirmed by the responses to a question concerning the most important factor in their recruitment; 64 percent of the ambitious Democrats said that they decided on their own as compared with 47 percent of the nonambitious, a pattern repeated, though less dramatically, among Republicans (58 percent to 47 percent respectively). For the nonambitious, self-recruit-

Table 4.3. Ideological Positions of Local Party Officials, by Ambition (in percentage)

Ideology	Democrats		Republicans	
	Ambitious	Nonambitious	Ambitious	Nonambitious
Very liberal	12	10	2	1
Somewhat liberal	25	27	2	2
Moderate	34	35	15	12
Somewhat conservative	20	23	44	47
Very conservative	9	5	37	38
(N)	(490)	(4909)	(326)	(4470)

ment is the most frequently mentioned pathway to involvement, but party channels stand out as being quite important to them, too (indeed, more so than for the ambitious). The ambitious activists are also much more likely to say that being on the local committee is very important to them personally. Finally, the ambitious in both parties are, not surprisingly, significantly more likely than the nonambitious to say that they plan to run for public office.

In short, these local party officials display fewer differences than anticipated in personal and political backgrounds, but they do differ on some key points. Most notably, in keeping with their personal political goals, the ambitious activists are more likely to come into party work through contact with elected officials, candidates for elective office, and their own initiative. They are also more likely to see their involvement as personally important and to plan, at least, to realize their desire for a political career by running for public office in the future.

Ideology and Issue Positions

Beyond being related, at least in a limited way, to some background differences among these local activists, we would expect to find that ambition is also related to ideological and issue orientations (Steed and Baker, 1975; Fishel, 1973; Wilson, 1962). However, in terms of general political philosophy and their positions on a series of issues salient at the time of the survey, the party officials' responses to questions reveal that they are largely undifferentiated by ambition for a political career. (See tables 4.3 and 4.4.) Ideologically, the two groups of Democrats are almost identically distributed, with roughly one-third in each of the three categories (liberal, moderate, and conservative), though with a slight tilt to the liberal end of the scale.

Table 4.4. Local Party Officials' Positions on Selected Issues, by Ambition (in percentage liberal responses)

Issue	Democrats		Republicans	
	Ambitious	Non-ambitious	Ambitious	Non-ambitious
Social				
Gov. assistance for women	88	87	58	51
Personal choice for abortion	76	73	43	43
School prayer	71	72	9	10
Environmental protection	85	84	67	63
Gov. aid for blacks/minorities	74	68	39	31
Support for women's equality	91	88	84	80
Affirmative action programs	28	21	6	3
Economic				
Fewer services to reduce gov. spending	72	74	28	25
Constitutional amendment to balance nat. budget	27	31	15	12
State tax increase for financial crisis	32	29	9	7
Gov. aid in jobs and living standards	54	45	16	12
Gov. health care assistance	92	90	52	51
Foreign policy/defense				
Increase defense spending	68	71	38	41
Continue cooperation with Russia	91	91	80	80

Similarly, the two groups of Republicans are virtually identical in their aggregate ideologies, with overwhelming majorities (exceeding 80 percent) of the ambitious and the nonambitious alike identifying themselves as conservative.

Just as ambition has little apparent connection to these activists' ideologies, it also has little apparent connection to their issue positions. As shown in table 4.4, on none of the fourteen issues are the differences between the ambitious and the nonambitious as great as 10 percentage points. If activist ambition affects party organizations, then, it is not likely to do so in the area of platforms or policy development; any significant party schisms on these points apparently stem from factors other than differences in the political outlooks of ambitious and nonambitious party officials.

Electoral Activities, Party Perspectives, and Communication Patterns

Even though the data on the issue positions and ideologies of these party activists do not support the initial expectation, the findings are perhaps not too surprising if we consider that ambitious activists might logically conform rather closely to the majority positions within their parties as long as such conformity is conducive to their aspirations. However, such congruence between the ambitious and the nonambitious would not be so logical with regard to such matters as levels of electoral and party activities. We would expect, for example, that the ambitious would exhibit higher levels of activity as a way to promote their office goals and help develop the skills associated with the development of a political career.

The figures in table 4.5 generally confirm this expectation. Among Democratic officials, the ambitious consistently demonstrate higher levels of involvement in the various political activities listed. This is especially evident for the last thirteen activities listed in the table, all of which deal with efforts to coordinate or utilize the listed activities (as opposed to the more personal, and perhaps singular, involvement in the first thirteen activities listed in the table). On only one of the activities (voter registration) do the performance levels of the nonambitious exceed those of the ambitious activists, and then only by 1 percent. Not only is the pattern of activity performance commonly higher among ambitious activists, but on a majority of the activities the differences are also rather sharp.

The same pattern holds for the Republican officials as well. Although the difference in level of activity between the ambitious and the nonambitious is less dramatic, ambitious Republicans, like their Democratic counterparts, show consistently higher levels of activity across the board.

Similarly, with regard to their levels of activity in different types of elections, the ambitious officials tend to be more active than the nonambitious. (See table 4.6.) For the Democrats, this difference is sharpest in local elections (where 77 percent of the ambitious indicated that they are "very active," as compared with 60 percent of the nonambitious) and in state elections (64 percent to 49 percent). The difference in activity levels in national elections is much smaller, but even here a slightly higher percentage of the ambitious than of the nonambitious said they are "very active." Ambition also differentiates the Republican officials in local and state elections, though not in national elections, with the ambitious being much more likely to be very active in local elections (69 percent to 51 percent) and somewhat more likely to be very active in state elections (60 percent to 50 percent). In short, ambition apparently contributes to producing an even higher level of political activity in both parties among a group already considerably more active than the population at large.

Table 4.5. Political Activities of Local Party Activists, by Ambition (in percentage performing the listed activities)

Activity	Democrats		Republicans	
	Ambitious	Non-ambitious	Ambitious	Non-ambitious
Contacting voters	88	84	86	85
Raising money	65	52	66	55
Voter registration	84	85	77	81
Campaigning	87	73	92	76
Public relations	88	74	84	71
Contacting new voters	80	74	72	74
Party meetings/business	87	82	90	83
Recruiting/organizing workers	77	67	78	68
County party organizational work	77	68	73	68
Increasing political info. for others	80	75	80	78
Policy formulation	70	56	69	58
Recruiting cands. for local office	76	62	75	66
Other nomination activities	58	43	55	44
Organized door-to-door canvassing	46	24	51	29
Organized campaign events	50	32	53	37
Arranged fund raising	42	28	49	31
Organized mailings	46	33	58	47
Distributed campaign literature	71	61	81	72
Organized phone campaigns	44	30	49	40
Purchased billboard space	9	4	10	6
Distributed posters and lawn signs	66	53	74	67
Conducted registration drives	31	21	30	24
Used public opinion surveys	19	8	20	12
Dealt with campaign media	40	21	45	26
Candidate consultation (before announcing)	82	69	76	62
Suggested candidate run	91	78	89	79

In contrast, and somewhat surprisingly, ambition does not make much difference with regard to a series of questions that tap the concepts of amateurism/professionalism and party organizational independence.[2] We could reasonably expect that ambitious activists, looking to develop a political career and thinking seriously about running for public office at some point, would be more willing than nonambitious activists to compromise on controversial issues for the sake of party unity and winning office. Similarly, we could expect the ambitious to be more inclined to say that good party workers support a candidate even if they disagree with him or her. However, these

Table 4.6. Campaign Activity Levels of Local Party Activists, by Ambition (in percentage)

Level	Democrats		Republicans	
	Ambitious	Nonambitious	Ambitious	Nonambitious
Local elections				
Very active	77	60	69	51
Somewhat active	18	27	22	31
Not very active	5	9	7	14
Not active at all	1	3	2	5
(N)	(489)	(4963)	(326)	(4420)
State elections				
Very active	64	49	60	50
Somewhat active	31	37	30	38
Not very active	4	11	8	9
Not active at all	1	4	2	3
(N)	(489)	(4879)	(327)	(4440)
National elections				
Very active	40	36	53	53
Somewhat active	36	34	32	31
Not very active	19	21	12	12
Not active at all	5	9	3	4
(N)	(483)	(4826)	(323)	(4422)

expectations receive almost no confirmation in the data. (See table 4.7.) In both parties the ambitious are a little more likely to support the professional (or pragmatist) position, but the differences are very small and insignificant. For example, 50 percent of the ambitious Democrats agree that party unity is more important than the free discussion of divisive issues, barely more than the 46 percent of the nonambitious Democrats agreeing with this point. Among the Republicans, the percentages are 35 percent and 32 percent, respectively. These slight variations, which also apply to the other items in table 4.7, lead to the broader conclusion that ambition makes virtually no difference among activists on these points. As an interesting aside, the relatively low percentages of Republicans who value party unity over the free discussion of divisive issues are somewhat surprising, inasmuch as they run counter to the stated goal of many Republican leaders who promote party cohesion. This contradiction undoubtedly reflects the entry into the GOP ranks of large numbers of issue-oriented activists (especially of the religious right) in recent years (see data in chapter 5).

As a final query about the relationship between ambition and activists'

Table 4.7. Local Party Activists' Views on Party Activities and Organization, by Ambition (in percentage)

View	Democrats		Republicans	
	Ambitious	Non-ambitious	Ambitious	Non-ambitious
Good party workers support candidate with whom they disagree				
Strongly agree	23	20	8	8
Agree	39	40	36	30
Disagree	27	31	42	44
Strongly disagree	10	9	14	19
(N)	(490)	(4892)	(326)	(4789)
Party unity is more important than free discussion of divisive issues				
Strongly agree	24	16	10	8
Agree	26	30	25	24
Disagree	37	43	51	52
Strongly disagree	13	12	14	16
(N)	(485)	(4789)	(325)	(4844)
Cands. should not compromise values even if necessary to win office				
Strongly agree	47	45	52	56
Agree	37	43	38	35
Disagree	13	11	8	7
Strongly disagree	2	2	2	2
(N)	(487)	(4844)	(323)	(4762)
Avoid controversial issues to ensure party unity				
Strongly agree	21	15	8	9
Agree	35	36	32	32
Disagree	35	41	43	46
Strongly disagree	10	8	17	14
(N)	(480)	(4762)	(324)	(4367)
Good party workers should remain neutral in primaries				
Strongly agree	24	18	19	18
Agree	30	31	26	29
Disagree	33	41	42	41
Strongly disagree	13	9	13	12
(N)	(485)	(4779)	(322)	(4368)

Table 4.7. continued

View	Democrats		Republicans	
	Ambitious	Non-ambitious	Ambitious	Non-ambitious
No state party direction of local party activity				
Strongly agree	24	18	18	15
Agree	37	45	35	42
Disagree	33	33	40	39
Strongly disagree	6	4	7	3
(N)	(481)	(4741)	(324)	(4580)
No national party direction of state party				
Strongly agree	24	18	16	13
Agree	38	46	39	44
Disagree	34	33	39	39
Strongly disagree	4	4	6	4
(N)	(469)	(4580)	(317)	(4236)

work within and perspectives on the party, we asked about their communication with others in the party organization. Not surprisingly, in light of the greater levels of activity by the ambitious party officials reported above, the ambitious again evince a greater tendency to communicate within and across party organizational levels. (See table 4.8.) This is especially the case for communications within the local committee, but it is also the case in communicating with the county chair. Neither type of activist in either party shows much communication with the state chair, state party committee members, or national committee members, but there is slightly greater participation in these activities by the ambitious than the nonambitious.

Ambition and Party Activists: The Special Case of the County Chairs

To wrap up our analysis, we controlled the data on party position to see if ambition operates differently among the county chairs than among the precinct officials. While space limitations do not allow a full presentation of the data, we can summarize briefly by noting that the patterns we have described previously are altered only slightly when ambitious county chairs are compared with nonambitious county chairs.

The main change is in the compression of differences between the am-

Table 4.8. Local Party Activists' Communication Patterns, by Ambition (in percentage)

Level of communication	Democrats		Republicans	
	Ambitious	Non-ambitious	Ambitious	Non-ambitious
Other party comm. members				
Very often	35	19	38	22
Often	43	47	44	50
Seldom	20	30	17	26
Never	2	3	1	2
(N)	(489)	(4878)	(327)	(4406)
County chair				
Very often	31	20	31	22
Often	36	38	38	39
Seldom	27	37	27	32
Never	6	6	4	8
(N)	(485)	(4752)	(322)	(4294)
State chair				
Very often	6	2	7	2
Often	20	10	13	11
Seldom	42	47	49	47
Never	33	41	31	40
(N)	(480)	(4789)	(325)	(4367)
State party comm. members				
Very often	11	3	9	4
Often	26	16	22	19
Seldom	41	47	47	48
Never	22	34	21	28
(N)	(485)	(4807)	(325)	(4370)
Nat. comm. members				
Very often	2	1	3	1
Often	10	4	11	6
Seldom	36	32	37	36
Never	52	62	50	56
(N)	(479)	(4729)	(320)	(4336)

Table 4.8. continued

Level of communication	Democrats		Republicans	
	Ambitious	Non-ambitious	Ambitious	Non-ambitious
Local gov. officials				
Very often	50	30	40	21
Often	35	42	37	41
Seldom	12	22	19	32
Never	3	6	4	7
(N)	(489)	(4871)	(325)	(4395)
State gov. officials				
Very often	26	10	18	7
Often	38	30	33	26
Seldom	28	44	39	48
Never	8	16	10	18
(N)	(482)	(4816)	(325)	(4383)
Nat. gov. officials				
Very often	7	2	7	3
Often	22	12	18	14
Seldom	40	44	42	48
Never	31	42	33	36
(N)	(487)	(4840)	(327)	(4399)

bitious and the nonambitious among the county chairs. For example, among Democratic county chairs the ambitious are slightly more likely to organize campaign events and telephone campaigns than are the nonambitious, but the differences are nowhere near the spreads of 18 and 14 percentage points on these activities reported for the full data set in table 4.5. Similarly, contrary to the results in table 4.5, there are no differences between the ambitious and the nonambitious Democratic county chairs in such activities as purchasing billboard space and dealing with the campaign media. In a few instances, the patterns themselves are reversed among the county chairs. For example, among Republican county chairs the nonambitious are proportionately more involved in state election campaigns than are the ambitious, in clear contrast to the figures in table 4.6 for the full data set. However, there is no systematic evidence of such pattern reversal, and the instances where it occurs are rare.

In short, ambition is an apparent factor in differentiating among county chairs in much the same ways it differentiates among precinct officials, but its influence is more muted and in some instances disappears altogether. We can speculate that once people rise to a higher position within the party organization they will have developed a greater commitment to work for the party (e.g., by participating in campaign activities, by communicating with others in the organization) regardless of their aspirations for a political career. Ambition might well show up more prominently as a differentiating factor among those who have, as a group, relatively less commitment to the party.

Discussion

The essential thrust of this analysis has been to explore the utility of extending ambition theory beyond the elected public office and into the political party environment. The data examined here suggest two broad conclusions. The first is primarily methodological inasmuch as it relates to the operationalization of ambition and its application to the study of party activists. The more stringent definition applied in this analysis seems to be more appropriate than the broader definition used in some previous analyses, and it does tend to discriminate more sharply among the activists. In the same way, it is more useful to examine party organizational activists (here precinct officials and county chairs) than state convention delegates when looking for the effects of ambition within the party. The argument is that state convention delegates are more likely to be occasional activists who are otherwise less involved in party work and hence are probably not as good a population for such an analysis. In any event, by using a different measure of ambition and a different group of party activists, it is possible to find ways in which ambition theory may be extended to political parties well beyond what was found in the earlier analyses of party convention delegates.

The second conclusion is that ambition does seem to differentiate the local party officials on some key points but not on others. There is little or no evidence here that ambitious activists differ from nonambitious activists on most standard background characteristics or on such matters as ideological or issue orientations. It is clearly not the case, then, that ambition is likely to manifest itself in such things as the development of party platforms or campaign strategies (at least insofar as such strategies might be affected by views on specific issues). Nor does ambition seem to matter significantly in terms of amateur versus professional orientations toward the party and its work.

Where ambition does make a difference is in the recruitment patterns, activities, and communication patterns exhibited by party leaders in both parties. The ambitious activists are more likely to have entered formal party organizational work through contact with elected officials and other candidates for office and through their own initiative, and they continue, once involved, to evince relatively higher levels of communication with others in the party organization, especially at the local level. Involvement in the party organization is more important to them personally than to the nonambitious, as well. Most important, from the standpoint of the party organization, these activists are more extensively engaged in a variety of activities of significance to the well-being of the party (both campaign and organizational-maintenance activities). While this involvement is more the case for precinct officials than for county chairs, the basic patterns generally hold at both organizational levels.

The picture that emerges from this exploratory analysis is that the ambitious activists are more intensely committed to the party, and they are more likely to be the catalysts of the local organization. Although a small number, they represent a thin stratum of officials who tend to push the local party organizations in the pursuit of their traditional functions. At a time when the party is frequently assumed to be losing its historic importance in the political system as it loses ground to competing organizations (e.g., PACs, the media, public relations firms), this is at least one group of activists who are inspired to work to hold the line and maintain the party.

Thus, while ambition theory has frequently been advanced as an important element in democratic political systems from the standpoint of accountability to the public, we find evidence, consistent with Schlesinger's longstanding thesis, that it is also important to party organizations. Political parties in the United States have never been famous for highly efficient, tightly knit organizations, but our data suggest that the levels of efficiency (or activity) they manage to attain, as well as the degree of organizational unity (e.g., through communication among levels and activists), are disproportionately a result of the presence of ambitious activists in the party ranks. Recognizing that viable political parties make valuable contributions to a democratic politics, we see here yet another way that political ambition may be important to democracy.

Part Two
Activities in Organizations

Those who study political parties have long noted the parties' contributions to the functioning of the larger political system. Indeed, many have argued that the parties are indispensable to the functioning of democratic political systems (e.g., Schattschneider, 1942: 1; Key, 1964: 200–201). While there may not be complete agreement on this point, there is general agreement that the extent to which parties contribute to the operation of democratic systems is closely related to their performance of certain key activities. As William J. Keefe (1980: 21) has noted, "The contributions of political parties to the maintenance of democratic politics can be judged in a rough way by examining the principal activities in which they engage." Within the context of the present study, then, it is important to examine the activities of these local party officials. In this section, the analytical focus shifts, therefore, from who the activists are, and how and why they are involved in local party organizations, to the functions local parties perform.

Political parties are thought to perform a variety of functions in democratic societies, among them the management of societal conflict by structuring disagreements within a partisan context (see, among others, Eldersveld, 1982: 6–7; Bibby, 1992: 13). In chapter 5, Robert P. Steed analyzes the ideological structures of the two parties to see if this traditional structuring function is still evident at the level of local party organizations. He is concerned with both intraparty and interparty patterns, and he discusses the possible implications of these patterns for other party activities.

As organizations, effective parties must be able to provide an ongoing presence *between* elections to ensure maximum success *during* elections. In chapter 6, Frank B. Feigert and John R. Todd explore the activities carried out by party leaders to maintain the party organization between elections. They compare Democrats with Republicans and county chairs with precinct officials in an effort to locate the centers of maintenance activities within the local party organizations.

The primary goal of American political parties, and the reason they seek to maintain themselves, is to win elections. In chapter 7, John A. Clark, Brad Lockerbie, and Peter W. Wielhouwer examine the variations in campaign activity performance among grassroots party activists. They analyze both levels and types of activities performed by county chairs and precinct officials and offer some interesting conclusions regarding the differential emphasis on managerial and retail or labor-intensive activities among these local officials.

A generation ago, Eldersveld (1964) characterized the relationship among party organizational units as "stratarchy," with little interaction between levels of the party. In chapter 8, David Brodsky and Simeon Brodsky reopen the question of intraparty communication. They are especially interested in testing Eldersveld's thesis with data gathered almost thirty years later, with a view toward ascertaining whether the stratarchy model remains applicable at a different time and a different place. They are also interested in the implications of intraparty communications for the party's ability to perform other functions related to such matters as contesting local elections and building stronger local organizations.

Much of the recent debate over the health of the political parties in the United States revolves around whether the parties continue to perform the activities they have traditionally done in the political system. The chapters in Part II go to the heart of this issue and offer a wide range of data and discussion relevant to understanding the place of the parties in contemporary American politics.

5
Parties, Ideology, and Issues
The Structuring of Political Conflict

Robert P. Steed

It is commonly asserted that a key party function in the United States—indeed, one of the party's main contributions to the operation of the political system—is the provision of programmatic structure to political debate and election campaigns. For example, Paul A. Beck and Frank J. Sorauf (1992: 14) note that "the American parties carry on a series of loosely related activities that perhaps can best be called education or propagandization. . . . They . . . represent the interests of and the issue stands congenial to the groups that identify with them and support them." John Bibby, in listing the various functions of the parties, notes that parties help provide voters with the means for sorting out candidates and issues and thereby help to channel the vote in meaningful ways (Bibby, 1992: 10–12).

There is more to the structuring function than just providing cues for the electorate, however. It can also be argued that as parties concern themselves with ideology, issues, and programs, such matters as candidate and activist recruitment, internal organizational cohesion, and levels of activism within the party will be affected as well. For example, just as voters respond to party cues during periods of partisan realignment, party activists respond by becoming more or less active, by dropping out of partisan politics altogether, or by switching parties; normally, partisan transformation is accompanied by a greater ideological polarization between the parties' elites and by some effort on the part of party activists to "reduce ideological and personal dissonances by reassessing where they belong politically" (Bowman, Hulbary, and Kelley, 1990: 54; also see Sundquist, 1983; Shannon, 1968: 175–176, 180–181; Sinclair, 1977; Abramowitz, 1979). In this context, studies of local party leaders in Florida (Bowman, Hulbary, and Kelley, 1990) and South Carolina (Steed, Moreland, and Baker, 1995) and research on state party activists (Moreland, 1990a; Abramowitz, 1979; Moreland, 1991b; Steed, Moreland, and Baker, 1990a) describe such party sorting as an element of southern party change in recent years.

On the other hand, political parties in the United States have been notoriously nonideological, historically, in comparison with parties in most other democratic nations (Beck and Sorauf, 1992: 433–435; Price, 1984: chap. 1; Eldersveld, 1982: 53–57.) Indeed, one of the key criticisms of American parties is that, from the standpoint of providing either efficient governance or democratic accountability, they are not sufficiently concerned with ideological and issue consistency, with the enunciation of clear positions on policy, or with the enactment of platforms into policies (see, e.g., Ranney, 1954; Beck and Sorauf, 1992: 446–454; Greenstein and Feigert, 1985: 143.) Whether or not American parties are sufficiently concerned with issue or ideological positions to perform their structuring function efficiently, therefore, remains a topic of debate.

An examination of local party functions, then, should logically include some attention to how much, and in what ways, local parties help to structure political conflict within an issue-ideological context. This chapter addresses two central questions related to this concern. First, do the local parties provide issue and ideological cues to assist the electorate in sorting out the whirl of political stimuli with which they are confronted? Second, does ideology serve to structure conflict within the parties? That is, is ideology a relevant variable for understanding actions and decisions within the local party organization?

Patterns of Ideological Differentiation

The first question seems to have a relatively simple answer. In spite of the charge that American parties are not very much concerned with ideology, a great deal of previous research has rather consistently shown partisan divisions in party platforms, congressional voting patterns, voter orientations, and party activists' orientations (see, for example, McClosky, Hoffman, and O'Hara, 1960; Kirkpatrick, 1975; Montjoy, Shaffer, and Weber, 1980; Jackson, Brown, and Bositis, 1982; Baer and Bositis, 1988: 100–107; Beck and Sorauf, 1992: 433–446; Steed, Moreland, and Baker, 1990b: 128–133; Budge and Hofferbert, 1990; Bibby, 1992: 72–74.) Our data on local party officials are consistent with these findings. As noted in passing in chapter 3, and as demonstrated even more clearly in table 5.1, there are rather sharp interparty cleavages between these two groups of activists with regard to their ideological self-placement. In each state, in each subregion (Rim South and Deep South), and in the region as a whole local Democratic activists are more liberal in the aggregate than Republican activists. Conversely, local Republican activists are significantly more conservative than their Democratic counterparts.

Similarly, throughout the region, perhaps reflecting their somewhat greater socioeconomic and demographic homogeneity, the Republicans are

Table 5.1. Ideological Positions of Local Southern Party Officials (in percentage)

	Democrats	Republicans
Alabama		
Liberal	30	3
Middle-of-the-road	32	11
Conservative	38	87
Georgia		
Liberal	33	2
Middle-of-the-road	33	12
Conservative	34	86
Louisiana		
Liberal	28	1
Middle-of-the-road	39	11
Conservative	33	88
Mississippi		
Liberal	34	3
Middle-of-the-road	35	12
Conservative	31	85
South Carolina		
Liberal	40	1
Middle-of-the-road	32	11
Conservative	28	88
North Carolina		
Liberal	40	2
Middle-of-the-road	37	12
Conservative	23	86
Arkansas		
Liberal	31	3
Middle-of-the-road	33	12
Conservative	36	85
Florida		
Liberal	46	3
Middle-of-the-road	35	18
Conservative	18	79

Table 5.1. continued

	Democrats	Republicans
Tennessee		
Liberal	30	2
Middle-of-the-road	44	14
Conservative	27	84
Texas		
Liberal	43	2
Middle-of-the-road	31	12
Conservative	26	86
Virginia		
Liberal	48	4
Middle-of-the-road	37	16
Conservative	15	80
Deep South		
Liberal	34	2
Middle-of-the-road	34	11
Conservative	32	87
Rim South		
Liberal	39	3
Middle-of-the-road	35	13
Conservative	25	84
Entire South		
Liberal	37	2
Middle-of-the-road	35	12
Conservative	28	85

much more ideologically homogeneous than the Democrats. In every state, at least 79 percent of the local Republican officials identify themselves as conservative; southwide, 85 percent of these activists consider themselves to be conservative. Although there are state-by-state variations, the local Democratic officials are much more evenly divided among liberals, moderates, and conservatives. In four states, conservatives slightly outnumber either liberals or moderates, but in the majority of states liberals are in the plurality among the Democrats. For the entire South, slightly over one-third (37 percent) are liberal, slightly over one-third (35 percent) are middle-of-the-road, and just under one-third (28 percent) are conservative.

At least on the surface, then, the parties in this study are offering different ideological images to the public. This divergence extends as well to their respective positions on a series of issues—more important in terms of con-

Table 5.2. Local Party Officials' Positions on Selected Issues, by Ideology (in percentage liberal responses)

Issue	Democrats	Republicans
Social		
Gov. assistance for women	88	51
Personal choice for abortion	74	43
School prayer	29	10
Environmental protection	84	64
Gov. aid for blacks/minorities	68	32
Support for women's equality	89	80
Affirmative action programs	21	3
Economic		
Fewer services to reduce gov. spending	73	25
Constitutional amendment to		
balance nat. budget	31	12
State tax increase for financial crisis	29	7
Gov. aid in jobs and living standards	46	12
Gov. health care assistance	90	51
Foreign policy/defense		
Increase defense spending	71	41
Continue cooperation with Russia	91	80

crete policy implications. As shown in table 5.2, there are sharp interparty variations in the patterns suggested by the ideological data on each of the fourteen issues examined. In a few instances (e.g., the question of contin- ued cooperation with Russia and support for equal treatment of women in the business world), the differences are fairly small, but on the vast majority of these issues they are quite sizable. For example, on nine of the issues the differences exceed 20 percentage points, and on seven they equal or exceed 30 percentage points.

In short, these two groups of local party officials differ in more than name only: they differ consistently and sharply in their specific political ori- entations. For both groups, the ideological labels have real political mean- ing and are consistent with the images the parties project to the public.

The Ideological Structure of the Democratic Party

The interparty variations described in the preceding section are, of course, an important element in structuring conflict for the electorate. Another aspect of this structuring function concerns the degree to which ideology affects the parties internally. Just as we assume that interparty ideological

Table 5.3. Personal Background of Local Democratic Party Officials in the South, by Ideology (in percentage)

Characteristic	Liberal	Moderate	Conservative
Age (years)			
25 or younger	3	3	3
26–35	7	8	6
36–55	46	42	36
56 or older	44	47	55
Gender			
Male	57	65	71
Female	43	35	29
Race			
White	75	82	85
African American	19	12	7
Hispanic	2	1	1
Other	4	5	7
Education			
Grade school	2	3	4
High school	16	21	28
Some college	24	31	30
College degree	19	17	17
Graduate degree	39	28	20
Family income			
Less than $10,000	4	4	4
$10,000–$19,999	10	10	12
$20,000–$29,999	14	16	17
$30,000–$39,999	16	17	16
$40,000–$49,999	14	14	16
$50,000–$59,999	12	12	12
$60,000–$69,999	9	8	7
$70,000 or more	20	20	16
State of childhood			
South	78	88	92
Non-South	22	12	8

Table 5.3. continued

Characteristic	Liberal	Moderate	Conservative
Religious affiliation			
Protestant	79	87	92
Catholic	11	9	6
Jewish	3	2	0
Nonbeliever	5	2	0
Other	2	1	1
Church attendance			
Every week	40	47	55
Almost every week	15	20	18
Once a month	13	10	9
A few times a year	23	19	15
Never	9	3	3
Fundamentalist?			
Yes	4	10	14
No	96	90	86
Born again?			
Yes	23	30	44
No	77	70	56
Bible is word of God			
Agree	49	68	82
Disagree	51	32	18

differences are important, we assume that intraparty ideological patterns should influence a host of internal party activities and decisions. In this and the next section, we shall examine, in turn, each party's internal ideological structure and explore some of the possible implications for the local party organization.

As shown in table 5.3, there are a number of systematic, and in some cases relatively significant, differences between the liberals and the conservatives who are active in the southern Democratic Party's local organizations. Conservatives tend more than liberals to have within their ranks higher percentages of older activists, males, whites, and native southerners. They also tend to be less well educated and slightly less affluent. With respect to religious denomination, more are Protestants (92 percent to 79 percent) and fewer are Catholics (6 percent to 11 percent); they attend church more frequently than the liberal Democratic activists; and they are more likely to consider themselves fundamentalists. Proportionately, almost twice as many conservatives as liberals say that they have had a born-again religious experience and that they believe the Bible is the literal word of God.

Table 5.4. Political Background of Local Democratic Party Officials in the South, by Ideology (in percentage)

Characteristic	Liberal	Moderate	Conservative
Years active in politics			
Fewer than 5	7	10	8
6–10	12	14	12
11–20	30	29	28
More than 20	50	48	52
Other political positions held			
Party position	34	29	22
Elective position	22	24	28
Appointive position	27	26	26
Parents or relatives active?			
Yes	50	53	51
No	50	47	49
Father's party identification			
Democrat	78	85	87
Republican	13	8	8
Independent	6	6	4
Other	2	1	1
1988 Presidential Vote			
Bush	4	17	38
Dukakis	94	80	57
Other	1	1	2
Did not vote	1	2	3
Party switcher?			
Yes	8	5	8
No	92	95	92

Interestingly, on all points examined here, moderate activists are ranged consistently between the liberals and the conservatives.

While the personal backgrounds of liberal and conservative Democratic party officials differ rather clearly, the political backgrounds are quite similar. (See table 5.4.) Indeed, liberals and conservatives are essentially undifferentiated in terms of the length of their political activity, activity by parents or other relatives, and party switching. There are slight differences with regard to their holding of other political positions, with a higher percentage of liberals having held some other party position and a higher percentage of conservatives having held an elective position. Conservatives are slightly more likely to have had a father who identified with the Democratic Party

Table 5.5. Local Southern Democratic Party Activists' National and State Party Identification, by Ideology (in percentage)

Identification	Liberal	Moderate	Conservative
National party			
Strong Democrat	88	68	52
Weak Democrat	6	16	17
Independent, Leaning Democrat	5	9	12
Independent	1	3	6
Independent, Leaning Republican	0	2	6
Weak Republican	0	1	2
Strong Republican	0	0	5
State party			
Strong Democrat	93	82	71
Weak Democrat	3	9	11
Independent, Leaning Democrat	4	6	10
Independent	0	1	3
Independent, Leaning Republican	0	1	2
Weak Republican	0	0	0
Strong Republican	0	0	2

(87 percent to 78 percent). The most striking item in table 5.4 concerns these activists' voting record in the 1988 presidential election. The conservatives were much more inclined to defect from their party's ticket than were the liberals: almost two-fifths (38 percent) report casting their ballot for George Bush as compared with only 4 percent of the liberals. Indeed, only 57 percent of the Democratic conservatives supported the Dukakis-Bentsen ticket!

These data on 1988 voting patterns suggest strongly that conservative Democratic activists in the South are, as other studies have suggested about southern conservatives in general, disaffected with their party, especially in the context of presidential elections (Sundquist, 1983; Bain, 1972; Black and Black, 1987: chaps. 11–12; Carmines and Stanley, 1990). This pattern receives further confirmation in the data in table 5.5, which show sharply different levels of identification with both the national and the state Democratic Party. While 88 percent of the liberal Democratic activists identify strongly with the national party, only slightly over half (52 percent) of the conservative Democratic activists indicate strong identification. Almost one-fifth of these conservatives say they are independents leaning Democratic or purely independent in their national party identification, and 13 percent are independents leaning Republican or even fully identified with the national Republican Party.

While the figures are not so negative for the Democratic Party at the state

**Table 5.6. Local Southern Democratic Party Activists' Feelings
toward the Political Parties, by Ideology (in percentage)**

Feeling	Liberal	Moderate	Conservative
Toward national Democratic Party			
Close	52	30	24
Neutral	39	55	49
Distant	9	15	27
Toward state Democratic Party			
Close	64	54	45
Neutral	31	40	43
Distant	5	6	12
Toward national Republican Party			
Close	4	4	13
Neutral	19	37	47
Distant	77	59	40
Toward state Republican Party			
Close	4	4	10
Neutral	20	34	44
Distant	76	62	46

level as at the national level, the pattern of weaker identification among
conservatives is still present. Only 71 percent of the conservative Democratic activists identify strongly with their party at the state level (compared
with 93 percent of the liberal Democratic activists), and a small portion
even identify themselves as strong Republicans at the state level.

Further evidence of southern Democratic conservatives' unhappiness
with the national party is presented in table 5.6. Only 24 percent say they
feel "close" to the national Democratic Party, less than half the proportion
of liberal Democratic activists responding in this manner. Moreover, while
relatively few of the liberal Democrats feel "distant" from their national
party, more than one-fourth of the conservatives feel "distant." Similarly, the
conservative Democrats feel proportionately closer to the national Republican Party than do the liberals (13 percent to 4 percent) and proportionately less distant from the national Republican Party (40 percent to 77 percent).

Both liberal and conservative Democrats feel closer to the state party
than to the national party, but again there are clear intergroup differences
along the lines noted above. Almost two-thirds of the liberal Democratic
activists feel close to the state party as compared with less than half of their

Table 5.7. Levels of Campaign Activity of Local Democratic Party Officials, by Ideology (in percentage)

Level	Liberal	Moderate	Conservative
Local elections			
Very active	64	60	60
Somewhat active	26	28	26
Not very active	8	9	9
Not active at all	2	3	5
State elections			
Very active	58	48	43
Somewhat active	34	38	38
Not very active	7	10	13
Not active at all	1	4	6
National elections			
Very active	48	29	27
Somewhat active	33	37	33
Not very active	15	24	26
Not active at all	4	9	14

conservative colleagues. And among the conservatives, 12 percent say they feel distant from their state party, more than twice the proportion among liberals. A considerably greater percentage of the liberal Democrats report feeling distant from the Republican Party in their home state as well (76 percent to 46 percent).

These different views toward the party are also reflected in the levels of campaign activity of these party officials. While there are virtually no differences in activity patterns at the local level, there are some rather clear differences at the state and national levels. (See table 5.7.) At both these levels of political involvement, liberal Democrats are more active than conservative Democrats, with the differences being sharpest at the level of national campaigns. In fact, only 60 percent of the conservative Democratic officials report that they are "somewhat" or "very" active in national campaigns (compared with 81 percent of the liberal Democratic officials).

Not surprisingly, these differences between liberal and conservative Democratic activists extend beyond their backgrounds, party orientations, and activity levels to their positions on a number of specific issues. As shown in table 5.8, there are sharp variations on each of the fourteen issues examined. In a few instances (e.g., the question of continued cooperation with Russia), the differences are fairly small, but on the vast majority of these issues, the differences are quite large. For example, on nine of the issues,

Table 5.8. Local Southern Democratic Party Officials' Positions on Selected Issues, by Ideology (in percentage liberal responses)

Issue	Liberal	Moderate	Conservative
Social			
Gov. assistance for women	96	87	74
Personal choice for abortion	86	74	56
School prayer	48	24	9
Environmental protection	91	85	75
Gov. aid for blacks/minorities	87	66	46
Support for women's equality	94	89	81
Affirmative action programs	36	15	10
Economic			
Fewer services to reduce gov. spending	86	74	55
Constitutional amendment to balance nat. budget	45	29	15
State tax increase for financial crisis	43	25	16
Gov. aid in jobs and living standards	60	41	34
Gov. health care assistance	96	90	83
Foreign policy/defense			
Increase defense spending	82	72	55
Continue cooperation with Russia	94	92	87

the differences exceed 25 percentage points, and on two (school prayer and government aid for minorities) they exceed 40 percentage points.

In sum, these two groups of local Democratic party officials differ in more than name only: they differ consistently and sharply in their specific political orientations. In the same way that ideological categories have meaning within the context of interparty politics, they also have meaning within the context of Democratic intraparty politics.

The Ideological Structure of the Republican Party

One key difference between the Republican and the Democratic activists is the greater homogeneity of the Republicans. Whereas the Democrats are rather equally divided into three ideological groups, the Republicans are overwhelmingly conservative. Indeed, liberals constitute only 2 percent of these local activists southwide.[1]

With regard to their background characteristics, liberal and conservative Republican activists differ slightly in terms of gender, race, income, and re-

Table 5.9. Personal Background of Local Republican Party Officials in the South, by Ideology (in percentage)

Characteristic	Liberal	Moderate	Conservative
Age (years)			
25 or younger	2	3	3
26–35	11	10	10
36–55	40	43	42
56 or older	47	45	45
Gender			
Male	54	53	66
Female	46	47	34
Race			
White	83	90	92
African American	13	5	1
Hispanic	0	1	1
Other	4	4	6
Education			
Grade school	3	1	1
High school	15	10	12
Some college	30	31	31
College degree	27	29	30
Graduate degree	25	30	25
Family income			
Less than $10,000	4	1	2
$10,000–$19,999	14	7	7
$20,000–$29,999	11	13	12
$30,000–$39,999	17	16	16
$40,000–$49,999	16	13	15
$50,000–$59,999	13	15	13
$60,000–$69,999	10	10	9
$70,000 or more	14	26	26
State of childhood			
South	72	66	74
Non-South	28	34	26

ligion. (See table 5.9.) There are virtually no differences in age, education, or state of childhood. There are proportionately more males and more whites in the ranks of conservative Republicans, and they tend to be somewhat more affluent. The sharpest variations come in the religious variables, however. Although these local Republican party officials are virtually the same denominationally, the conservatives are slightly more likely to attend

Table 5.9. continued

Characteristic	Liberal	Moderate	Conservative
Religious affiliation			
Protestant	85	83	89
Catholic	10	13	8
Jewish	2	2	1
Nonbeliever	3	2	1
Other	1	0	1
Church attendance			
Every week	44	40	53
Almost every week	20	18	16
Once a month	11	14	9
A few times a year	19	23	17
Never	5	5	4
Fundamentalist?			
Yes	7	8	20
No	93	92	80
Born again?			
Yes	23	18	32
No	77	82	68
Bible is word of God			
Agree	46	51	72
Disagree	54	49	28

church every week. They also are more likely to be fundamentalists and to consider themselves born-again Christians. They differ most dramatically from the liberal Republican activists in their professed belief that the Bible is the word of God (72 percent to 46 percent). In short, Republican activists do not differ among themselves along political ideological lines to nearly the same degree as the Democratic activists; the major exception involves various religious variables.

Similarly, local Republican party activists differ only slightly on a number of political background factors. (See table 5.10.) Conservatives and liberals report similar levels of parental political activity, have been involved in politics for similar periods of time, and evince similar patterns of parental party identification. The most noticeable differences in table 5.10 relate to the types of political positions that these activists have held previously (conservatives being more likely than liberals to have held other party positions) and to their votes in the 1988 presidential election (liberals being more likely to have defected from the Bush-Quayle ticket). Also, liberals are

Table 5.10. Political Background of Local Republican Party Officials in the South, by Ideology (in percentage)

Characteristic	Liberal	Moderate	Conservative
Years active in politics			
Fewer than 5	17	13	15
6–10	17	14	16
11–20	30	30	29
More than 20	35	42	40
Other political positions held			
Party position	25	36	36
Elective position	16	18	20
Appointive position	19	22	24
Parents or relatives active?			
Yes	49	50	44
No	51	50	54
Father's party identification			
Democrat	53	48	50
Republican	34	40	37
Independent	10	11	11
Other	3	1	1
1988 Presidential vote			
Bush	84	96	99
Dukakis	13	3	0
Other	1	0	1
Did not vote	3	1	0
Party switcher?			
Yes	36	30	29
No	64	70	71

slightly more likely to be party switchers, a point that is rather surprising inasmuch as the Republican Party is clearly conservative and would seem, therefore, to be more attractive to conservatives who might be considering a party switch.

Not so surprisingly, just as the local conservative Democratic party officials indicate less attachment than their liberal colleagues to their party, the local Republican party officials who are liberal evince less attachment to the Republican Party than their more conservative colleagues. (See table 5.11.) At both the national and state levels, liberal Republican activists are considerably less likely than conservative Republican activists to report

Table 5.11. Local Southern Republican Party Activists' National and State Party Identification, by Ideology (in percentage)

Identification	Liberal	Moderate	Conservative
National party			
Strong Democrat	4	1	0
Weak Democrat	1	1	0
Independent, Leaning Democrat	4	1	0
Independent	3	3	1
Independent, Leaning Republican	16	12	6
Weak Republican	11	9	3
Strong Republican	62	73	89
State party			
Strong Democrat	4	1	0
Weak Democrat	3	1	0
Independent, Leaning Democrat	2	0	0
Independent	1	4	1
Independent, Leaning Republican	18	14	9
Weak Republican	12	10	6
Strong Republican	60	69	84

strong identification with the Republican Party, and a small percentage profess to identify themselves as Democrats. In the same vein, a much smaller percentage of these liberal Republicans say that they feel "close" to the Republican Party (at both the state and the national levels). (See table 5.12.) While they are not much more likely than conservative Republicans to feel close to the Democratic Party, they are considerably less likely to feel distant from the Democratic Party.

This lower level of enthusiasm for their party is perhaps reflected in the lower levels of activity by liberal Republican activists in state and national election campaigns. (See table 5.13.) Although almost equal percentages of liberal and conservative Republicans say they are very active in local elections, a relatively larger percentage of conservatives report high levels of activity in state and national elections (53 percent to 37 percent and 55 percent to 38 percent, respectively).

Finally—and again as with the Democrats—we find that the patterns of difference between liberal and conservative Republican Party officials extend to their positions on the specific issues examined in the survey. As shown in table 5.14, the proportion of liberals giving a conservative response is consistently lower on each of the fourteen issues. While a majority of conservatives responded conservatively on eleven of the fourteen issues, a majority of liberals responded conservatively on only five of the issues.

Table 5.12. Local Southern Republican Party Activists' Feelings toward the Political Parties, by Ideology (in percentage)

Feeling	Liberal	Moderate	Conservative
Toward national Democratic Party			
Close	4	2	2
Neutral	39	29	10
Distant	57	69	89
Toward state Democratic Party			
Close	7	3	2
Neutral	41	38	20
Distant	53	59	78
Toward national Republican Party			
Close	46	49	68
Neutral	37	44	26
Distant	17	8	6
Toward state Republican Party			
Close	47	52	71
Neutral	36	42	24
Distant	18	6	5

Although the differences are relatively narrow in a few cases (a balanced budget amendment and a state tax increase to meet a financial crisis), the differences are commonly much wider and on six issues exceed 30 percentage points. Ideological divisions within the party, then, are associated with a slight break in the conservative homogeneity of the Republican Party in the South.

Summary and Conclusions

These data clearly show that the ideological orientations of local party officials help to structure political activity and discourse both between and within the parties. The initial part of the analysis indicates that these activists differ clearly, in the aggregate, in their ideological self-identifications, with the Democrats being more liberal and the Republicans more conservative. This differentiation appeared, as well, in their collective positions on the issues included in the survey.

The parties have not become homogeneous groupings at the polar extremes of the ideological spectrum, however. Within each party there are liberals, conservatives, and moderates who exhibit some systematic differ-

Table 5.13. Levels of Campaign Activity of Local Republican Party Officials, by Ideology (in percentage)

Level	Liberal	Moderate	Conservative
Local elections			
Very active	51	50	53
Somewhat active	39	31	30
Not very active	8	15	13
Not active at all	2	4	4
State elections			
Very active	37	45	53
Somewhat active	47	41	36
Not very active	13	11	8
Not active at all	3	3	2
National elections			
Very active	38	43	55
Somewhat active	37	34	30
Not very active	18	17	11
Not active at all	6	6	4

ences in backgrounds (both socioeconomic-demographic and political), party orientations, and issue positions. The potential impact of these internal divisions is much greater for the southern Democratic Party than for the southern Republican Party, mainly because conservatives constitute such an overwhelming majority within the ranks of the Republicans. Although liberal Republicans differ (in some ways quite sharply) from conservative Republicans, their potential for influencing events within the party in the near future is muted by their small numbers. Moderate Republican activists are numerically greater than liberals (constituting 12 percent of our sample), and they, too, differ from the conservatives, usually falling somewhere between the two more extreme groups; however, their potential impact is also likely to be very limited in the face of the preponderance of conservatives in the party's activist ranks. For the Republicans, therefore, the most likely source of internal conflict probably lies in whatever divisions may exist within the ranks of the conservatives (e.g., economic conservatives vs. social conservatives such as those associated with the religious right; see, for example, Baker, Moreland, and Steed, 1989; Baker, Steed, and Moreland, 1991).

For the Democrats, the picture is quite different. Here the three ideological groups are much more evenly balanced, with each group being represented in numbers capable of having some sizable impact on the party. Un-

Table 5.14. Local Southern Republican Party Officials' Positions on Selected Issues, by Ideology (in percentage conservative responses)

Issue	Liberal	Moderate	Conservative
Social			
Gov. assistance for women	15	25	53
Personal choice for abortion	30	31	62
School prayer	61	80	92
Environmental protection	14	23	39
Gov. aid for blacks/minorities	38	47	72
Support for women's equality	9	10	21
Affirmative action programs	78	94	98
Economic			
Fewer services to reduce gov. spending	46	56	78
Constitutional amendment to balance nat. budget	79	81	89
State tax increase for financial crisis	85	88	94
Gov. aid in jobs and living standards	66	80	90
Gov. health care assistance	20	32	52
Foreign policy/defense			
Increase defense spending	39	43	62
Continue cooperation with Russia	6	9	22

der these circumstances, the differences examined in the previous analysis reflect internal divisions of some importance. The variations across ideological groupings on such matters as campaign activity levels, issue preferences, voting patterns, and feelings of attachment to the party (especially the national Democratic Party) are particularly significant. Problems associated with these divisions have been evident in elections over the past two decades, as southern Democrats have struggled, with varying degrees of success, to hold their coalition together in the face of increased competition from the Republicans.

There is little evidence to suggest that this ideological fragmentation of the Democratic Party will cease in the near future. Over the longer term, however, we might speculate that the party will become less divided. For one thing, we can speculate that, since the conservatives are slightly older, generational replacement might well change the configuration of the party in a more moderate-to-liberal direction. Along the same lines, if African Americans continue to become more involved in southern party politics— approaching their levels of involvement, for example, in Democratic state conventions in the South—the ranks of liberal Democrats will grow. While this growth does not automatically translate into more liberal positions on all issues and under all circumstances, there will likely be a more general push toward that end of the ideological scale. Also, in-migrants constitute a larger proportion of the liberal Democrats than of the conservative Democrats; continued population change in the region is likely, therefore, to contribute to an increase in the liberal segment within the party.[2] Finally, the high levels of disaffection among Democratic conservatives makes them ripe for defection—if not *to* the Republican Party, then at least *from* the Democratic Party. To the extent that such party sorting through defection materializes, the conservative segment of the party will shrink.

Our concern in this book is with political parties in general, not southern parties alone. Much of the discussion, however, revolves around the peculiar circumstances of southern party development in recent decades, and this naturally raises the question of how much our findings can be generalized to parties outside the region. This is a special concern in the discussion of ideology inasmuch as the dramatic rearrangement of the southern party system in the post–World War II era has, as suggested at the beginning of the chapter, heightened the ideological differences between the region's parties. While the response to this concern must be more speculative than empirical, it would seem rather safe to assume that the broad patterns we have examined in this chapter are likely to be found in parties outside the South as well. While the specific manifestations of both the interparty and intraparty ideological cleavages are likely to differ (e.g., conservative disaffection within the Democratic Party is probably less likely to show up in distant feelings toward the national party), it is still quite likely that these divisions are related to systematic differences of importance to the parties; in turn, these ideological cleavages contribute to the parties' ability to structure political conflict. Certainly, while not congruent with the responsible party model of ideological parties, our data suggest that this is, nevertheless, a function that contemporary parties perform to a substantial degree.

6
Party Maintenance Activities

Frank B. Feigert
John R. Todd

That parties exist between campaigns is obvious, but this might seem to come as a surprise to party scholars. A recent classic work on party organization correctly points out that "public policy performs party maintenance functions. The law ordains that there shall be at least the shell of a party organization and generally invests the officers of this organization with functions of public significance. Public policy assures the minority party in the states of continued existence even at very low levels of electoral success" (Cotter et al., 1984: 149).

If there is an activity focus in party scholarship, it conventionally centers on campaigns, examining how, and to what extent, party organizations and their activists are oriented to campaigns for public office (e.g., Abramowitz et al., 1983; Bass and Westmoreland, 1984; Hedges, 1984; Hopkins, 1986; Marvick and Nixon, 1961; Marvick, 1983). An earlier strain of scholarship focuses on how effective campaigns are in terms of stimulating the vote (e.g., Cutright and Rossi, 1958; Katz and Eldersveld, 1961; Rossi and Cutright, 1961; Wolfinger, 1963). This led to two related fields of inquiry, those of (1) recruitment and (2) incentives to party and campaign activity.

The first is illustrated, in part, by analyses such as those of Bowman and Boynton (1966b); Jackson, Brown, and Brown (1978); Marvick and Nixon (1961); and Hulbary and Bowman (chapter 1 of this book). The second, a rather well-developed line of research, is seen in such diverse works as those by Abramowitz et al. (1983); Bowman, Ippolito, and Donaldson (1969); Conway and Feigert (1968, 1974); Ippolito (1969a); Miller, Jewell, and Sigelman (1987); and Roback (1980a, 1980b). Much of this latter research stems from the seminal organizational theory work of Clark and Wilson (1961). Shaffer and Breaux, in chapter 2 of this book, explore the question of incentives for southern grassroots activists. Certainly, the party's ability to engage in interelection (i.e., party maintenance) activities would provide a means to extend the incentives otherwise offered. For example, the solidary incentive need not be offered only during campaign season. Indeed, to be effective, the solidary incentive is arguably best offered on a continuing basis. For that matter, a range of incentives, it has been suggested, "would appear to facilitate maximizing party effectiveness in performing both campaign and non-campaign tasks" (Conway and Feigert, 1974: 709).

The Importance of Party Maintenance

Arguably as important, or more so, are those non-campaign-related activities in which members of the party organization engage in the interelection period. Clearly, for reasons of cost-effectiveness (Schlesinger, 1984), the formal party organization cannot be re-created, de novo, for every campaign.[1] Regardless of the degree of activity, on a continuum from intense to passive, party officers occupy positions that are not totally refilled for every election. Indeed, more than three-fourths of all respondents in our eleven-state survey held their positions prior to the most recent party election. If the party is to be more than an empty shell, one that is filled only every two years or so to assist campaigns for various offices, the organizational apparatus must be maintained. This includes offers of incentives to remain active and continuing activist recruitment to replace those who have left. Such questions, hardly glamorous, have rarely been addressed. In the context of political parties there have been exceptions to this point, including Bowman and Boynton (1966a); Burrell (1986); Crotty (1968a); and Ippolito and Bowman (1969). Conway and Feigert (1974, table 5) show that only 11 percent of the precinct workers they surveyed admit to interelection activity. On the other hand, 63 percent report working one to four hours a week and 18 percent report working five to ten hours a week in nonelection times. Clearly, the party is not at all an empty shell, and it is the nature and extent of such activities that we explore in this chapter. Given the rapidly changing nature of southern politics, with an emerging Republican Party, we would expect to find our GOP activist sample quite given over to party maintenance activities. "Over time, the electorally weaker party has shown the greatest organizational effort" (Cotter et al., 1984: 157). We might also expect that Democrats, facing a challenge, would similarly engage in such activities, not only to maintain but also to revitalize their organizations. Hence, we might expect to find a higher degree of activism in the South than elsewhere, an expression of what Rosenau (1974) has felicitously described as "citizenship between elections."

Data

In dealing with responses to survey questions related to party maintenance, we consider those party functions rated "important" by our sample of southern party activists, as well as the correlates. The basic question asked was: "In your current party position, which of these activities are among the important things you do?" Of the thirteen activities then listed, six are considered relevant to party maintenance: raising money; participating in party meetings and business; recruiting and organizing workers; working in the county party organization; increasing political information for workers; and formulating policy.

Our analysis in this chapter considers these activities, along with certain attitudinal variables as they relate to party maintenance. The variables include an ideological self-description in response to the question "What about your political beliefs? Do you consider yourself: very liberal, somewhat liberal, middle of the road/moderate, somewhat conservative, or very conservative?" In a related part of the survey, activists were asked for responses, ranging from "strongly agree" to "strongly disagree," to a series of three statements about party unity: (1) Party organizational unity is more important than are divisive issues; (2) Sometimes it is necessary to avoid controversial positions for the sake of party unity; and (3) To build a political party, it is better to work from the top down (e.g., utilizing presidential elections to increase party voter registration) rather than from the bottom up (e.g., concentrating on running candidates for city/county governing bodies or the state legislature).

Why do we consider such questions? As Cotter et al. point out in reference to state and local organizations, "Traditionally, the hallmark of American party organization has been fragmentation" (1984: 156). American parties have seldom been known for a sustained high degree of ideological coherence. It is our expectation that answers to these questions, along with personal political philosophy, address the possibility that ideological purism could be counterproductive to efforts directed at party maintenance, not to mention party building.

Clearly, we might expect differences to emerge based on political party, especially since the Republicans have shown themselves to be strongly resurgent, not only in terms of campaigns and election results but in other respects as well (see, for example, Black and Black 1987, 1992; Welch and Brown, 1979.) For instance, there has been relatively rapid development of a cadre of Republican Party activists, available at each election period and clearly so in the intercampaign period as well. It should be noted that there are clearly some interstate differences in this respect, as not all GOP organizations had achieved parity with their Democratic counterparts at the time this study was undertaken.[2]

Findings

Party Activities

In table 6.1 we see the results of our first cut at how well the organization maintains itself in the months and years between campaign periods. As noted, respondents were asked to rate listed activities according to degree

Table 6.1. Party Maintenance Activities Rated Important, by Party (in percentage)

Activity	Democrats	Republicans
Raising money*	53.2	56.2
Participating in party meetings and business	82.9	83.2
Recruiting and organizing workers	68.1	68.4
County party organizational work	69.2	67.8
Increasing political information for workers*	75.6	78.6
Policy formulation	57.2	58.7
Activity index (No. of activities rated important)*		
0	9.7	6.4
1	11.5	9.2
2	13.3	12.8
3	14.9	15.7
4	13.6	16.5
5	14.8	15.6
6	22.2	23.8
(N)	(5601)	(4857)

*p < .01.

of importance. Somewhat surprisingly, we see that there are few party differences regarding such activities and that there is general and high agreement that such activities must be performed, however unglamorous or out of the public eye they might be. Each activity is rated as important by more than half of our sample, regardless of party. Two activities, money raising and increasing political information for party workers, statistically distinguish the two parties from one another, although the differences of roughly 3 percent suggest that this may be an artifact of the very large sample size. When we combine responses into a cumulative activity index, party differences emerge more clearly, principally because Democrats are slightly less willing than Republicans to rate maintenance activities as important. However, for the most part, such differences appear to be minimal.

When we control for position within the party (table 6.2), a clearer picture emerges, one that is not totally unexpected. All intraparty distinctions are statistically significant. County leaders are considerably more likely to view each activity as important, quite likely because their positions lead them to see such maintenance activities as functional for a healthier party organization. There are strong similarities between Democrats and Republicans of comparable position (precinct leaders and county chairs), suggesting that views of such activities are more a function of position than of

**Table 6.2. Party Maintenance Activities Rated Important,
by Party and Position (in percentage)**

	Democrats		Republicans	
Activity	County chairs	Precinct officials	County chairs	Precinct officials
Raising money	71.7	50.6	72.9	53.6
Participating in party meetings and business	89.2	82.0	85.4	82.8
Recruiting and organizing workers	83.5	66.0	87.0	65.6
County party organizational work	86.5	66.9	87.3	64.8
Increasing political information for workers	83.4	74.5	82.4	78.0
Policy formulation	66.2	56.0	65.0	57.8
Activity index (No. of activities rated important)				
0	4.7	10.3	2.3	7.0
1	4.7	12.4	5.4	9.8
2	7.4	14.1	8.2	13.4
3	10.0	15.4	9.0	16.7
4	12.1	13.8	17.2	16.3
5	19.7	14.2	19.5	15.0
6	41.4	19.8	38.5	21.7
(N)	(619)	(4986)	(1611)	(4246)

party. This is shown even more clearly in our cumulative activity index. Roughly a quarter of the county chairs are likely to describe three or fewer such activities as not important, and the median number for chairs of both parties is five. On the other hand, roughly half of the precinct officials (52.2 percent Democrats, 46.9 percent Republicans) view maintenance activities as not important.

Querying the activists about which party maintenance activities are most important (table 6.3), we find that Republicans are more inclined to so describe each of these activities (except for participating in party meetings) than are Democrats. However, these differences are rather small for the most part, and such evaluations are at a relatively low level. The greatest difference is only 4 percent, as Republicans are slightly more inclined to evaluate the increasing of political information for workers. It seems that party is not a significant predictor variable in terms of attitudes toward maintenance activities.

Table 6.4, again, shows just how much more such views are dependent on one's position within the party than on party itself. County chairs, with

**Table 6.3. Selected Maintenance Activities Rated Most Important,
by Party (in percentage)**

Activity	Democrats	Republicans
Raising money	4.0	5.0
Participating in party meetings and business	9.4	8.3
Recruiting and organizing workers	4.9	5.5
County party organizational work	5.5	6.5
Increasing political information for workers	7.4	11.4
Policy formulation	2.4	4.8

Note: Values do not total 100 percent because campaign-related activities were included in the question.

a few exceptions, are more inclined than are precinct officials to rate *each* of the maintenance activities as most important. The exceptions (for both parties) are participating in party meetings and business and formulating policy. Republican county chairs are also less likely to give high importance to the task of increasing political information for workers.

What is intriguing about tables 6.3 and 6.4 can be inferred from the footnote to each. The basic question addressed to the party workers asked them to rate as "most important" not just the six maintenance activities but seven campaign-related activities as well. The seven included contacting and registering voters, nominating activities, and campaigning itself—the most obvious sorts of party activity, associated with conventional images of the party

**Table 6.4. Party Maintenance Activities Rated Most Important,
by Party and Position (in percentage)**

| Activity | Democrats | | Republicans | |
	County chairs	Precinct officials	County chairs	Precinct officials
Raising money	7.0	3.6	5.1	5.0
Participating in party meetings and business	7.7	9.6	5.9	8.7
Recruiting and organizing workers	6.5	4.7	12.2	4.6
County party organizational work	15.0	4.3	16.4	5.0
Increasing political information for workers	7.7	7.4	8.8	11.8
Policy formulation	1.8	2.4	3.4	5.0

Note: Values do not total 100 percent because campaign-related activities were included in the question.

as existing primarily to fulfill an electoral function. In table 6.3, one-third of the Democrats cited maintenance activities as most important, as did two-fifths of the Republicans. As would be expected, we find in table 6.4 that county chairs are much more likely than are precinct officials to have such orientations (45.7 percent vs. 32.0 percent for Democrats, 51.8 percent vs. 40.1 percent for Republicans). It is somewhat remarkable that such behind-the-scenes activity is valued so highly, inasmuch as it lacks public recognition as well as the glamour and excitement of campaigns. Clearly, what many people might consider to be the humdrum minutiae of party politics are valued by our sample of southern activists. This may be so for instrumental reasons, suggesting that activists recognize a need for a vital organization even in noncampaign periods. It could also be a rationale for the solidary rewards the party offers on a continuing basis. The distinctions between the parties that we have noted may also account, in some part, for recent Republican successes in the South.

Attitudinal Correlates

Do these orientations reflect some underlying attitudinal dimension? We examine this question in table 6.5 in two lights. The first is self-ascribed political philosophy, ranging from very liberal to very conservative. One might expect that commitment to the party organization would be driven by those who are more ideological in their outlooks. In this view, the party might be seen as a vehicle for achieving the purposive incentives associated with ideology. Hence, we might expect that those who are ideologically more extreme would be more inclined to actualize their ideology by having a higher activity index rating. This expectation is scarcely met. While those who describe themselves as very liberal or very conservative are more inclined to view party maintenance activities as important than are the other three groups, the differences are marginal at best and fail to achieve statistical significance, even granting the large numbers involved.

On the other hand, religiosity may account in part for these orientations. Nicely associated (gamma = .294, p < .00000) with political philosophy in our sample is a constructed variable, the "piety index." When asked whether they considered themselves "born again," "fundamentalist," "evangelical," or "charismatic" in their religion, more than 9 percent describe themselves in two or more of these terms. Hence, we have constructed a simple additive index of the extent to which respondents describe themselves in these terms, based on the number of terms selected for self-characterization. Controlling for party, the strong association increases. There is a slight difference, with Republicans (gamma = .347) having a slightly stronger correlation than do Democrats (gamma = .306). It is interesting that this background attitudinal variable, seemingly less proximate to political activ-

Table 6.5. Selected Correlates of Index of Party Maintenance Activities (in percentage)

Activity index (No. of activities rated important)	Correlate				
	Personal political philosophy*				
	Very liberal	Somewhat liberal	Moderate	Somewhat conservative	Very conservative
0	7.3	6.7	8.7	8.1	6.9
1	9.6	9.6	11.6	10.3	9.7
2	11.6	13.2	13.0	13.2	13.3
3	14.6	15.4	16.1	15.7	14.2
4	14.8	14.7	14.4	15.6	15.3
5	16.4	15.6	14.6	15.2	15.6
6	25.5	24.7	21.7	21.8	25.0
(N)	(560)	(1556)	(2471)	(3478)	(2130)
	Piety index**				
	0	1	2	3	4
0	7.6	9.2	8.0	4.6	8.8
1	9.5	11.4	14.3	9.3	11.8
2	13.5	12.1	14.4	14.6	13.2
3	16.0	13.9	17.9	14.9	14.0
4	15.6	13.7	15.4	16.9	17.6
5	15.5	15.0	12.5	16.2	15.4
6	22.3	24.6	17.5	23.5	19.1
(N)	(5549)	(3945)	(526)	(302)	(136)

Note: See text for details on piety index.
*p = .11.   **p = .00001.

ity than political philosophy or ideology, is significantly (p = .00001) but only weakly and inversely associated (gamma = −.018) with our index of party activity. Hence, it seems that one's political philosophy may be more strongly related to views of party maintenance activity than is intensity of religious views.

If religious views can be associated with party activity, however weakly, one might expect that party unity could be at risk. In table 6.6 we test differences between Democrats and Republicans and then between activists of both parties on three questions relating to party unity. We see that on all three questions there are significant differences between the two parties. Popular images of the Democrats as a disorganized and fractious group notwithstanding, we see greater dissension within the GOP on such questions.

Table 6.6a. Views on Party Unity, by Party (in percentage)

Question	Democrats	Republicans
Party organization and unity are more important than free and total discussion of issues which may divide the party*		
Strongly agree	16.5	8.0
Agree	29.5	24.1
Disagree	42.4	51.6
Strongly disagree	11.6	16.3
Controversial positions should be avoided in a party platform to insure party unity*		
Strongly agree	15.3	8.8
Agree	35.5	31.5
Disagree	40.7	45.9
Strongly disagree	8.5	13.7
To build a political party, it is better to work from the top down (e.g., utilizing presidential elections to increase party voter registration) rather than from the bottom up (e.g., concentrating on running candidates for city/county governing bodies or the state legislature)*		
Strongly agree	8.0	6.9
Agree	19.0	19.7
Disagree	49.7	45.4
Strongly disagree	23.3	28.0

*$p = .00000$.

On the first question, more than two-thirds (67.9 percent) of GOP activists are willing to stress divisive issues ahead of party unity, outweighing the Democrats (54 percent). On the second question, three-fifths (59.6 percent) of Republicans disagree with the avoidance of controversial positions, as compared with less than half (49.2 percent) of Democrats. On the third question, regarding the source of party building, each party is strongly inclined to build the organization from the bottom up. We may conclude that the significant difference noted is an artifact of the very large numbers involved in our analysis (see table 6.6a).

When we examine these data by party and position, a slightly different picture emerges. Among Democrats, county chairs and precinct officials show significant differences only on our third statement, dealing with party building. Even so, although statistically significant the differ-

Table 6.6b. Views on Party Unity, by Party and Position (in percentage)

Question	Democrats		Republicans	
	County chairs	Precinct officials	County chairs	Precinct officials
Party organization and unity are more important than free and total discussion of issues which may divide the party*				
Strongly Agree	16.5	16.5	10.1	7.7
Agree	32.4	29.1	25.9	23.8
Disagree	40.9	42.6	52.2	51.5
Strongly Disagree	10.1	11.8	11.8	16.9
Controversial positions should be avoided in a party platform to ensure party unity**				
Strongly Agree	16.5	15.1	8.6	8.8
Agree	36.9	35.3	32.8	31.3
Disagree	39.2	40.9	47.1	45.8
Strongly Disagree	7.3	8.7	11.4	14.1
To build a political party, it is better to work from the top down (e.g., utilizing presidential elections to increase party voter registration) rather than from the bottom up (e.g., concentrating on running candidates for city/county governing bodies or the state legislature)***				
Strongly Agree	7.9	8.0	5.0	7.2
Agree	16.2	19.4	19.3	19.8
Disagree	46.7	50.1	45.4	45.4
Strongly Disagree	29.2	22.5	30.3	27.6

*$p = .308$.
**$p = .471$.
***$p = .003$.

ences are essentially inconsequential. Similarly, Republicans are differentiated on the first question, whether party unity is more important than divisive issues. Even here there is little difference, although precinct officials are slightly more disposed than are county chairs to disagree with the statement (68.4 percent vs. 64 percent). There are no differences worth mentioning within either party on the avoidance of controversy in order to maintain party unity, although Republicans are more willing to take controversial positions.

There remains yet at least one avenue worth exploring in terms of party unity, and that is to return to our use of the piety index. Bear in mind that the index itself taps a dimension of intensity of personal religious views, inasmuch as respondents are increasingly willing to describe themselves in such pietistic terms as "born again," "fundamentalist," "evangelical," or "charismatic" (the base being no such self-description). The piety index, we have seen, is significantly associated with and correlated with personal political philosophy as well as views toward party maintenance activity, more so for Republicans than for Democrats. Table 6.7 relates this index to responses to our three statements on party unity. Disagreement with either of the first two statements suggests that the respondent places a greater premium on the issue or position taken than on party unity. It is important to note that a majority of activists (64.0 percent and 55.7 percent, respectively) in the combined sample of both parties are willing to disagree on these questions. However, we should also recall from table 6.6 that differences between the two parties are rather pronounced: 54.0 percent and 49.2 percent for Democrats versus 67.9 percent and 59.6 percent for Republicans. Hence, the appearance of high commitment to ideological purity that supposedly characterizes our sample is, to some extent, a function of party. For those willing to describe themselves in terms of only one pietistic term, there is a sharp drop in issue or position-taking purism from those unwilling to describe themselves thus. However, from this point a monotonic increase in these qualities is evinced, rising from the lows of 52.2 percent (divisive issues) and 47.3 percent (controversial positions) to 83.3 percent and 84.3 percent.

On the third question, that of party building, we found little difference of consequence in table 6.6 except for that between county chairs and precinct activists among Democrats. Similarly, there is little variation in the combined sample, although the same monotonic increase previously noted also emerges.

Summary and Conclusions

What lessons can be derived from this analysis? While it is true that party scholars have largely ignored questions of party maintenance, it is also true that a vital party must be more than an empty vessel refilled every two years or so for a campaign, in which activists are solely candidate-centered, using the party label solely as a convenience for campaign purposes. Rather, we find that approximately half of our sample of activists see their party organizations very much in need of intercampaign activity, apparently including their own commitment to the time and effort such activity

Table 6.7. Views on Party Unity, by Placement on Piety Scale (in percentage)

	Piety scale placement				
Question	0	1	2	3	4
Party organization and unity are more important than free and total discussion of issues which may divide the party*					
Strongly agree	10.9	16.5	8.6	3.0	2.3
Agree	25.2	31.3	23.2	16.8	14.4
Disagree	48.8	42.2	51.2	51.3	63.6
Strongly disagree	15.2	10.0	17.1	28.9	19.7
Controversial positions should be avoided in a party platform to insure party unity*					
Strongly agree	11.3	15.2	6.5	4.1	4.5
Agree	32.9	37.5	29.2	15.5	11.2
Disagree	45.7	38.3	47.6	47.0	53.7
Strongly disagree	10.0	9.0	16.7	33.4	30.6
To build a political party, it is better to work from the top down (e.g., utilizing presidential elections to increase party voter registration) rather than from the bottom up (e.g., concentrating on running candidates for city/county governing bodies or the state legislature)*					
Strongly agree	6.5	9.4	7.2	4.5	3.1
Agree	17.0	22.8	21.3	15.6	17.1
Disagree	49.0	46.1	46.0	45.5	48.1
Strongly disagree	27.6	21.6	25.5	34.4	31.8

Note: See text for details on piety index.
*$p = .00000$.

requires. Whether the remainder in either party are truly active themselves, including during election season, is beyond the scope of the present analysis.

Certain differences emerge, inasmuch as Democrats are somewhat less inclined either to applaud or to participate in activities contributing to party maintenance. This may reflect their former dominant party status. Although the South has historically been described as a "one party" region, this statement applies to voter behavior and the consequent partisan composition of government. However, in an organizational sense, party maintenance was irrelevant for the once-dominant Democrats (Key, [1949] 1984). As expected, attitudes on party maintenance are also quite dependent on party position, since county chairs show a higher activity index, connoting an awareness of the need to maintain the party in the so-called off-season.

In examining the background of such attitudes, we have focused on two variables, those of personal political philosophy and religious pietism. The former of these is statistically unrelated (p = .110, gamma = .005) to attitudes toward party maintenance. Hence, at first blush, it would seem that neither party's organization can be described as a battleground between liberals and conservatives. However, it must also be pointed out that the range of political philosophy is fairly evenly distributed among Democrats, where it is apparently not a factor entering such views. On the other hand, there is such a skew in favor of conservatism in our Republican sample that any results would be meaningless.[3]

It is when we examine religiosity, as measured by our additive index, that we find some potential for understanding the attitudes displayed. Bearing in mind that such self-descriptions are not restricted to either party but *are* related to political philosophy, we find that they are nicely related to views on party unity, in an inverse manner. That is, the more likely one is to view oneself in such terms as "born again," "fundamentalist," "evangelical," or "charismatic," then the lower the premium placed on party unity.

These data suggest that southern parties are more active in the interelection period than might otherwise be surmised. Both parties have a corps of individuals apparently willing to devote the time and energy to activities, out of the public view, that contribute to the parties' ongoing, as well as increased, success. On the assumption that such views can be translated into action, it would seem that the foot soldiers of southern party organizations, more so for Republicans, are more likely to be those we can describe as pietistic and professing Christians. In short, if the intensity of view they have in religious affairs is consistent with political action, those sustaining the southern parties when campaigns are not under way will be more intense and committed, thus possibly leading to party building.

This is not to be taken as an argument that the Christian right has necessarily taken over the southern party organization. Nonetheless, the extent to which the Christian Coalition has emerged shows remarkable parallels with the rise of the GOP in the South. This has been variously depicted as a struggle between a euphemistic "old guard" and a new breed. However, we certainly see that such conflict can be institutionalized within the formal party organization, including interelection periods when the party is typically considered dormant. In this light, we can view the rise of southern Republicanism as something of a struggle between the necessarily more pragmatic county chairs and the more pietistic precinct officials, taking place within a framework essentially devoid of philosophical dissension regarding public policy. Whether this will lead to a new orthodoxy beyond public affairs remains to be seen, as would its consequences for both the party and the public it nominally serves.

7
Campaign Activities

John A. Clark
Brad Lockerbie
Peter W. Wielhouwer

At the most basic level, the goal of political parties is to win elections. Models of political behavior focus on partisanship, issues, and candidates as determinants of vote choice in the electorate (e.g., Asher, 1992, for a summary). In addition, the campaign activity of local party organizations has been shown to increase the likelihood of participation. Aside from the candidates it nominates or the issue positions it advocates, the political party can influence electoral outcomes by waging a campaign for votes.

In this chapter, we examine patterns of campaign activity by grassroots party activists in the South. Some scholars have treated activists as informants about the activities of the party organization (e.g., Cotter et al., 1984). Our data, with multiple respondents per county organization, allow a more complex view of individual activists; in the organizational context, some people choose to be more active than others. We find differences in activity levels between county chairs and precinct committee members. In addition to the level of activity, there are differences in the *types* of activities being performed by different strata of the party. Both organizational and individual variables are related to the performance of campaign activities.

Organizational Vitality and Party Campaign Activity

One measure of an organization's vitality might be the amount of activity it undertakes in support of the party's candidates (Burrell, 1986). Unlike more elaborate measures of organizational strength (e.g., Gibson et al., 1983, 1985), campaign activity indicates what a party *does* rather than its bureaucratization or organizational structure.[1] Moribund parties might be led by people who fill slots in the hierarchy but do little to further the election of the party's candidates. Vital party organizations ought to exhibit higher levels of activity from county and precinct activists.

One of the pillars of the party-in-decline school has been the alleged demise of local party organizations. While it is true that urban machines have

all but disappeared, it is less clear whether such organizations ever existed
in most urban and nonurban locales, particularly in the South (Beck and
Sorauf, 1992: 82; Mayhew, 1986). Due in part to the growth of entitlement
programs and civil service reform, patronage is less important than it once
was. Similarly, nominations are no longer tightly controlled by party organizations. Still, there is little beyond conjecture to demonstrate the disappear-
ance of local parties.

In contrast, the evidence available on local party activity reveals that
many organizations display greater vitality than the party-in-decline school
would have us believe. Summarizing the campaign efforts of grassroots activists in five cities, Crotty (1986a: 29) observed that "all of the local parties
engaged in each of the activities to a significant degree; and the intensity of
effort invested in the individual activities is impressive, again higher than
might have been assumed." Today's local parties may not act like old-style
machines, but that does not mean that they are failing to perform important
tasks in their communities.

Unfortunately, there is no national baseline from which to judge the
change in party activity across time. In fact, the first direct estimates come
from a national survey of county party chairs in 1979–80. In a comparison
with the best available data on previous activity, Gibson and his colleagues
(1985: 155) concluded that "local party organizations have *not* become less
active and less organized over the last two decades" (emphasis in original).
Four years later, it appeared that most parties exhibited either an increase
or no change (but not a decline) in the performance of campaign activities
(Gibson, Frendreis, and Vertz, 1989).

While Gibson and his colleagues (1985) uncovered little party organizational activity in the South as the 1980s began, the national committees of
both parties identified the region as strategic to their electoral fortunes.
The Republicans in particular sought to strengthen first state party organizations, then local parties too (Huckshorn, 1994). The Democrats were
forced to respond to this new electoral threat. Democratic county organizations increased their campaign efforts more in the South than in any other
region between 1980 and 1988 (Smith, 1989).

Local party organizations may be more vital, but to what end? Students
of political parties have long been interested in the effects of party activity
on the behavior of the mass public. Early research led to differing conclusions. Katz and Eldersveld (1961), for example, discovered that the strength
of the local Republican leadership influenced the mobilization of voters in
heavily Democratic Wayne County (Detroit), Michigan, while Democratic
leaders appeared to have no effect. Crotty (1971) reached similar conclusions concerning the relationship between local Republican organizational
activity and election outcomes in then mostly one-party North Carolina.

More recent research has expanded our understanding of the impact of party campaign activity. Frendreis, Gibson, and Vertz (1990) found weak and inconsistent effects of party campaigning on election outcomes. Republican activity was related to the likelihood of running a complete slate of candidates, which in turn affected vote totals for higher-ticket offices. In one midwestern city, the party canvass mobilized party supporters, who in turn displayed their political preferences for their friends and neighbors (Huckfeldt and Sprague, 1992). The activity of the local party organization did not directly alter the behavior of many voters, but it did indirectly influence the electoral outcome.

Using the American National Election Studies of 1952 through 1990, Wielhouwer and Lockerbie (1994) found that the effects of party contacting are more pronounced now than they were several decades ago, when the parties were supposedly stronger. In most instances, it is the party out of the presidency that has a greater impact on mobilization. These findings suggest that the presence of active grassroots party organizations can counteract a lack of control over the operation of government. Like a second-place car rental agency, the out-party must "try harder" to win control of public office. In places where the party is electorally weak, organizational effort can provide a foundation for future growth.

Perhaps more now than in the past, southern grassroots parties are capable of influencing electoral outcomes with their campaign activity. And, as the South becomes more competitive below the presidential level, it becomes more important to understand the role of party activists and party organizations. Several empirical questions remain, however. For instance, how active are grassroots party organizations in the conduct of campaign activities? Is there specialization among party activists? Is there an organizational presence at the local level capable of conducting an election campaign? Were those observers who proclaimed the decline of grassroots parties premature in lamenting their demise?

Activity Performance by Grassroots Activists

One of the primary characteristics of sophisticated organizations is the division of labor within the organization to promote specialization (March and Simon, 1958). If party organizations are to be considered at all sophisticated, there must be evidence that responsibilities are divided among activists. For our purposes, there ought to be differences in the activities performed by county chairs and precinct committee members. We address this issue in two ways. First, we examine activists' assessments of the most important activity they performed. Second, we look at the number of campaign activities they performed. In both instances, there is evidence of specialization.

Just what activities do these party leaders think are important? Chairs are

Table 7.1. Most Important Party Activity, by Position and Party (in percentage)

	Democrats		Republicans	
Activity	Chair	Member	Chair	Member
Contacting voters	10.9	16.9	7.8	18.2
Raising money	7.0	3.6	5.1	5.0
Registering voters	15.2	28.8	9.1	18.4
Campaigning	9.0	9.1	5.9	9.0
Public relations	9.0	4.9	7.1	4.4
Contacting new voters	1.0	1.8	1.0	1.3
Party meetings/business	7.7	9.6	5.9	8.7
Recruiting party workers	6.5	4.7	12.2	4.6
Organizational work	15.0	4.3	16.4	5.0
Information for others	7.7	7.4	8.8	11.8
Policy formulation	1.8	2.4	3.4	5.0
Recruiting candidates	8.8	5.9	17.1	8.4
Other nomination activities	0.3	0.5	0.2	0.4
(N)	(599)	(4662)	(591)	(4011)

much more likely to emphasize managerial activities, while precinct committee members place a higher value on the retail efforts of politics. More than 15 percent of the chairs selected organizational work as their most important activity, while only 5 percent of the precinct leaders selected this option. Similarly, almost 13 percent of the chairs selected getting local candidates to run as their most important activity, while just over 7 percent of the nonchairs made this selection. In contrast, 24 percent of the members made registering voters their top priority, compared with just over 12 percent of the chairs. More than 17 percent of the members and less than 10 percent of the chairs selected contacting potential voters as their most important activity.

Some differences emerge when we break the chair/member distinction down by party, as shown in table 7.1. Democratic chairs rank registering voters as their most important activity, with organizational work in second place. Republican chairs, however, rank getting candidates to run as their primary activity, with organizational work again a close second. Recruitment is clearly a more important duty for Republican chairs. Recruiting party workers or candidates was the top priority of 29 percent of Republican chairs, compared with about half as many Democrats. It appears that southern Republicans must continue to emphasize party building at the grassroots level, while their Democratic counterparts can rely on their traditional

Table 7.2. Activities Engaged in, by Position and Party (in percentage)

	Democrats		Republicans	
Activity	Chair	Member	Chair	Member
Organized canvassing	29.7	25.8	31.9	30.6
Organized campaign events	66.7	29.9	70.0	33.8
Arranged fund raising	57.2	25.4	60.6	28.1
Sent mailings	40.5	33.0	53.8	47.1
Distributed literature	72.9	60.5	78.7	71.4
Organized phone banks	45.6	29.1	56.8	38.6
Purchased billboards	8.4	4.5	9.2	5.4
Distributed posters	70.8	52.2	79.7	65.3
Contributed money	77.2	59.8	85.4	72.9
Registration drives	35.1	20.3	33.6	23.0
Utilized surveys	12.8	9.1	16.5	12.5
Dealt with media	60.9	18.0	64.0	22.6
(N)	(619)	(4981)	(611)	(4246)

electoral strength to flush out potential candidates and workers. It is important to note that there is a substantial divergence of opinion among the chairs as to their top priority; no single activity was named by more than 18 percent as their most important duty.

There is greater agreement among precinct committee members of both parties regarding their most important responsibilities. Registering voters was named by 29 percent of the Democrats and 18 percent of the Republicans, followed by contacting voters (17 percent and 18 percent, respectively). Unlike county chairs, these activists view their role as operating on the front lines of politics, advancing the parties' goals through direct contact with potential voters.

Similar patterns of specialization are present in the campaign activities performed by grassroots party activists. Table 7.2 shows relatively few differences across parties. Republicans are more likely to have organized telephone campaigns, sent mailings to voters, and distributed lawn signs and posters. For the most part, however, these differences are relatively minor. The major differences that exist are within the parties rather than across parties; position in the party hierarchy appears to account for a great deal of variation. Chairs are much more likely to have engaged in organizational and managerial activities than are the other activists. Except for organizing door-to-door canvassing, in which relatively few engaged, those activities that involved a managerial task were much more likely to have been performed by the chairs. Chairs were more than twice as likely as members to have organized campaign events and arranged fund-raising events. Chairs were approximately one and one-half times as likely as members to have organized telephone campaigns, almost three times as likely as members to have dealt with campaign media. There does appear to be a strong differentiation of activities across levels within these party organizations. Even in those activities that are not organizational or managerial, such as distributing campaign literature and contributing financially, chairs tend to be more active than members.

In looking over the patterns of activity presented here, an intuitive categorization seems to emerge. Some of the activities are managerial; that is, they are likely to be geared to establishing or running political campaigns at the local level. These activities include organizing door-to-door canvassing, organizing campaign events, arranging fund-raising activities, organizing telephone campaigns, conducting registration drives, utilizing public opinion surveys, and dealing with campaign media. Each activity requires some political expertise or substantial managerial skills. Other activities seemed to be more hands-on and labor intensive. Such activities include sending mailings to voters; distributing campaign literature, posters, or lawn signs; and contributing money to campaigns.

On the basis of this categorization, we created two separate additive indexes for analysis.[2] The *managerial* activity index ranges from zero to seven and includes those variables discussed here. Figure 7.1 reveals the percentage distribution of respondents on this index; the comparisons of interest are Democrats versus Republicans, and chairs versus members. Figure 7.1 reveals that there is little difference between Democrats and the GOP in the number of activities performed (although the mean for Democrats is 1.74 activities, and for Republicans it is 2.07): pluralities of both groups perform no managerial activities, and 71 percent of Democrats and 64 percent of Republicans perform two or fewer of these activities. There is, however, a substantial difference between chairs and rank-and-file activists (the member mean is 1.72 activities, and the chair mean is 3.21): the modal number of managerial activities is zero for members and three (in the more normal distribution) for chairs; while 44 percent of members perform two or more of these activities, 45 percent of chairs perform four or more. In sum, chairs are more likely to perform managerial activities than are precinct committee members.

The *labor-intensive* index ranges from zero to four. Figure 7.2 shows the percentage distribution of each group in the performance of these activities, as discussed previously. The distributional patterns are similar in appearance for all four groups, with the modal categories at the high end of the scale. The Republican mean is 2.62 labor-intensive activities; the Democrats' mean is 2.12. The percentage of Republicans performing no activities is 9.4, which is 10 percentage points lower than for the Democrats; similarly,

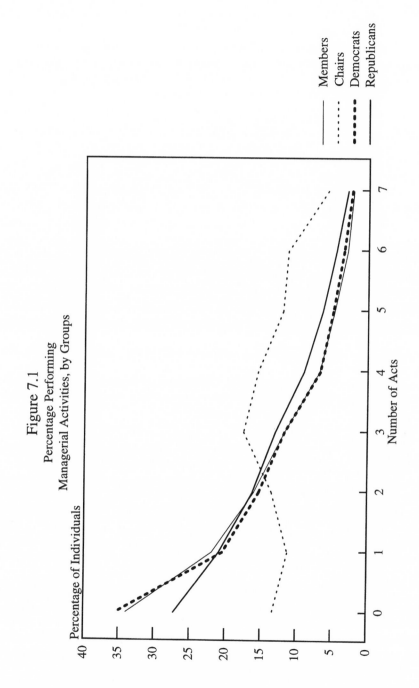

Figure 7.1
Percentage Performing
Managerial Activities, by Groups

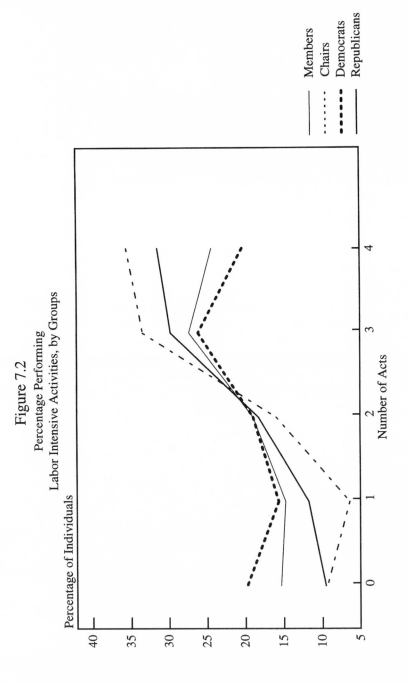

Figure 7.2
Percentage Performing
Labor Intensive Activities, by Groups

the percentage of GOP activists performing all four activities is 31.3, which is 11 percentage points higher than for the Democrats. While there was about a 1.5-point difference between chairs and members on the managerial index, this gap narrows in the labor-intensive activity index: the mean for chairs is 2.79 activities, while members performed a mean of 2.31 activities.

Explaining Activity Levels

We are interested in the extent to which we can explain the variations in the managerial and labor-intensive activity indexes. To this end, we apply multivariate analyses to these two dimensions to ascertain whether items other than role differentiation can explain the patterns of activity. Two organizational characteristics and up to ten individual-level political and sociodemographic characteristics are utilized as independent variables.

Independent Variables

Unlike survey respondents from the mass public, our grassroots activists consciously participate in politics within the context of a party organization. Just as they affect the organization, so too should their perceptions of the organization's effectiveness influence the level of commitment they make to the party. Two organizational variables were included in the analysis. First, we constructed an index of the change in party organizational health, based on activists' responses to a battery of party health questions. Respondents were asked to compare their county party today with the organization five to ten years ago in terms of overall strength, campaign effectiveness, fund-raising ability, candidate recruitment, and development of the organizational skills of workers. The responses were coded on a series of five-point scales, each ranging from "significantly weaker" to "significantly stronger." The components were added together, forming an index with a possible range of 0 to 20, with higher scores representing stronger party health. Our expectation is that where the party is perceived as gaining strength, individuals will be motivated to perform more activities. These effects are likely to be more pronounced for members than for chairs. Chairs are key elements in local parties and have greater responsibility for the party's overall vitality, whereas organizational weaknesses are likely to take their toll on the rank and file, who might be more likely to withdraw in the absence of a healthy organization.

Second, perception of the amount of factionalization in a local party organization is included in the equation because this may affect the performance of campaign activities. Factionalization might affect precinct members more (through disenchantment and frustration) than it affects those further up the party hierarchy, from whom we would expect a higher level of commitment. On the other hand, the competition for control of the local party organization might stimulate members to be more active.[3] We measure factionalization with a four-point scale, where 3 represents a "fairly high" amount of factionalization, and 0 represents none.

In addition to these organizational attributes, individuals bring various political predispositions to bear on their party activity. One of the most vexing questions for parties scholars is the relationship between attitudes toward the party and the performance of campaign activities. Wilson (1962) and Wildavsky (1965) noted that some activists were primarily concerned with winning elections, while others were principally motivated by issues and ideology. The professional/amateur or pragmatist/purist distinction has been examined from a variety of perspectives (see chapter 2 of this book). Ideological or purposive motivations can lead to initial involvement in party affairs (e.g., Clark and Wilson, 1961), but many people need other incentives to maintain participation in party organizations (Wilson, 1962; Dodson, 1990). Our expectation is that party officials with an orientation favorable to party organization and party unity will be more active than those whose issue concerns outweigh their concerns about winning. We measure the pragmatist/purist dimension with a trichotomy constructed from four items relating to party norms.[4] Issue purists were scored with a 3, those with more pragmatic orientations were given a score of 1, and those in the middle were coded 2.

Not unrelated to issue purism is the ideological predisposition of the individual activist. Activists whose personal ideologies match most closely the views held by the national party organizations have a greater stake in the electoral success of the party. The distinction may be especially important among Democrats in the South, since they have traditionally anchored the conservative wing of their party. We measure ideology using the respondent's self-placement on a five-point scale ranging from "very liberal" to "very conservative." In the chair and member equations, the scale is recoded so that conservative Republicans and liberal Democrats receive high scores. Additionally, each party equation includes a dummy variable separating chairs from members, and the chair and member equations contain a dummy variable testing for different intercepts between Democrats and Republicans.

The literature on political participation often focuses on a variety of sociodemographic characteristics to explain participation in the general public (Verba and Nie, 1972; Rosenstone and Hansen, 1993). Our respondents have already crossed the threshold into political activity as evidenced by their party offices. However, we include a variety of sociodemographic characteristics as control variables and as a way to compare activity levels among activists with those of the mass public. Such variables include age, gender,

Table 7.3. Multiple Regression Results for Managerial Activity Index

Independent variable	Republicans	Democrats	Chairs	Members
Intercept	3.06 (.33)**	2.77 (.26)**	3.97 (.62)**	1.71 (.21)**
Party health	.03 (.01)**	.02 (.01)**	.12 (.01)**	.01 (.00)*
Factionalism	.18 (.04)**	.13 (.03)**	.14 (.07)*	.15 (.03)**
Ideology[a]	.02 (.04)	-.13 (.03)**	.25 (.07)**	.09 (.02)**
Chair	1.33 (.09)**	1.34 (.09)**	—	—
Democrat	—	—	.43 (.16)**	-.11 (.06)*
Issue purism	-.26 (.05)**	-.29 (.04)**	-.46 (.09)**	-.24 (.03)**
Age	-.02 (.00)**	-.02 (.00)**	-.02 (.00)**	-.02 (.00)**
Female	.40 (.07)**	.20 (.06)**	.28 (.15)**	.32 (.05)**
Years in county	-.00 (.00)	-.01 (.00)**	-.00 (.00)	-.00 (.00)*
Education	-.01 (.03)	.10 (.03)**	-.00 (.06)	.06 (.02)**
Income	.11 (.02)**	.06 (.02)**	.08 (.03)**	.09 (.01)**
African American	-.08 (.23)	.13 (.09)	.08 (.36)	.14 (.09)
Hispanic	—	.21 (.22)	—	.44 (.22)*
R²	.12	.14	.14	.07
(N)	(3556)	(3956)	(999)	(6542)

Note: Entries are unstandardized ordinary least squares coefficients (standard errors in parentheses).

[a]For the Democratic and Republican equations, higher ideology scores indicate increased conservatism; for the chair and member equations, higher ideology scores indicate ideological extremism (defined in terms of the ideological tendencies of the national party organizations).

*p ≤ .05.

**p ≤ .01.

length of residence in the county, levels of education and income, and race (ethnicity).

Multivariate Analysis

We estimate eight Ordinary Least Squares regression equations; the results are presented in tables 7.3 and 7.4.[5] As with figures 7.1 and 7.2, the comparisons of interest are between Democrats and Republicans and between chairs and members. Table 7.3 presents four equations for the managerial activity index: one equation for each of the parties, one for chairs, and one for members. We adopt the same approach in table 7.4. By presenting the equations in this manner, we should be able to ascertain whether the items hypothesized previously as important behave similarly for both parties and across positions within the party organization. Also, we will be better able to see if there are the differences we expect. By using multivariate regression, we are able to control for the possibility that some of our independent

Table 7.4. Multiple Regression Results for Labor-Intensive Activity Index

Independent variable	Republicans	Democrats	Chairs	Members
Intercept	3.10 (.22)**	2.93 (.19)**	2.99 (.37)**	1.85 (.15)**
Party Health	.03 (.00)**	.01 (.00)	.04 (.01)**	.01 (.00)**
Factionalism	.09 (.02)**	.07 (.03)**	.11 (.04)**	.07 (.02)**
Ideology[a]	.11 (.03)**	-.16 (.02)**	.14 (.04)**	.16 (.02)**
Chair	.31 (.06)**	.39 (.07)**	—	—
Democrat	—	—	.06 (.10)	-.18 (.04)**
Issue purism	-.14 (.03)**	-.15 (.03)**	-.14 (.06)**	-.14 (.02)**
Age	-.00 (.00)	-.01 (.00)**	-.01 (.00)*	-.00 (.00)**
Female	.21 (.04)**	.08 (.05)	.19 (.09)**	.15 (.03)**
Years in county	-.00 (.00)	-.00 (.00)**	-.01 (.00)*	-.00 (.00)**
Education	-.04 (.02)	.06 (.02)**	-.06 (.04)**	.04 (.02)*
Income	.05 (.01)**	.05 (.01)**	.03 (.02)	.06 (.01)**
African American	.10 (.15)	-.23 (.07)**	-.25 (.21)	-.17 (.06)**
Hispanic	—	-.09 (.17)	—	.12 (.16)
R²	.05	.08	.09	.07
(N)	(3556)	(3956)	(999)	(6542)

Note: Entries are unstandardized ordinary least squares coefficients (standard errors in parentheses).
[a]For the Democratic and Republican equations, higher ideology scores indicate increased conservatism; for the chair and member equations, higher ideology scores indicate ideological extremism (defined in terms of the ideological tendencies of the national party organizations).
*p ≤ .05.
**p ≤ .01.

variables are correlated. This statistical procedure measures the influence of each independent variable on the dependent variables while simultaneously taking into account the influence of the other variables.

The multivariate analysis does not change our finding that chairs are more active than precinct members, particularly on the managerial index. In the party equations, being a GOP chair increases the number of managerial activities performed by 1.33 when other factors are controlled, while for Democrats this increase is 1.34. The magnitude of the relationship is substantially smaller on the labor-intensive index, although the coefficients are still significant. The comparable difference is captured in the intercepts of the chair and member equations. Even when other influences are controlled, the managerial skills required of county chairs create a division of labor within local parties.

One relationship that does change in the multivariate analysis is the party of the respondent. In the bivariate case, it appeared that Republicans were slightly more active than Democrats on both indexes. When other factors are controlled, Democratic chairs score almost half a point higher on the managerial index, but there is no difference between Republican and Democratic chairs on the labor-intensive index. Among precinct leaders, there is a statistical (but not substantive) difference indicating that Republican precinct members are slightly more active on both indexes.

The party health coefficients show that grassroots activists are more likely to perform managerial activities when they perceive improvement in the health of their local party organization, but the statistical significance is matched by substantive significance only in the chair's managerial index. Even in this single equation, it would take the maximum change on all five components of the index in order to result in a prediction of just two more managerial activities.

The amount of factionalization also significantly affects the number of activities performed in each model; higher levels of factionalization are associated with more active parties, particularly for managerial activities. It would appear that conflict within a local party, rather than driving activists out through disenchantment, acts as a catalyst for increased activism, perhaps in a competition for control of that party.

Our measure of issue purism bears a strong negative relationship to the performance of campaign activities. Activists with an orientation for issues rather than for winning are less active than their pragmatic counterparts. The distinction is more dramatic for the managerial index than for labor-intensive activities, and especially for chairs rather than precinct leaders. Finding chairs with a strong desire to win elections seems especially important for vital local parties (see also Norrander, 1986).

The effect of ideological self-placement is different across parties. Among Republicans, changes on the ideological spectrum do not produce changes in the number of managerial activities performed, but conservatives are more active on the labor-intensive index than are the relatively few moderates in the GOP. For Democrats, however, the negative coefficients indicate that liberals perform more activities on both indexes. The ideology scale for Democrats was reversed in the chair and member equations so that partisan differences in ideology did not cancel each other out. The effect of ideology is stronger for chairs than for the other three models, but all four coefficients are statistically significant and in the expected direction. Ideology is a motivating force, if a moderated one, in the performance of campaign activities.

In contrast to the mass public literature, activity levels of grassroots activists decrease with age in seven of the eight models.[6] The coefficients are small, but they suggest that new blood is necessary to revitalize the party from time to time. Keep in mind that our respondents are already active, and so have crossed the difficult threshold barring most people from participation. Women are typically more active than their male colleagues. Income is relatively important in most instances, while educational attainment has differential effects. On both indexes, education is positively related to activity performance for Democrats and precinct members, but not for Republicans or county chairs. Long-time residents perform fewer activities, but the coefficients are quite small and, for Republicans, not significant.

Conclusions

The results presented here lead us to some interesting conclusions.[7] There are substantial differences in the participation levels of activists across parties and positions. These differences can be partially explained by a combination of organizational, political, and sociodemographic variables. First, there is a division of labor within local party organizations. Chairs are more active than precinct committee members. The difference is especially great for activities that require coordination or management skills. In this way, parties act like somewhat sophisticated, complex organizations. If one looks at the perceptions of the health of the party organizations, one can see that those members who believe the party is healthy are more likely to participate in both managerial and labor-intensive activities. Somewhat surprisingly, greater factionalism leads to greater rates of activity. Perhaps because each faction is striving for control, members in each faction work harder to achieve a better position for laying claim to positions of authority and power within the organization. Factionalism, provided it does not go too far, may actually be beneficial for the health of the party organization. It may keep the party organization from settling into a torpor.

Among the individual-level political variables, issue purism and ideological extremism work in opposite ways. Those who are issue purists are less likely to be active in the party organization's activities. Perhaps because the issue purists are unwilling to compromise their positions, they are unwilling to assist those who deviate from what they perceive to be orthodoxy. In contrast, ideologues are among the more active party members, at both the managerial and labor levels. To some extent this probably diminishes the effect of nonparticipation by the issue purists. Some of those who are at the extremes of their respective parties are willing to put aside their differences to work for the good of the party.

The sociodemographic items also have something to say about the health of party organizations. Younger members tend to do more work; the better a party is at recruiting young members, the more activities are likely to be undertaken. Women tend to do more of the work of the party organizations for both Democrats and Republicans. A concern for both parties might be whether their activity levels will drop as more and more women enter the workplace.

Finally, it appears that today's southern grassroots parties are capable of contesting elections, although we cannot speak to their bureaucratic development from these data. We can say that these organizations maintain a measure of vitality conspicuously missing from earlier treatments of southern politics (e.g., Cotter et al., 1984; Mayhew, 1986). At midcentury, the South was once characterized by a dearth of party organizational activity and a nearly complete absence of Republicans (Key, [1949] 1984). Now most organizations are active in campaigns, and the emergent Republican activists tend to be more involved than their Democratic counterparts. Such changes speak volumes about the alleged decline of party organizations. If such organizations can emerge in the South, perhaps we have been too quick to dismiss their importance in other parts of the country.

8
Communication Patterns

David Brodsky
Simeon Brodsky

Scholars and pundits have devoted considerable attention to the health of
America's political parties. Since the late 1960s, some analysts, including
Burnham (1969, 1970) and Broder (1972), have reported a pattern of party
decline. Others, such as Eldersveld (1986) and Cotter et al. (1984), have
reported evidence of resurgent local and state parties. How can we account
for these differing conclusions? Baer and Bositis (1993) suggest that the
problem lies in the divergent conceptual and operational definitions that
guided the research reported to date. Thus, those studies that relied on
measures of partisan identification and voter perceptions of the parties generally offered negative assessments of party health. In contrast, studies that
relied on such factors as the presence of professional staff and success at
fund-raising generally offered optimistic assessments of party health.

This chapter assesses an alternative indicator of party health, the communication patterns reported by local party executive committee members.
First we seek answers to the following questions: Do local officials "talk" with
each other? With state party officials? With national party officials? Then
we examine the effects of such variables as party position, partisan affiliation, and race on communication patterns. Finally, we consider what the
reported communication patterns have to say about the health of the parties as organizations.

Literature Review

A Legacy of Weak Party Organizations

In order to understand party organizations in the modern South, we must
first address the organizational precursors to today's parties. Key ([1949]
1984) observed that the dominance of the Democratic Party, characterized
by the single-party state, left a legacy of weak party organizations. The inability of the Republican Party to challenge the Democrats successfully at
the polls had profound consequences for both party organizations. For the

Republicans, the inability to attract and elect candidates left little incentive to build a strong organization. For the Democrats, the absence of any serious Republican threat at the polls removed one of the primary motivations for developing highly institutionalized party structures. Hence, in many southern states "no-party" politics was a more apt conceptualization than one-party politics (see, e.g., Blair, 1986). Candidate-centered politics in the South was the norm long before any so-called party decline set in. Indeed, Democratic candidates frequently turned on each other, often to the detriment of the party organization. Thus, Democratic dominance perhaps provided the seeds for later weakness.

Despite the prevalence of decentralized party organizations in the South and elsewhere, some studies found relatively centralized and hierarchical structures, especially when state party organizations tied themselves to powerful political machines (Bibby, 1990). Although the South offers several examples of such arrangements (e.g., Long in Louisiana and Byrd in Virginia), E. H. Crump's Memphis-based machine provides an especially clear illustration of how a state party system became intricately linked to a local machine. Crump's ability to form statewide alliances through the judicious use of patronage allowed him to dominate Tennessee politics for roughly twenty years (Bass and DeVries, 1976; Swansbrough, 1985; Majors, 1986). Furthermore, his ability to deliver Shelby County Democrats allowed his preferred candidates to begin their primary contests with roughly 20 percent of the necessary vote already secured (Key, [1949] 1984).

Recent party research affords us some insights into the specific effects of institutional transformation on party organizations in the South. First, the Republican state party organizations have become dramatically stronger, as measured by such factors as staff size, services provided to candidates, and voter mobilization programs (Cotter et al., 1984). Second, the Democratic state party organizations have lagged behind their Republican counterparts. Third, despite their success at the state level, the Republicans have generally failed to develop strong local parties in the region. And finally, despite (or perhaps because of) their traditional dominance of local politics in the South, the Democrats also have failed to develop especially strong local parties.

Communications and Complex Organizations

Students of complex organizations have pointed to the central role that communication plays in the life of such organizations (e.g., Etzioni, 1961; Blau and Scott, 1962; Crozier, 1964; Simon, 1976). Indeed, Arrow (1974) concluded that the successful functioning of an organization depends, to a great extent, on effective channels of communication. Students of political parties have reached similar conclusions. For example, Duverger (1954), in his classic work on parties, suggests that an understanding of the linkages of the constituent units that form the party must precede an understanding of the parties themselves. Similarly, Eldersveld (1964: 377) concludes "that the actuality and character of communication in the political party are significant for the maintenance of the party as a viable socio-political sub-system of action."

The early party studies found little evidence of hierarchical structures and centralized power. For example, Schattschneider (1942: 129) concluded that "decentralization of power is by all odds the most important single characteristic of the American major party; more than anything else this trait distinguishes it from all others." Later scholars shared Schattschneider's conclusion. Eldersveld's (1964) study of Detroit's party organizations led him to describe the overall party system as a pattern of nonhierarchical relationships—a *stratarchy*. Within this structure, each level of organization acts in a relatively autonomous manner, exercising power with little interference from higher levels of the party.

Some recent party theorists suggest that the case for stratarchy may be somewhat overstated. Schlesinger (1985) argues that party "nuclei" have incentive to work together in the face of declining partisanship among the electorate. The result is a more fully integrated party structure built around the desire to capture individual offices. Indeed, Baer (1993) suggests that mutual cooperation serves as a defining characteristic of the modern, institutionalized party. Schwartz (1990) uses the image of a party network to describe the complex interactions between various partisan actors.

Empirical research has found evidence to support these theories. For example, Huckshorn et al. (1986) found that the national party organizations and their state counterparts cooperate in a variety of activities designed to further the goals of the entire party. Similar relationships exist among state and local party organizations (Cotter et al., 1984; Gibson, Frendreis, and Vertz, 1989) and among party and campaign organizations (Trish, 1994). While contact between various strata of the party is not the same as cooperation, it does seem to be a necessary condition if integration is to occur.

Communication Patterns of Party Activists

Although the literature concerned with political parties has grown substantially since Eldersveld (1964) completed his study of Wayne County activists, his picture of communications by local party activists remains one of the most complete available. First, Eldersveld observed a great deal of variability in the communication patterns reported by the Wayne County party activists. Second, he found the frequency of communications decreased as one moved from the precinct or ward level to the county and state parties.

Table 8.1. Local Activists' Reported Frequency of Communication with Other Party Officials (in percentage)

Party level	Very often	Often	Seldom	Never
National committee	1.3	5.6	34.3	58.8
State chair	2.7	10.7	46.8	39.8
State committee	4.3	18.2	47.2	30.3
County chair	21.8	38.3	33.9	6.0
County committee	22.0	47.9	27.6	2.6

Note: Based on responses to the questions: "How often do you communicate with other party committee members? County party chair? State party chair? State party committee members? National committee members?"

Third, Eldersveld found that the extent and style of communication had observable effects on the transfer of information and on the development of ideological consensus.

Our study measured *frequency of communication* based on responses to a question about party organization: "How often do you communicate with: Other party committee members? County party chair? State party chair? State party committee members? National committee members?" Possible responses were (1) "very often," (2) "often," (3) "seldom," and (4) "never."

While the more recent party research suggests that party integration has increased in recent years (e.g., Huckshorn et al., 1986; Cotter et al., 1984; Schlesinger, 1991), this research provides little evidence of increased communication by grassroots activists. Consequently, we anticipated that our data would support Eldersveld's (1964) finding of relatively low levels of communication, with the frequency of communication declining as we moved from contact within the local party to communication with the state and national party organizations. The data presented in table 8.1 confirm our expectations. The proportion of local party activists who chose "very often" or "often" to describe the frequency of their communications with the various leadership strata declined from 69.9 percent for other county executive committee members and 60.1 percent for county chairs to 22.5 percent for state committee members and 13.4 percent for state party chairs. Fewer than one in ten local party activists reported frequent (very often or often) contact with national committee members. Conversely, the proportions of activists who indicated they never communicated with other levels of the party increased from 2.6 percent for contacts with other county committee members to 58.8 percent for communications with national committeemen or national committeewomen. More important, the pattern of decreasing communications as we moved up the party hierarchy gener-

Table 8.2. Percentage of Local Activists Reporting Frequent Communications with Other Party Officials, by Selected Sociodemographic and Political Variables

Independent variables	County committee	County chairs	State committee	State chairs	National committee	(Average N)
Race						
White	70.0	60.9	22.0	12.8	6.6	(8686)
Black	70.2	54.3	26.0	18.1	9.9	(774)
Gender						
Male	69.7	60.7	22.3	13.3	6.3	(6247)
Female	70.7	59.2	22.9	13.5	7.9	(3539)
Church attendance						
Weekly or more	67.1	59.2	19.0	12.3	5.7	(4778)
Less than weekly	72.5	60.7	25.6	14.3	7.9	(5028)
Party						
Democratic	67.5	58.6	21.3	13.2	6.2	(5275)
Republican	72.5	61.8	23.7	13.6	7.7	(4678)
Position						
Chair	87.3	91.2	44.2	35.6	9.6	(1152)
Member	67.5	56.7	19.5	10.3	6.6	(8800)
Switched party?						
Yes	69.4	58.3	23.0	12.1	7.1	(1701)
No	69.9	60.6	22.3	13.4	6.7	(8050)

Note: Percentage of respondents who answered "very often" or "often" to the questions: "How often do you communicate with other party committee members? County party chair? State Party chair? State party committee members? National committee members?"

ally held when we controlled for the effects of race, gender, frequency of church attendance, party, position, and party switching. County chairs represented the only partial exception to the pattern of declining communications, as the chairs in the sample reported slightly higher levels of contact with their fellow chairs than they reported with local executive committee members.

We anticipated finding that the frequency of contact reported would vary among different subgroups within the sample of party activists. Although the data set contained a number of variables that might lead to different communication patterns among the party activists, we focused on six factors suggested by the research literature on organizational behavior, political participation, and political parties. The data displayed in table 8.2 allow us to assess the accuracy of our expectations.

Gender and Race

Gender and race figure prominently in the vast body of research seeking to identify the correlates of political participation.[1] For example, Conway (1991), Tate (1991), and Rosenstone and Hansen (1993) found gender differences in voting, with males generally participating at higher levels than females. Similarly, Caldeira, Patterson, and Markko (1985), Bobo and Gilliam (1990), Conway (1991), Hirlinger (1992), and Verba et al. (1993) found racial and ethnic group differences in levels of political activism, with higher levels of participation generally found among whites.

We expected that whites would report more regular contact than blacks. An examination of the data failed to confirm our expectations. With the exception of contact with county chairs, blacks reported more frequent communications than whites with officials at each level of the party organization. The black advantage over whites ranged from less than 1 percent in the case of contact with other executive committee members to 5.3 percent in the case of contact with state party chairs. The historical exclusion of blacks from local parties in the South and the efforts of the national party organizations (especially the Democrats) to increase the presence of blacks in the party, especially when taken in conjunction with increased interaction between the national and state parties, might help explain these unexpected findings.

Although we anticipated that men would report higher levels of communication than women, the differences between males and females did not meet our expectations. First, the gender differences in the reported frequencies of communication were quite small, ranging from a high of 1.6 percent for contact with national committee members to less than 1 percent for contact with state party chairs. Second, and perhaps more important, women reported more frequent communications at all but one level, contact with county chairs.

Frequency of Church Attendance

Current research points to the potential impact of frequency of church attendance on the frequency of political participation. Although Verba et al. (1993) concluded that religious attendance alone does not have a significant impact on political participation, research reported by Brady, Verba, and Schlozman (1995) pointed to the possible indirect effects of church attendance in developing the skills essential for political participation. This finding may explain the positive correlation between frequency of church attendance and political participation found by Tate (1991), Rosenstone and Hansen (1993), and others. On the other hand, many religious conservatives have only recently become engaged in politics, particularly on the side of the Republican Party (Rozell and Wilcox, 1996; Oldfield, 1996). As such, they may be less well integrated into the party structure.

Following the political participation literature, we expected that activists who attended church at least once a week would report more frequent contacts than party officials who attended church less often. The data did not confirm this expectation. To the contrary, those who attended church frequently (i.e., at least once a week) reported less frequent contact than other activists. Moreover, this pattern held across levels of the party organization. This evidence gives support to the alternative explanation, that religious activists may not be well connected within the party network.

Party

The recent literature on the state of the parties suggests that the Democratic and Republican parties differ along several key dimensions. For example, Cotter et al. (1984) and Huckshorn et al. (1986) reported substantial differences in the level of organizational development and in the extent of intraparty integration, with more highly developed and integrated parties among the Republican parties. Freeman (1986) concluded that the parties have substantially different political cultures, with the Republicans having a more hierarchical orientation. Wekkin (1985) likens the state of the Democratic intraorganizational interactions to Deil Wright's (1982) "overlapping authority" model of intergovernmental relations and that of Republican intraorganizational contact to Wright's "inclusive authority" model of intergovernmental relations. It seems reasonable to expect that such differences might also lead to differences in intraparty communication, with higher levels of communication reported by Republican activists.

When we turned our attention to the effects of party on the frequency of communications, we found, as expected, that Republican activists reported more frequent communications with each level of the party organization. The most pronounced differences between the parties appeared at the local level, where the Republicans enjoyed a 3.2 percent advantage in the frequency of communications with county chairs and a 5.0 percent advantage in contact with other county committee members.

Position

Much of the research on the behavior of individuals within organizations (e.g., Etzioni, 1961; Olson, 1965; Romzek, 1990; Robertson and Tang, 1995) and political participation (e.g., Rosenstone and Hansen, 1993; Harris, 1994) suggests that occupants of the higher positions within an organization, as well as individuals with high levels of commitment to the organization, will play more active roles in their organizations. Similarly, Eldersveld (1964) found that party chairs reported more frequent contact than executive committee members with other party officials, a finding he attributed, in part, to the organizational demands placed on the chair and to the chair's position within the party structure. Thus, we anticipated finding more frequent communications reported by the chairs in the sample.

As expected, chairs reported higher levels of contact than members at each level of the party organization. But did these chair-member differences remain constant at each level of the party hierarchy? The data in table 8.2 show that the magnitude of this difference varied, being least evident at the national level (3.0 percent) and most pronounced at the state level (24.7 percent for state committee members and 25.2 percent for state party chairs) and in the frequency of contact with other county chairs (34.5 percent).

Switchers

We also expected more frequent communications from activists who switched parties, largely because we assumed that switchers would have a high level of commitment to their new home and, consequently, higher levels of involvement in their new party (Clark et al., 1991; Prysby, 1990). We determined whether or not a respondent had switched parties by the response to the question: "Have you ever been affiliated with a different political party?"

Our analysis of switchers and stalwarts failed to identify any substantial differences in the communication patterns of activists who changed parties and those who maintained their party loyalty. Stalwarts reported slightly more contact at the local level and with state party chairs, while switchers reported a bit more contact with state and national committee members.

Communication Styles of Party Activists

In addition to the extent of communication between levels of the party, our data allow us to examine the styles of communication exercised by party activists. Eldersveld (1964) identified four primary types of communicators: *cosmopolitans,* who maintain wide contacts throughout the party structure— including the precinct level, the state party, and the national party; *elite associates,* who maintain contacts in the upper echelons of the party but who have little contact at the precinct and ward levels; *localists,* who interact exclusively at the district, ward, and/or precinct level; and *isolates,* who have no significant contacts with any part of the party structure.

We based our measure of *styles of communication* on responses to the five-part question "How often do you communicate with: Other party committee members? County party chair? State party chair? State party committee members? National committee members?" Isolates, or noncommunicators, included all individuals who responded "seldom" or "never" to the questions. Isolates, therefore, reported low levels of communication with all ranks of party officials. Localists included individuals who responded either "very often" or "often" to one of the questions assessing communication with local party officials and who reported "seldom" or "never" communicating with state or national (i.e., nonlocal) party officials. Elite associates communicated "very often" or "often" with state or national party officials and "seldom" or "never" with local party officials. Cosmopolitans responded "very often" or "often" to at least one question regarding nonlocal communication *and* "very often" or "often" to at least one question regarding local communication.

When we examined the communication styles of the southern party activists, we found the following distribution: isolates, who reported virtually no contact with other party officials, accounted for 22.1 percent of the sample; localists, officials who indicated frequent contact with other county activists but minimal contact with state and national officials, made up 49.8 percent of the sample; elite associates, grassroots party officials who reported frequent contact only with state and national party leaders, accounted for 1.1 percent of the sample; and cosmopolitans, county executive committee members who indicated frequent contact with officials of the state or national parties as well as with local party committee members or chairs, comprised 27.0 percent of the sample.

Race

We anticipated that race might affect communication style, in that blacks might report lower levels of communication than whites. The data presented in table 8.3 largely failed to confirm our expectations. First, as expected, the proportion of black activists classified as isolates (little or no contact) exceeded the comparable proportion for whites, although by a very small margin. Second, again as expected, the percentage of white activists classified as localists surpassed the comparable proportion for blacks (42.9 percent). However, contrary to expectation, the proportions of blacks classified as elite associates and cosmopolitans exceeded the comparable proportions of white activists in each classification.

Gender

Our expectation of lower levels of participation among female activists led us to anticipate finding larger proportions of women among the isolates and localists in the activist sample. The data, however, yielded a somewhat different picture, with only slight gender differences in the percentage of activists found in each style. For example, half of both females and males manifested a localist communication style, while one-fourth of both females and males exhibited a cosmopolitan style.

Table 8.3. Activist Communication Styles, by Selected Sociodemographic and Political Variables (in percentage)

Independent variables	Isolate	Localist	Elite associate	Cosmo-politan	(N)
Race					
White	22.0	50.7	1.0	26.3	(8541)
Black	22.5	42.9	1.6	32.9	(750)
Gender					
Male	22.0	50.0	1.1	26.9	(6164)
Female	22.0	49.8	1.0	27.2	(3457)
Church attendance					
Weekly or more	24.4	51.2	0.8	23.6	(4637)
Less than weekly	19.9	48.7	1.3	30.1	(4958)
Party					
Democratic	23.8	49.6	1.1	25.5	(5160)
Republican	20.3	50.0	1.0	28.7	(4613)
Position					
Chair	3.9	40.5	0.3	55.3	(1168)
Member	24.6	51.0	1.2	23.2	(8604)
Switched party?					
Yes	22.4	49.3	1.0	27.3	(1673)
No	22.0	50.1	1.1	26.9	(7911)
(Total N)	(2163)	(4865)	(103)	(2642)	

Church Attendance

We expected that church attendance would affect communication styles, with frequent attendees less likely to place among the isolates and more likely to have demonstrated a cosmopolitan style. The results of our analysis did not confirm our expectations. Indeed, frequent attendees predominated among the isolates and the localists, while those who reported attending church less regularly proved more likely to place among the elite associates and the cosmopolitans.

Party

The edge in organizational integration reputedly enjoyed by the Republicans led us to foresee a higher percentage of cosmopolitans among Republican activists and higher percentages of isolates and localists among Democratic activists. Although the data confirmed these expectations in the case of isolates and cosmopolitans, the magnitude of the differences between the parties proved smaller than we anticipated. In the case of localists and elite associates, we found virtually no difference; majorities of both Republicans and Democrats reported little or no contact with either state or national party officials.

Position

We also predicted position in the local party organization would affect communication style, with chairs more likely than members to have a cosmopolitan style and members more likely than chairs to be either isolates, localists, or elite associates. The data shown in table 8.3 support each forecast. First, the proportion of cosmopolitans among the chairs was more than double the comparable percentage for other local activists. Indeed, cosmopolitans accounted for a majority of chairs but for only one in four members. Second, one in two members and, somewhat surprisingly, two in five chairs reported a localist style. Third, while isolates accounted for one in four members, fewer than one in twenty chairs fit this style. Finally, members outnumbered chairs among elite associates, but by only a very small margin.

Switchers

We anticipated that the commitment of activists who switched parties at some point in their careers would lead to more frequent communication with other party officials. The data failed to support this expectation. We found virtually no difference in the distribution of styles among those who switched and those who maintained their party identification.

Discussion and Conclusions

The data presented here point to several conclusions regarding communications among southern grassroots party activists and other party officials. First, a sizable minority of local party activists rarely communicate with each other or with other party officials. Second, the communications that do take place have a decidedly local focus, as grassroots party activists indicated relatively infrequent contact with state and national party officials. Third, position within the party structure clearly affected the frequency of contact with other party leaders. Thus, county party chairs reported more frequent communications than county executive committee members, especially contact with state committee members and chairs. Fourth, the frequency of communication varied by party; Republican activists reported more contact at all levels. Fifth, the higher levels of interaction with state and national party officials found among black grassroots officials suggest that the parties, at these levels, have enjoyed greater success than their local counterparts in involving minority group members in party activities. Sixth, although the ranks of local party officials contained fewer women than we might reasonably expect, the comparable communications patterns for men and women suggest that gender has little effect on the level of involvement in party affairs. Finally, the absence of any significant differences in the frequency of communications reported by party loyalists and switchers indicate that the parties have successfully incorporated newcomers into their ranks.

The data reported in this chapter also allow us to reach some tentative conclusions regarding the health of the southern parties as institutions.[2] First, the relative infrequency of communications across levels of the party hierarchy suggests that even though state and national parties (both Democrats and Republicans) have become more highly integrated institutions (Huckshorn et al., 1986), they remain essentially stratarchical organizations characterized by a lack of control from above (Eldersveld, 1964). Second, the paucity of reported contact also implies that the southern parties may have fallen short in transmitting the shared organizational cultures observed by Freeman (1986) among national party elites. Third, the relatively high levels of interaction among activists at the local level may bode well for the parties' ability to contest elections and engage in party-building activities successfully (see also Clark and Lockerbie, 1993). And last, the communications data indicate that the parties have succeeded, at least to some extent, in incorporating female and minority activists (albeit in relatively small numbers) into their communication networks.

Our findings concerning communication patterns may also speak to the competitive balance between the two parties. The relatively small interparty differences in the frequency of communications may indicate that the southern Democratic parties have narrowed the organizational edge attributed to their Republican counterparts. However, the consistent Republican advantage in communications with each level of the party organization suggests that the Democrats still have a way to go in building fully integrated party structures.

Part Three
Party and the Environment

Political parties do not exist in a vacuum; rather, they both influence and are influenced by the environment in which they operate (Harmel and Janda, 1982; Blank, 1980; Beck and Sorauf, 1992; Price, 1984; Epstein, 1967; Keefe, 1980). As the preeminent linkage organizations in democratic societies, parties act as intermediaries connecting citizens with their government (see, e.g., Lawson, 1980; Eldersveld, 1982: chap. 1; Bibby, 1992: 5–7). A portrait of local party organizations must, therefore, include a look at the relationship between the party and its environment. Samuel J. Eldersveld (1964: 304–305) summarizes this relationship from the perspective of party leaders:

> The political party leader has to contend with an "environment" which includes many objects—the "other party," current political issues, the social structure and organized groups in the community most relevant for politics, the governmental apparatus he seeks to control, the mass media available to him. In addition, part of the leader's environment is "atmosphere," more abstract understandings about the game of politics, and how it is to be played. Thus, there are certain moral norms and operational proprieties to be observed and of which he must be conscious. These concern particularly the proprieties of alternative competitive strategies and activities open to him. . . . But, in addition, abstract understandings about the character of the political order are also involved. In a "democratic" society expectations develop which require a party leader to conform to a particular set of values concerning human relations, group process, and governmental behavior patterns. These value expectations may vary specifically from one democratic culture to the next. . . . Thus, a great range of environmental conditions and political norms, with variable content, may exist in political systems. The party is seeking to maximize its support and status in this environment. The party

leader is aware of the milieu and brings it to his work, or subsequently develops, a basic set of perspectives about his personal relationship to the milieu in his capacity as a political agent.

The four chapters in Part III expressly address elements of environmental interaction with local organizations and activists. In light of the dramatic changes that have swept the region in the post–World War II period, the South provides an excellent laboratory for examining this relationship, and it provides a useful foundation for generalizing to the party-environmental nexus. In chapter 9, John McGlennon finds that the traditional one-party factionalism of southern politics (Key, [1949] 1984) has evolved into new divisions in a two-party system. He explores factionalism with a view toward identifying its impact on the local parties in such matters as its potential for damaging these organizations.

The linkage between party and citizenry is, of course, one that can be answered empirically (McClosky, Hoffman, and O'Hara, 1960; Kirkpatrick, 1975). In chapter 10, David Breaux, Stephen D. Shaffer, and Patrick Cotter combine the Mississippi and Alabama subsamples of the grassroots activist study with mass-level data from the two states. Following the approach pioneered by McClosky et al., they compare the party activists' ideological patterns and belief systems with those of the general public and offer insights into the parties' abilities to attract mass support and to contest state-level elections.

The difference between state and national political parties is evident in Republican domination of recent presidential elections in the South compared with slower gains at other offices (Black and Black, 1992). Robert P. Steed and Lewis Bowman (chapter 11) examine the relationship between strength of party attachment at the state and national levels and other aspects of party involvement. They explore the relationship between strength of party attachment and various traditional functions that parties perform and then examine some of the correlates of party attachment with special attention to those related to the party's external environment.

Finally, party organizations are influenced by changes taking place in the world around them. In chapter 12, Rosalee A. Clawson and John A. Clark draw on the party elite theory of democracy (Baer and Bositis, 1988) to examine the impact of women and blacks on the political parties. They are particularly interested in examining whether the inclusion of women and blacks in the ranks of organizational activists has altered the parties' respective issue orientations in appreciable ways.

Taken together, these chapters underscore the importance of the relationship between the parties and their environment and thereby remind us that an understanding of contemporary local parties requires continuing attention to their environmental context.

9
Factions in the Politics of the New South

John McGlennon

Factional division has been recognized as an important part of southern politics ever since the days of V. O. Key, when candidate-centered Democratic factionalism substituted for interparty competition. Factions provided what limited competition occurred in southern elections, as the Huey Long supporters battled the anti-Longs in Louisiana, the Talmadge adherents contested the anti-Talmadges in Georgia, the Byrd machine was challenged by the anti-organization Democrats in Virginia, and so on (Key, [1949] 1984; Heard, 1952; Rae, 1994; Steed et al., 1980). The existence of ongoing, predictable factions in some southern states provided structure for the Democratic primaries that substituted for competitive general elections (Key, [1949] 1984; Bass, 1991: 74ff).

More recently, the reemergence of factional politics in the once-dominant Democratic Party has provided opportunities for a growing but still minority Republican Party. The increasing influence of African American voters and more liberal nonnative southerners within Democratic primaries led to a deep schism in the once segregationist, conservative party (Baker et al., 1990; Moreland et al., 1987).

With party competition now in full bloom, the Republicans in the South have the luxury of enough partisans to allow for some disagreement over nominees and policies. In a party with little apparent ideological diversity, the gradations of distinctiveness may be subtle, but they can be a source of intense intraparty warfare (e.g., Black and Black, 1987: 136–140).

The sources of the factional division may vary from state to state or from year to year, but its existence has been evident in almost all of the states of the region. In contemporary southern politics, these divisions are based on a number of different factors, from geography to issues to personality.

In this chapter, we will examine the existence of factionalism in the two parties of the South, seeking to identify sources of factionalism as well as variations in these sources across the parties and across the states. We will then consider whether factional dispute within the major parties appears to make a significant difference in the way the political parties go about their business of nominating candidates and working for those candidates in the general elections.

Factionalism in Political Parties

Discussions of the American political party system have noted the tendency for our decentralized brand of party organization to exhibit factionalism. Factionalism in American state parties is based not on one main source, such as ethnicity or ideology or region. It is found in all of these sources and more: in personality, issues, and style, to name just a few. Factionalism in American state parties can be long-lasting, or it can be temporary; it can be basic to the functioning of the party or relatively innocuous in its effects on party fortunes. But given the need of our parties to develop broad coalitions of support in order to win elections, and given the low level of centralized authority that the party leadership can exercise, it is inevitable that factionalism will be present in parties (Key, 1958: 318–328; Eldersveld, 1964: 29; Baer and Bositis, 1988: 100–102).

Historically, factionalism has played a greater role in southern elections for two reasons, both directly tied to the lack of an effective opposition party. In the first instance, the voters of the one-party Democratic South did not have party as a cue to voting. With every candidate sharing the same party label, candidates made appeals to voters on other grounds, such as their ideology, their stand on important issues, their regional affiliation (e.g., highland vs. delta, country vs. city) and even local pride (V. O. Key's "friends and neighbors voting"). Factionalism offered some hope for a candidate to build support in blocs, not one voter at a time.

Factionalism also offered voters a way of cutting through the field of contenders in the decisive Democratic primary in order to focus on those who represented what the voter favored or disliked. It could serve as something of a substitute for two-party politics, especially in those cases where there were durable, persistent factions that structured the competition within the primary, as in the Georgia and Louisiana of Key's day.

Since the Democrats were effectively uncontested throughout most of the South for the first half of the twentieth century, and since virtually all southerners identified themselves as Democrats, there was neither any incentive nor any ability to control or limit the impact of factionalism. Whether the winning candidate for governor, member of Congress, or county commissioner was a liberal or conservative, a "big mule" or a "redneck," the victor was still a Democrat, and the party still held the office.

In competitive party systems, such as have emerged across the South in recent years, the impact of factionalism within a party is much more important. Although the various sources of factionalism are still likely to be found in both parties, the presence of an opposition party does offer an option to dissatisfied party voters: deserting their party in the general election. Thus, a faction that is consistently defeated in party-nominating contests may temporarily or permanently move to the other party. And since party disputes are often played out in full public view, party activists must worry about the impact of their internal divisions on the electability of their candidates in competitive general elections.

Factionalism can play an important role in many aspects of party operation. A fair amount of attention has been devoted to the question of how nomination contests affect party fortunes in general elections (Beck and Sorauf, 1992: 241–244; Johnson and Gibson, 1974; Buehl, 1986; Stone, 1986; Kenney and Rice, 1984, 1987; Kenney, 1988; McNitt, 1980). Not every primary or convention fight for nomination is the result of factionalism, but often the factions of a party are highly visible in supporting competing candidates for party designation. Factionalism may have other impacts as well, in ways that can be equally, if not more, important to parties. Divisions in a party may limit the effectiveness of the party's fund-raising, recruitment, precinct operations—in fact, virtually all of the regular activities of the party. It may also create tension between elected officials and the party organization. This chapter will identify the sources of factionalism in southern state parties and examine the impact of factionalism on perceptions of party effectiveness and organizational strength.

Factionalism in the Two Parties

As with the other chapters, the data for this chapter are drawn from the Southern Grassroots Party Activists Project. The project surveyed county and precinct-level party officials in the eleven states of the South. Our respondents were asked several questions directly about the nature and degree of factionalism in their own state parties. They were asked to designate which of five types of factionalism were present in their state party: factionalism based on ideology, on personal followings, on geographical divisions, on one or two issues, and on time lived in the state—new vs. old residents.

Ideological division was expected to be a potentially serious problem for Democrats, as they are more widely representative of varying political philosophies. Overwhelming numbers of Republicans identified themselves as "very conservative" or "somewhat conservative," and virtually no members of the party defined themselves as liberals. On the other hand, Democrats had significant numbers of conservatives and moderates as well as the more dominant liberals (for a fuller discussion of ideology among these party activists, see chapter 5).

Republicans in a few southern states saw the emergence of ideological tension as early as the 1960s and 1970s. Moderate "Mountain Republicans" in Virginia, Tennessee, and North Carolina were not always comfortable with the highly conservative former Democrats who were beginning to dominate their parties. In Arkansas, Winthrop Rockefeller single-handedly built the GOP into a competitive party for a few years, based on his own moderate, antisegregationist approach (Appleton and Ward, 1994). But by and large, the Republican state parties in the South emerged during the last few decades as highly conservative organizations.

While ideology in general can be an important source of factional dispute, issues can prove as significant a factor in dividing partisans. In particular, an issue that mobilizes voters to become active in a party and its nominating contests can be a source of tension with party members who have a broader and longer affiliation with the party. In the recent past, issues such as civil rights, Vietnam, women's rights, abortion, religious expression, gun control, taxes, and government policy toward homosexuality have mobilized activists, both pro and con, to participate in one party or the other.

The impact of individual personalities is another source of potential factionalism, one with a long history of divisiveness in the one-party South. Personality-based factionalism in southern politics did not disappear with the passing of such figures as Huey Long, Eugene Talmadge, and Harry Byrd.

Factional divisions identified with personalities are often thinly disguised ideological schisms (e.g., the Jesse Helms vs. James Holshouser conflict in the North Carolina GOP, and the John Connally vs. Ralph Yarbrough factions of the Texas Democrats). Nevertheless, personal loyalty is sometimes a more convincing explanation for contesting wings within a party. Certainly the split among Virginia Democrats between backers of Charles Robb and Douglas Wilder did not have its base in ideology.

The potential for conflict between recent migrants to southern states and party activists who are natives makes it worthwhile to investigate whether factionalism is evident on this basis. All of the southern states have seen some in-migration, although the amount and type varies widely. In those states with a lot of migrants, it is reasonable to expect more factional splits between old-timers and newcomers.

Finally, geography has been a significant source of factionalism in southern states in the past, and it is worth examining whether precinct officials of either party see this as a significant problem today. Key cited the conflict between metropolitan and rural voters, Miami versus the rest of Florida ([1949] 1984: 92), and the Delta versus the Hills in Mississippi (230–238) as just three examples of geographical factionalism.

Key makes it clear that the geographical division he cites is distinct from the "friends and neighbors voting" that delivered large majorities to candidates in their home counties, being a more persistent division based on the particular economic interests or social composition of regions within a state.

Table 9.1. Level and Sources of Factionalism in Southern Democratic and Republican Parties (in percentage)

Level/source	Democrats	Republicans
Level of factionalism		
Fairly high	19.9	16.8
Moderate	54.3	47.2
Low	15.4	27.4
None	10.4	8.6
Source of factionalism[a]		
Personal followings	77.3	73.6
Ideology	61.5	59.4
Issues	57.7	63.7
Geography	57.1	36.4
Old vs. new residents	49.0	40.1

[a]Percentage of total members citing each category.

Respondents were asked whether each of these five types of factionalism was present in their state party (see table 9.1), but not whether they were part of such a faction. However, a number of other questions allow enough of a classification of respondents to indicate which side of a factional divide would be the likely choice of the respondent. The activists were asked for their attitudes toward the importance of issues or ideology vs. maintaining party unity for electoral success. Finally, the respondents were asked to evaluate the current strength of the party organization in their own state.

Intraparty Evaluations of Factionalism

In this section, we examine each party to determine the level of factionalism in general and the prevalence of each type of factionalism. We examine both the regionwide existence of factionalism and the levels within individual states.

Democrats

Nine out of ten southern Democratic activists recognized the presence of factionalism in their party, and a total of three-quarters judged it to be either "fairly high" (20 percent) or "moderate" (the majority).

The sources of factionalism as cited by Democrats were as follows: personal followings of candidates or officials (named by 77 percent of those noting factionalism), ideology (62 percent), "one or two issues" (58 per-

Table 9.2a. Democratic Factionalism: Source of Factionalism, by Level of Factionalism (in percentage)

Source	Democrats who rate factionalism high	All Democrats who cite each source	Difference[a]
Personal followings	81.2	77.3	3.9
Ideology	73.4	61.5	11.9
Geography	57.2	57.1	0.1
Issues	53.0	57.7	-4.7
Old vs. new residents	48.9	49.0	-0.1

[a]Difference is determined by subtracting the percentage of all Democrats citing the presence of the source of factionalism from the percentage of Democrats who perceived a high level of factionalism citing the same source of factionalism.

cent), geography (57 percent), and old vs. new residents (49 percent). Most Democrats who acknowledged factionalism named more than one source within their party (table 9.2).

If factionalism is present to a high or moderate degree in a party, is that the result of numerous factions or of the intensity of a single factional divide? If a high level of factionalism is the result of many different factors creating cleavages in a party, the problem might not be as serious as a persistent, stable division over a single cause or two.

The relationship between respondents' evaluations of the degree of fac-

Table 9.2b. Democratic Factionalism: Degree of Factionalism, by State (in percentage)

State	High level of factions	High + moderate levels of factions
Alabama	21.0	79.0
Arkansas	15.6	72.2
Florida	23.5	75.6
Georgia	17.4	70.7
Louisiana	24.1	84.4
Mississippi	22.6	74.7
North Carolina	28.9	79.4
South Carolina	17.7	74.0
Tennessee	19.6	74.0
Texas	20.5	72.7
Virginia	11.4	66.5

Note: Level of factionalism determined for first category by number of respondents citing a "high" level of factionalism; for second category, by adding "high" and "moderate" responses.

tionalism in the party and the recognition of each type of factionalism is inconsistent. In the case of each of the first four types listed previously (issue-based, geographical, old vs. new, and personal), respondents' identification of the source of factionalism is unrelated to the respondents' perception of whether the overall level of factionalism in the party is high or low (table 9.2). On the other hand, the recognition of ideology-based division is in direct relation to the evaluation of the degree of party factionalism. The more likely one is to see schisms based on ideology, the higher the perception of the level of factionalism, suggesting that activists see ideology as a more serious form of factionalism than other types.

The perceived level of factionalism varied substantially from state to state among Democrats, both in terms of the percentage of Democrats who rated the level "fairly high" and in terms of the combination of "fairly high" and "moderate" ratings. The two methods of measuring provide slightly different state rankings. Using the "fairly high" rating, North Carolina and Virginia Democrats are the most and least factional state parties, respectively. Louisiana, Florida, and Mississippi cluster toward the top of the scale, with Alabama, Texas, and Tennessee in the middle and South Carolina, Georgia, and Arkansas having relatively low levels.

Using the broader measure of factionalism, Virginia still scores the lowest, by a significant margin, but Louisiana moves ahead of North Carolina as the most factional state among Democrats, with Alabama close behind. The parties in Florida, Mississippi, Tennessee, and South Carolina are next, followed by Texas, Arkansas, and Georgia.

Republicans

Virtually the same percentage of Republicans see the presence of factionalism in their party, but the divisiveness is pegged at a lower level—not surprising in a group that has only recently reached competitive organizational strength and that is more racially and ideologically homogeneous. Only 64 percent of Republicans (vs. 74 percent of Democrats) rate factionalism as fairly high or moderate.

Like the Democrats, Republicans were most likely to see "personal followings" as the main source of factionalism, but the GOP activists saw "one or two issues" as the next most likely source of conflict in the party, followed by ideology, old vs. new activists, and geographical factions. Those who saw a fairly high level of factionalism were considerably more likely to cite ideology than other activists were and somewhat more likely to perceive conflict based on personal followings and old/new splits. They were less likely to perceive a division over issues (see table 9.3).

Republicans also varied substantially from state to state in their perceptions of factionalism. Again, the two measures of factionalism—"high" cita-

Table 9.3a. Republican Factionalism: Source of Factionalism, by Level of Factionalism (in percentage)

Source	Republicans who rate factionalism high	All Republicans who cite each source	Difference[a]
Personal followings	78.4	73.6	4.8
Ideology	68.8	59.4	9.4
Geography	37.6	36.4	1.2
Issues	60.9	63.7	-2.8
Old vs. new residents	47.6	40.1	7.5

[a]Difference is determined by subtracting the percentage of all Republicans citing the presence of the source of factionalism from the percentage of Republicans who perceived a high level of factionalism citing the same source of factionalism.

tions alone and in combination with "moderate" citations—differ a bit in results. Louisiana and Florida Republicans see the highest levels of factional division by far. Alabama and Mississippi (especially) have the fewest activists who see high rates of conflict. The remaining states fall between the extremes and rank as follows, from high to low: Georgia, North Carolina, Virginia, Arkansas, Texas, South Carolina, and Tennessee.

In the broader categorization—moderate to high—Florida and Louisiana reverse their order at the top of the factionalism scale, followed by Georgia, North Carolina, Texas, Arkansas, Virginia, Alabama, South Caro-

Table 9.3b. Republican Factionalism: Degree of Factionalism, by State (in percentage)

State	High level of factions	High + moderate levels of factions
Alabama	11.5	61.0
Arkansas	17.9	63.7
Florida	27.4	75.7
Georgia	21.5	71.1
Louisiana	27.6	73.4
Mississippi	8.3	49.9
North Carolina	19.5	69.2
South Carolina	14.7	60.8
Tennessee	13.2	57.1
Texas	16.2	66.7
Virginia	18.5	62.2

Note: Level of factionalism determined for first category by number of respondents citing a "high" level of factionalism; for second category, by adding "high" and "moderate" responses.

lina, and Tennessee. Mississippi Republicans distinguished themselves as the only state party, Democratic or Republican, of which more than half saw factionalism as low.

Interparty Comparisons

As the preceding discussion indicates, factionalism is generally viewed as a concern in both parties, though somewhat more frequently among Democrats than Republicans. Both parties see factionalism of several varieties, and the largest numbers in both parties believed that their organization was affected by divisions over personal followings. Ideology and splits over one or two issues were the next highest concerns for Democrats, reversing the order of the Republicans. Democrats were much more likely than Republicans to see geography and old-timer/newcomer conflicts.

Those who believed that their party was confronted by high levels of factionalism tended to have a somewhat different view of the kinds of factionalism in the party than did those who rated the factionalism as moderate to low. Among Democrats, those citing high levels of factionalism were substantially more likely to see ideology as a source of division. They had a slightly greater tendency to note the presence of personal followings, but were less likely to find geographical, issue-based, or old/new divisions than their fellow partisans. In the GOP, those who rated factionalism as high also saw ideological conflict more frequently, as well as old/new division and splits based on personal followings. The Republicans were only slightly more likely to cite geographical division, and they less frequently mentioned issue-based schisms.

These evaluations reflect the overall nature of party politics in the region. The ideological tension seen by Democrats is consistent with the fact that the party's membership includes sizable components of conservatives, moderates, and liberals. The substantial minority of Democratic conservatives were somewhat less likely to perceive ideological factionalism in their party than were liberals. More surprisingly, a Republican Party with little ideological diversity still sees ideology as a major source of factions.

Still, both parties' members identified personal followings as the most common source of conflict. At least two-thirds of the respondents of each party in each state who saw factionalism in their party identified alignment with a particular candidate as a cause.

The greater tendency of Democrats to cite both geography and old/new tensions reflects the longer existence of the party organization, which may bear the marks of the geographical factionalism of the V. O. Key era. The party may retain vestiges of conflicts that do not have as much import in contemporary politics.

Impact of Factionalism on Party Effectiveness

Although it is clear that factionalism is present in all the southern parties, the impact of this division is less clear. What effect do party members attribute to the presence or absence of intraparty dispute? Our data do not provide a direct answer to this question, but they support the conclusion that party activists *think* that factionalism inhibits the party in fulfilling its major responsibilities.

As a general rule, it should be the case that those activists who see party factionalism as high are more likely to see the party impeded in its efforts at organizational development. Not only should this apply across the board, but it stands to reason that those parties with the highest level of factionalism (as perceived by its members) should be seen as the weaker parties organizationally.

Democrats who rated party factionalism as "fairly high" were twice as likely as other Democrats to view their party as "significantly weaker" than it was five to ten years ago (see table 9.4). Although Republicans generally rated the change in party organization over the last decade very positively, the party members who saw high factionalism were also twice as likely to rate the party as weaker.

This negative evaluation of party strength applied to the individual items on which the respondents were asked to comment as well. Among both Democrats and Republicans, perceiving a high level of factionalism in the party resulted in a more negative view of the party's changes in campaign effectiveness; fund-raising; candidate recruitment; development of volunteer skills; and use of the mass media, opinion polls, and computer technology.

The fact that those who saw factionalism as a serious force in their party's politics also rated their party lower in terms of current organizational effectiveness is important. If party activists see factionalism both as an important force in their party and as an inhibitor of party functions, the effects can be mutually reinforcing. The more divided the factions of a state party, the more likely that the party may have a hard time convincing the activists of one faction to work with the other faction on party-building activities.

Fund-raising events, candidate recruitment activities, and use of computer technology can all be seen as potential weapons in intra- as well as interparty competition. Certainly both parties in many of the southern states have gone through bitter battles for control of the party machinery and have faced charges that the winning faction had used or would use the party machinery unfairly.

Do the state parties that perceive high levels of factionalism correspond to the parties viewed as having relatively low levels of organizational improvement over the past decade? In examining this question, let us look at

Table 9.4. Level of Factionalism and Evaluation of Party Effectiveness (percentage rating party "significantly weaker")

	Democrats		Republicans	
Function	Highly factional	All Democrats	Highly factional	All Republicans
Overall organization	27.3	13.6	10.8	4.6
Campaign effectiveness	20.8	10.0	8.7	3.8
Fund-raising ability	20.1	10.4	6.9	3.3
Recruiting ability	19.7	10.1	8.3	4.3
Development of worker skills	19.8	9.3	9.8	3.9
Party use of media	14.9	7.6	9.2	3.9
Party use of polls	15.6	8.8	10.1	4.7
Party use of computers	15.9	10.9	7.9	4.9

the individual state party evaluations of party effectiveness, considering the Democrats and Republicans separately.

The relatively recent movement of the GOP into a competitive position organizationally, as well as the eroding position of the once dominant Democrats, leads to an imbalanced perception of party effectiveness. All state Republican parties were judged by their activists to be significantly stronger overall than they had been a decade ago. Almost all state Democratic parties were seen as somewhat weaker than they had been ten years earlier.

Within each party, the difference between the most improved and the least improved organization was significant. Using a measure in which the percentage of party activists describing their own party organization as slightly or significantly weaker was subtracted from the percentage of activists calling their party stronger, among Republicans the range was from 79.2 percent (South Carolina) to 28.9 percent (Tennessee). Among Democrats, Virginia had the most positive evaluation (20.3 percent) with Louisiana trailing all others (-27.8 percent).

But when organizational improvement is compared with the perceived levels of factionalism in each state party, there is not a clear relationship. While in some states it appears that the presence or lack of factionalism may have an impact on the activists' sense of party strength, in other states factionalism seems not to matter (see table 9.5).

Perhaps factionalism operates differently in different situations, serving as an indicator of success in some cases, as when a newly expanded electoral coalition brings increased strength even while causing tensions within the party. In other cases, factionalism may grow out of either finger pointing

Table 9.5. Intraparty Perceptions of Factionalism and Party Strength

	Democrats	Republicans
High factionalism	North Carolina	Louisiana
	Louisiana	Florida
	Florida	Georgia
	Mississippi	
	Alabama	
	Texas	
Moderate factionalism	Tennessee	North Carolina
	South Carolina	Virginia
	Georgia	Arkansas
		Texas
Low factionalism	Arkansas	South Carolina
	Virginia	Tennessee
		Alabama
		Mississippi
States in descending order of increased strength[a]	Virginia	South Carolina
	Arkansas	Alabama
	Georgia	Texas
	Tennessee	North Carolina
	Alabama	Arkansas
	Florida	Mississippi
	Texas	Louisiana
	North Carolina	Florida
	Mississippi	Georgia
	South Carolina	Virginia
	Louisiana	Tennessee

[a]Rankings based on percentage of respondents rating their party stronger than five or ten years ago minus those rating it weaker.

over political setbacks or the struggle to pick up the pieces of an unsuccessful party.

Conclusion

Southern political parties reflect the diverse coalitions that make up the increasingly competitive electorates of the eleven states of the Confederacy. The region's history of factionalism as a substitute for two-party politics has given way to a different form of division within a vastly changed party system.

The presence of factionalism itself does not guarantee a fractured or weakened party. Factional division appears to be an accepted part of the American party system, and it may be particularly prevalent in a system undergoing the kind of dramatic change experienced by the southern parties in recent decades. And given that the type of person attracted to party politics generally has strong feelings about candidates, issues, and ideology, the causes of factionalism are likely to be the motivational force for activism.

If factionalism is inevitable in party organizations, its impact seems to depend on how strong the divisions are. Most party activists do not find that factionalism alone hampers organizational effectiveness. But those who see a high level of factionalism are also less likely to cite improvement in their party's operations. The challenge to the party lies in recognizing that factionalism is a normal part of party life but that its intensification can have damaging consequences for party activities.

For the parties most affected by factionalism, the challenge is balancing the competing forces in the party in a way that prevents factionalism from reaching the high levels that seem to bring problems. But factionalism is likely to be the result of, not the cause of, dynamics in the electorate. Candidates, issues, ideology, and other factors play themselves out among the parties' membership and result in party conflicts. Parties will bear the brunt of their civil wars, but they would seem powerless to prevent them.

10

Mass/Elite Linkage

David Breaux
Stephen D. Shaffer
Patrick Cotter

Beginning with Franklin D. Roosevelt's presidential victory in 1932, the Democratic Party dominated the nation's political landscape for a period of thirty-six years. During this time, Democrats won every presidential election except that of Dwight D. Eisenhower, a war hero sufficiently nonpartisan that both parties sought him as their standard bearer. Except for two two-year periods, Democrats also continuously controlled both houses of Congress. One likely reason for this period of Democratic dominance and GOP weakness is that Republican activists and candidates were believed to be considerably more conservative in their policy views than were voters— most of whom were in the political center.

By the late 1960s and early 1970s, it was clear that the period of Democratic dominance had come to an end. The region in which this change was most evident was the South. Only once since 1968 has the traditionally one-party Democratic South voted Democratic in a presidential election. Republican congressional gains culminated in GOP capture of a majority of U.S. House and Senate seats in Dixie in the 1994 landslide. (However, Democrats continued to control most state and local offices below the governorships.) Again it is the policy views of party activists and candidates that are thought to be the source of this political change. Now, though, Democratic activists and candidates are believed to be substantially more liberal than is the electorate as a whole. As a result, voters may be abandoning the Democrats and fleeing to the more conservative Republican Party.

This chapter examines the current party system in the South, a critical region of the nation, by comparing mass and elite attitudes on public policy issues in two Deep South states (Alabama and Mississippi). We begin by exploring the extent to which the public and the party activists differ in the ideological coherence of their belief systems, and we then turn to an examination of policy distances between the populace and party activists in both states. A major objective is to ascertain the extent to which either or both parties may be ideologically cohesive to such an extreme degree that they risk electoral retaliation by being out of touch with average citizens.

Theoretical Insights from the Literature

In "Issue Conflict and Consensus among Party Leaders and Followers," McClosky, Hoffman, and O'Hara (1960) found that in the late 1950s domestic economic policy differences between Democratic and Republican Party activists (national convention delegates) were much greater than were differences between partisans in the general population, who tended to hold more centrist views. Indeed, Republican activists at that time were so conservative that their supporters in the population were actually closer in policy to the other party's activists. Subsequent studies in the 1960s confirmed the conservative nature of Republican campaign activists and political activists in general, while Democratic activists tended to reflect the more centrist views of the less active segment within both parties (Nexon, 1971; Verba and Nie, 1972). In "Electoral Myth and Reality," Converse, Clausen, and Miller (1965) suggested that the conservative views of political activists (those who wrote letters to newspaper editors or public officials) led Barry Goldwater in 1964 to overestimate the electoral appeal of his right-wing message.

By the late 1960s the party system was undergoing a dramatic transformation, as Vietnam, the civil rights movement, and urban riots polarized the nation. Ladd and Hadley (1975) found that the more politically active college-educated segment of *both* parties had polarized, with college Democrats moving even further to the left of their party's supporters in the electorate than college Republicans were to the right of their party rank and file. Examining campaign activists, Shaffer (1980) found a similar liberal divergence of Democratic activists from less active partisans, at least on civil rights and civil liberty issues. By 1972 Kirkpatrick (1975) was able to stand McClosky on his head, as she found that Democratic national convention delegates that year were the "odd men out." Democratic activists were much more liberal than the rank and file in either party, making the Democratic rank and file closer to the other party's activists than they were to the leaders of their own party. A study by Backstrom (1977) of the Congress elected in 1970 came to similar conclusions. Nie, Verba, and Petrocik's (1976: 202–204) longitudinal study of campaign activists illustrates the leftward movement of Democratic activists in the late 1960s and early 1970s, though they argue that Republican activists generally remained to the right of their citizenry party as well. Kagay's (1991) study of 1988 national convention delegates also illustrates how activists were more polarized on issues than either the public as a whole or the mass membership of either party and that the group of activists closest to the general public varied from issue to issue.

Related to the policy distance between mass and elites is the question of the structure of belief systems in both groups. Philip Converse's 1964 classic, "The Nature of Belief Systems in Mass Publics," found little evidence of ideological thinking in the general populace. A correlation matrix of policy issues yielded almost nothing in the way of organization—no significant "constraint" or correlation between different policy items. Elites in the form of congressional candidates demonstrated much more political sophistication and constraint than did the masses. Jennings (1992: 434–435), using data collected in the 1970s and 1980s, reached a similar conclusion: "Overall, it is patent that political party elites have a vastly more constrained and stable set of political preferences and perspectives than does the mass public in general, a conclusion that applies whether the test is a demanding one based on opinions about policy issues or a less stringent one based on appraisals of sociopolitical groups and prominent political actors."

Low constraint does not, of course, mean a total absence of organization among belief elements within the mass public. Several studies have examined what factors influence the level of ideological constraint among citizens. Stimson's (1975) factor analytic approach illustrated the importance of cognitive ability (measured by education and political information), as citizens highest in cognitive ability tended to use a smaller number of dimensions (factors) to structure their policy views than did less sophisticated voters. Furthermore, their principal dimension tended to be a left/right one that encompassed a wide range of issues, while the multiple dimensions of the less sophisticated reflected narrower issue domains such as race, social, economic, and women's issues. Nie, Verba, and Petrocik (1976) also found somewhat greater issue constraint among the college educated and the more politically interested (measured by campaign interest) compared with high school dropouts and the politically uninterested. They also stressed the importance of the political environment and the ideological nature of presidential candidates, finding much greater issue constraint in the public beginning in 1964 than in the 1950s, though other researchers have argued that differences in the wording and formatting of questions over time may account for these temporal changes (see, for example, Bishop, Tuchfarber, and Oldendick, 1978).

Methodology of Studying Belief Systems

The elite examined in this study are samples of county chairs and county executive committee members of the two major parties. The elite sample size is 1,153 for Mississippi and 1,040 for Alabama. Data from the party activists were collected through mail surveys conducted in the spring of 1991, as described in the introduction to this book. The public samples are drawn from two independently conducted statewide surveys. The Alabama data were collected through a telephone survey conducted by Southern Opinion Research in the spring of 1991. The Mississippi survey was conducted by Mississippi State University in April 1992. The public sample size is 558 for Mississippi and 519 for Alabama.[1] Identically worded policy questions were employed in all public and elite surveys, though the Mississippi survey eliminated issues if the wording of queries was likely to change over a year's time, as in the cases of defense spending and attitudes toward Russia. Since our primary consideration is a comparison of elites and masses, we omitted these issues as well from the Mississippi activists' factor analysis. Issue items were recoded to range from a score of 1 (most liberal) to 4 (most conservative); in the case of ideological self-identification, a score of 5 represented most conservative.

Belief systems were studied through factor analysis. The only identical indicator of cognitive ability included in both of the public surveys was formal education, so factor analyses for residents of Alabama and Mississippi were conducted separately for less educated (i.e., less than high school diploma) and more educated (i.e., college graduates). Activists of all educational levels were aggregated in conducting separate "elite" analyses for each state. In each case, a principal components analysis was conducted, and varimax rotation was employed when necessary to interpret the resulting factors. Public-elite issue proximity was examined by a comparison of means. The results of the factor analyses are found in the six tables in the appendix at the end of this chapter.

Belief Systems of Southern Elites and Masses

In the contemporary South, economic issues play a central role in people's political belief systems. In every factor analysis, nearly every issue loading most highly on the first factor that emerged contained an important economic component. Furthermore, among the issue items these economic concerns were the most highly related to ideological self-identification. Core economic issues that often emerged were jobs, medicine, and social services. Economic concerns of African Americans and women that also comprised the first factors were affirmative action and socioeconomic issues as they affected each subgroup—African Americans and women. The interrelationships of attitudes on economic and racial concerns suggest a barrier to improved racial relations, as whites may perceive that minority gains are made at their own economic expense.

A hierarchy of attitudinal constraint and political sophistication emerged in both states: the less-educated respondents among the populace had the least sophisticated belief systems, college-educated masses had more sophisticated structures, and party activists were the most sophisticated. The same seven items loaded most highly on the first factor in four analyses—namely, the college-educated public and aggregated activists' samples from both states. The seven items were as follows: MEDICINE, SOCIAL SERVICES, AFFIRM-ATIVE ACTION, BLACK SOCIOECONOMICS, WOMEN SOCIOECONOMICS, IDEOL-OGY, and JOBS.[2]

Different results are found in the analysis of less-educated respondents. The first factor emerging from the less-educated Mississippi citizens included the same items as in the college analysis, except for the omission of jobs, medicine, and social services (the first two loaded on a second "economics" factor and social services loaded on a minor factor) and the inclusion of abortion and women's rights. A varimax rotation was required to interpret the Alabama public high school dropout analysis properly, and even then only four items loaded highly and positively on the first factor—JOBS, MEDICINE, WOMEN SOCIOECONOMICS, and WOMEN'S RIGHTS. Ideology is not even related to the items in this factor, as its average correlation with factor 1 issue items is −.06.

Not only does the analysis of less-educated citizens contain fewer issues in the dominant factor 1, but these items are less constrained than they are for more sophisticated individuals. In Alabama, constraint among the factor 1 items steadily grows as one moves from less to more sophisticated persons, while in Mississippi constraint is lowest among the least sophisticated and is equally high among college graduates and party activists. The average correlation coefficient among all of the items comprising factor 1 is .27 for Alabama high school dropouts, .30 for Alabama college graduates, and .41 for Alabama activists (table 10.1). Constraint also grew in the Mississippi analyses, from .33 for high school dropouts to .45 for college graduates and party activists.

Another indication of more sophisticated belief systems among the more politically aware is provided by examining the average correlation coefficient between ideological self-identification and the issue items comprising factor 1 in each sample. This average correlation increases steadily in both samples as one moves from high school dropouts up to party activists. In Mississippi, the correlation between ideology and factor 1 issue items increases from .25 for less-educated respondents to .39 for more-educated citizens to .44 for party activists. In Alabama, the correlation changes from −.06 for the less educated to .24 for college graduates to .39 for party activists. Hence, the political belief systems of more-educated, and especially more politically active, southerners appear to be structured more along liberal and conservative self-identification lines than is the case for less-educated citizens.

Other evidence of a greater coherence of the belief systems of more politically aware individuals is provided by the smaller number of factors that emerge for them and the greater variance in the issue items explained by the dominant factor. Among less-educated Alabamians, only 15 percent of

Table 10.1. Factor Analysis of Mass and Elite Policy Views in Two States

Sample examined	Average correlation among items loading on factor 1	Average correlation between ideology and issue items in factor 1	No. of factors emerging	Percentage of variance in items explained by factor 1
Alabama				
Public, high school dropouts	.27	-.06	6	15
Public, college graduates	.30	.24	6	25
Party activists	.41	.39	4	29
Mississippi				
Public, high school dropouts[a]	.33	.25	4	28
Public, college graduates[a]	.45	.39	3	41
Party activists[a]	.45	.44	2	44

[a]These Mississippi analyses omitted six issue items that were not included in the statewide public surveys. These items were DEFENSE, RUSSIA, PRAYER, ENVIRONMENT, BALANCED BUDGET, and TAX INCREASE.

the issue item variance is accounted for by the first factor, and five other factors also emerge (table 10.1). More-educated Alabamians also exhibit six factors, but the first explains 25 percent of the variance in the issue items. Among Alabama party activists, only four factors emerge, and the first explains 29 percent of the variance. Among less-educated Mississippi respondents, four factors emerge, and the dominant one accounts for 28 percent of the variance. For college graduates in the Magnolia State, three factors emerge, and the first one explains 41 percent of the variance in the issue items. Only two factors emerge for Mississippi party activists, and the major one explains 44 percent of the variance.

Beyond the first factor in each analysis, other factors typically load on only one or two issues each. Among Alabama activists, three minor factors emerge: a school prayer/balanced budget dimension; a women's rights/Russia relations dimension; and a defense spending/isolationism dimension. Among Mississippi activists, the minor factor pertained to women's issues. Similar issue-specific dimensions characterize the minor

Table 10.2. Policy Views of Mississippians

	Public			Party officials	
	All	Democrats	Republicans	Democrats	Republicans
Issue	A	B	C	D	E
Women socioeconomic	2.06	1.92	2.27	1.85	2.41
Abortion	2.56	2.49	2.61	2.29	2.78
Defense spending	—	—	—	2.29	2.77
Social services	2.28	2.18	2.41	2.07	3.03
School prayer	—	—	—	3.36	3.52
Environment	—	—	—	1.98	2.30
Balanced budget	—	—	—	2.96	3.32
Tax increase	—	—	—	2.80	3.27
Blacks socioeconomic	2.18	1.91	2.52	2.13	2.89
Public jobs	2.20	1.95	2.57	2.40	3.22
Women's rights	1.84	1.85	1.91	1.84	2.07
Isolationism	.73	.64	.88	.78	1.37
Russia relations	—	—	—	2.00	2.15
Affirmative action	2.94	2.61	3.27	2.79	3.57
Health care	1.87	1.72	2.10	1.71	2.56
Ideology	3.49	3.34	3.70	2.91	4.19

Note: Cell entries are means with scales ranging from 1 for most liberal and isolationist to 4 for most conservative and internationalist, except for ideology, where 5 is most conservative.

factors emerging from the public high school dropout and college-educated analyses in each state.[3]

Issue Proximity between Masses and Elites

Despite the popular image of southern conservatism, the results of the Alabama and Mississippi surveys show that the citizens of these two states are generally centrist on specific public policies. Residents of both states fall to the left of the center of the scales on some issues and to the right on others.[4] In both states, voters are somewhat to the left of center on economic issues such as health care, jobs, and social services in general. They are also, on balance, willing to use government to improve the social and economic positions of women and African Americans and to provide equal rights to women (tables 10.2, 10.3). Residents in both states are to the right of the center of the scale on affirmative action and, in Alabama, on school prayer, a tax increase, a balanced budget amendment, and defense spending. Though the Mississippi survey omitted identically worded questions on these last four items, previous public surveys have shown strong support

Table 10.3. Policy Views of Alabamians

Issue	Public All A	Public Democrats B	Public Republicans C	Party officials Democrats D	Party officials Republicans E
Women socioeconomic	1.95	1.82	2.03	1.94	2.47
Abortion	2.40	2.36	2.43	2.21	2.81
Defense spending	2.67	2.70	2.76	2.47	2.85
Social services	2.13	2.05	2.19	2.15	2.91
School prayer	3.27	3.33	3.27	3.31	3.46
Environment	1.97	2.00	1.92	1.92	2.21
Balanced budget	2.95	2.93	2.97	3.03	3.35
Tax increase	2.86	2.78	2.96	2.84	3.31
Blacks socioeconomic	2.26	2.07	2.37	2.38	2.86
Public jobs	2.42	2.18	2.53	2.50	3.19
Women's rights	1.90	1.88	1.85	1.93	2.07
Russia relations	2.00	1.99	1.91	1.96	2.12
Affirmative action	2.95	2.66	3.17	3.14	3.57
Health care	1.93	1.77	2.08	1.74	2.53
Ideology	3.25	3.19	3.27	3.07	4.21

Note: Cell entries are means with scales ranging from 1 for most liberal and isolationist to 4 for most conservative and internationalist, except for ideology, where 5 is most conservative.

among the state's residents for school prayer, a balanced budget amendment, and defense spending. Ideological self-identification scores summarize these conflicting views, as average Alabamians are only slightly to the right of center, while the typical Mississippian falls between the moderate and the somewhat conservative categories.

As is presumably the case outside the region, the results of the Alabama and Mississippi surveys also show that Democrats and Republicans have different policy positions. In particular, as shown in tables 10.2 and 10.3, Democratic Party identifiers in the public in most cases hold more liberal views than do Republican identifiers, though usually the differences are not great.[5] Differences between the citizenry parties are more evident in Mississippi than in Alabama—for example, a .36 ideological difference for Mississippi vs. a mere .08 in the latter state (tables 10.4, 10.5). On every issue included in both public surveys, ideological differences between the public parties are greater in Mississippi than in Alabama.

The primary source of the greater ideological polarization of the citizen parties in Mississippi appears to lie in the greater conservatism of Mississippi Republicans, though the overall mean of this group still remains to the left of the somewhat conservative category. On every one of the nine

Table 10.4. Differences in Policy Views between Mississippi Groups

Issue	Polarization		Proximity to partisan public		Proximity to average voter	
	Rep. public–Dem. public C-B	Rep. officials–Dem. officials E-D	Dem. officials–Dem. public D-B	Rep. officials–Rep. public E-C	Dem. officials–All public D-A	Rep. officials–All public E-A
Women socioeconomic	.35	.56	-.07	.14	-.21	.35
Abortion	.12	.49	-.20	.17	-.27	.22
Social services	.23	.96	-.11	.62	-.21	.75
Blacks socioeconomic	.61	.76	.22	.37	-.05	.71
Public jobs	.62	.82	.45	.65	.20	1.02
Women's rights	.06	.23	-.01	.16	0	.23
Isolationism	.24	.59	.14	.49	.05	.64
Affirmative action	.66	.78	.18	.30	-.15	.63
Health care	.38	.85	-.01	.46	-.16	.69
Ideology	.36	1.28	-.43	.49	-.58	.70

Note: Cell entries are differences between group means.

Table 10.5. Differences in Policy Views between Alabama Groups

Issue	Polarization		Proximity to partisan public		Proximity to average voter	
	Rep. public–Dem. public C–B	Rep. officials–Dem. officials E–D	Dem. officials–Dem. public D–B	Rep. officials–Rep. public E–C	Dem. officials–All public D–A	Rep. officials–All public E–A
Women socioeconomic	.21	.53	.12	.44	-.01	.52
Abortion	.07	.60	-.15	.38	-.19	.41
Defense spending	.06	.38	-.23	.09	-.20	.18
Social service	.14	.76	.10	.72	.02	.78
School prayer	-.06	.15	-.02	.19	.04	.19
Environment	-.08	.29	-.08	.29	-.05	.24
Balanced budget	.04	.32	.10	.38	.08	.40
Tax increase	.18	.47	.06	.35	-.02	.45
Blacks socioeconomic	.30	.48	.31	.49	.12	.60
Public jobs	.35	.69	.32	.66	.08	.77
Women's rights	-.03	.14	.05	.22	.03	.17
Russia relations	-.08	.16	-.03	.21	-.04	.12
Affirmative action	.51	.43	.48	.40	.19	.62
Health care	.31	.79	-.03	.45	-.19	.60
Ideology	.08	1.14	-.12	.94	-.18	.96

Note: Cell entries are differences between group means.

issue scales included in both public surveys, Mississippi Republicans have
somewhat more conservative views than do Alabama Republicans (tables
10.2, 10.3). No consistent differences emerge between the two states' Democratic citizenry parties, however. One possible explanation for the greater
conservatism of Mississippi Republicans may be the greater conservatism of
that state as a whole, as deeper social divisions reflected in a greater African
American population (36 percent of Mississippi compared with 25 percent
for Alabama) and more widespread poverty may have stimulated conservative white flight to the more conservative party nationally.

Turning to party officials, Democrats in both states are ideologically fairly
close to the middle of the road, while Republicans are to the right of the
somewhat conservative category.[6] On most issues in both states, Democratic
grassroots officials are to the left of the issue scale midpoints, while Republican officials are to the right (tables 10.2, 10.3). Very few significant differences emerge within the parties when comparing across the states, as differences between Mississippi and Alabama Democrats and Mississippi and
Alabama Republicans are usually less than one-tenth of a scale point.
Hence, state boundaries do not appear to affect the ideological nature of
the Democratic and Republican activist parties.

The more conservative views of Republican grassroots activists compared with Democrats in both states are quite evident in the second col-
umns of tables 10.4 and 10.5. On every issue in both states, Republican activists hold more conservative views than do Democrats. On the ideological
self-identification scale, the mean score for Republicans is more than one
category to the right of Democrats. It is also quite interesting to note that
on every issue (except affirmative action in Alabama), the differences between the elites are greater than the differences between the masses. For
example, relative to the .36 and .08 ideological mean differences between
the citizenry parties in Mississippi and Alabama, the 1.28 and 1.14 gaps between the elite parties in each state are quite marked.

What accounts for greater ideological polarization between partisan
elites compared with the masses? We should remember that party activists
tend to have higher educational levels than those not active in politics. In
Mississippi, for example, over half of the grassroots party activists hold college diplomas, compared with only about 15 percent of the overall adult
population. Our factor analyses demonstrated how the belief systems of
more educated (and presumably more politically interested and involved)
persons tend to be more structured along ideological lines, with their policy
views showing greater constraint compared with the less educated. The
clear liberal-conservative differences between the national parties in presidential elections are especially likely to be discerned by more politically involved people, thereby generating an ideological sorting out of activists into
the parties that better represent their policy views.

Having shown that party elites are more ideologically polarized than are the rank and file, we need to examine further whether one or both of the parties are contributing to that polarization. Interestingly enough, despite the accusation of out-of-touch Democratic "liberalism" in presidential elections, it appears that if any party organization is out of touch with its partisan supporters in the public, it is the Republican Party (a point generally consistent with a similar analysis for the entire South as reported in Hadley, Maggiotto, and Wekkin, 1993). In both Mississippi and Alabama, Republican Party officials are more conservative than are Republican identifiers in the population on every issue (tables 10.4, 10.5). On ideological self-identification, for example, Alabama Republican officials are nearly one category to the right of the Republican citizenry, while Mississippi Republican elites are half of a category to the right of their party's supporters.

The Republican Party organization in these Deep South states is so conservative that the most bitter intraparty fights have been between conservatives and moderate conservatives, rather than between the right wing and a coalition of liberals and moderates. The battle between Gerald Ford and Ronald Reagan for the 1976 Republican presidential nomination was so divisive among party leaders in Mississippi that it destroyed the unit rule (whereby the state party had traditionally cast all of its votes for one candidate), as the state's delegation cast 16 votes for Ford and 14 for Reagan. Historically, GOP gubernatorial nominees and businessmen Gil Carmichael and Jack Reed have typified the moderate conservatives in Mississippi, with Carmichael pushing such reform measures as the Equal Rights Amendment, gun control, and a new state constitution, and Reed backing a tax increase to improve education. Mississippi Governor Kirk Fordice, who had worked for Barry Goldwater and Ronald Reagan as a grassroots party activist, exemplifies the conservative wing of the Republican Party, favoring tax cutting, school prayer, and privatization of government services.

Democratic Party officials, on the other hand, are much closer ideologically to their party's rank and file. In Alabama, for example, Democratic elites are to the left of their citizenry party on seven issue items and to the right of them on eight scales (table 10.5). On one of the items, ideological self-identification, Democratic officials are to the left of Democrats in the public by only .12 of one category. Mississippi exhibits a similar pattern, as Democratic elites are to the left of their citizenry party on six issue items and to the right on four. However, one of these six leftward-leaning issues is ideological identification, where activists are to the left of citizens by a somewhat greater amount than in Alabama—.43 of one category.

Before Democratic officials in the Deep South grow electorally overconfident thanks to their apparently greater responsiveness to their public's partisans, we should examine whether different patterns in responsiveness emerge for different kinds of issues. In both states, there are three issues on which Democratic elites are more conservative than are Democratic public identifiers—JOBS, BLACK SOCIOECONOMICS, and AFFIRMATIVE ACTION. Much of this Democratic elite conservatism may be attributed to the views of white Democrats, as previous research on Mississippi activists, for example, found wide racial divergence on these three issues of special concern to disadvantaged minorities (Shaffer and Breaux, 1995). For a party so dependent on the electoral support of African American voters, Democratic officials have to be concerned that racial splits within their own organization could lead to problems in the general election.

Yet an even greater problem faces the southern Republican Party. When comparing each party's grassroots activists with the policy views of the entire adult population, we find that the Republican organization is much more out of touch with the public. In both Alabama and Mississippi, Republican officials have more conservative views than the aggregated population on every issue examined (tables 10.4, 10.5, last column). On ideological self-identification, Alabama GOP elites are .96 of one category to the right of the state populace, while Mississippi elites are .70 of one category to the right of the citizenry as a whole. Especially troublesome is that the two specific issues on which Republicans in both states are most out of touch with the public are jobs and social services (health and education). These are popular economic issues, and Republican Party neglect of such important bread-and-butter concerns could leave southern officials with the same kinds of electoral problems that helped torpedo President Bush's reelection bid.

Democratic officials, in contrast, are generally much closer to the views of average citizens. In Alabama, Democratic elites are slightly to the left of the aggregate population on eight issues and slightly to the right on seven (table 10.5). On ideological self-identification, elites are only .18 of one category to the left of the populace. Mississippi Democratic elites have somewhat greater problems in representing their state's average voters, however, as they fall to the left on seven issue scales and to the right on only two (no difference exists on one). One of these seven leftward biases is on ideological self-identification, where Democratic officials are more liberal than aggregated citizens by .58 of one category—a distance that is nevertheless somewhat smaller than that facing the Republican Party (table 10.4).

Why are Mississippi Democratic officials somewhat less representative of their state's population than are Alabama Democrats? In both states, Republicans are slightly to the right of the somewhat conservative ideological self-identification category, while Democratic officials are ideologically close to the center. But remember that the average Alabama resident claims to have fairly centrist views, while Mississippi residents fall somewhat between the moderate and somewhat conservative categories (tables 10.2, 10.3). Hence, Alabama Democratic officials virtually mirror their public's views, while Republican elites are out in right field. Mississippi Democratic activists are slightly too moderate for the average citizen, though Republican elites are—by an even greater amount—too conservative for residents.

Increasing electoral successes for Republicans in the South could intensify intraparty conflict over just how conservative the party should be. There have been a number of instances of conflict within the Republican Party in Mississippi, for example, during the 1990s. Governor Fordice, frequently in the middle of these squabbles, even threatened at one point to campaign against the "pseudo-Republicans running up and down the [state senate] aisles" (Steed, Moreland, and Baker, 1994: 68). Though Republican Party leaders succeeded in mending the fences, these episodes suggest that greater electoral prosperity may lead southern Republicans to start acting like Democrats.

Conclusions

In some important respects, political patterns in the Deep South states of Mississippi and Alabama reflect the emergence of a New South. Average residents and party officials in these states reflect the political patterns that characterize American politics in general. More educated and politically active citizens possess more sophisticated belief systems that encompass economic and racial issues structured along liberal-conservative lines. Such politically aware southerners have more constrained belief systems, with more ideologically consistent views on policy issues, than do other citizens.

As in the rest of the nation, the Deep South political parties represent different philosophies, with Republicans taking the more conservative position. Defying Independent George Wallace's claim in 1968 that "there's not a dime's worth of difference between the two parties," issue differences between party activists are greater than those between party supporters in the general population. Given such differences, parties run the opposite risk of presenting candidates that may be ideologically out of touch with the state electorates.

Regarding which party organization appears to be especially out of touch with citizens, we seem to have come full circle back to the classic McClosky work. The Republican Party is now significantly more conservative than both states' populations, while the Democratic Party appears more in line with residents, especially in Alabama. Lacking longitudinal data, we can only speculate as to whether the current pattern of elite/mass public ideological issue orientations has been a long-term phenomenon or a cyclical one; nor can we do more than speculate about the applicability of these findings to the other southern states. If a long-term characteristic of the southern parties, as suggested by some of the intraparty strife among Mississippi Republicans during the 1990s, the mass/elite linkage may help to explain why Democrats have continued to dominate state and local offices below the governorship throughout much of the old Confederacy.

Another possibility is the cyclical version presented by Nie, Verba, Petrocik, Shaffer, and Kirkpatrick, whereby ideological presidential candidates tend to stimulate heightened political activism among their ideological soul mates in their respective parties. Hence, Goldwater produced a heightened conservative bias among Republican campaign activists in 1964, while McGovern produced a significant liberal bias among Democratic activists in 1972. The two-term presidency of conservative Ronald Reagan may have attracted ideological soul mates to the southern Republican parties, and the fruits of that selective self-recruitment may remain years after he has left office. Thus the GOP may find that it is only temporarily the party most out of step with the public. Even such dissonance need not be electorally fatal. As the elections of Ronald Reagan as president in 1980, Guy Hunt as governor of Alabama in 1986, and Kirk Fordice as governor of Mississippi in 1991 demonstrate, public dissatisfaction with a particular candidate or such societal conditions as a bad economy can sometimes reduce the salience of ideological considerations to insignificance. Perhaps the most likely explanation is some combination of the long-term and cyclical perspectives.

In the 1994 GOP landslide that swept across the nation, Alabama and Mississippi were islands of relative stability, as all congressional incumbents were reelected, and Democrats retained bare majorities of each state's congressional delegation. Perhaps the more moderate to moderate-conservative orientation of Democratic congressmen, compared with northern Democrats and even with some party colleagues in other southern states, better reflected the values of their constituents and helped them to withstand the GOP sweep. Among white Democratic congressmen, four sported moderate conservative voting records (Montgomery, Parker, Taylor in Mississippi, and Browder in Alabama, based on ADA and ACU pressure group ratings), and two had strictly moderate records (Bevill and Cramer in Alabama). The only Democrats championing liberal roll call records were African Americans representing majority black districts that have voted Democratic in recent presidential elections (Hilliard in Alabama and Thompson in Mississippi).[7]

The strength of this "big tent" philosophy of southern Democrats is most evident in state elections, where Democrats continue to control 66 percent and 70 percent of Alabama's state legislative seats and 71 percent and 74 percent of Mississippi's delegation (state senate and house, respectively). Both states are typical in this respect of the Deep South as a whole, as even after the 1994 GOP landslide Democrats retained control of 68 percent of state house seats and 70 percent of senate seats in these five states. Democrats are not quite as dominant in the state legislatures of the Rim South states, where they control 57 percent of state senate seats and 59 percent of house seats.

Another factor aiding members of Congress of both parties in 1994 was incumbency itself. Even with clearly conservative voting records, all three GOP members of Congress from Alabama easily won reelection, with 67–79 percent of the vote. Spencer Bachus (6th District) was initially elected in 1992 after redistricting had made his territory heavily Republican with a 90 percent white population. Sonny Callahan (1st), a former Democratic state legislator, switched to the GOP in 1984 and was first elected to Congress with a bare 51 percent vote in Reagan's landslide reelection year. Business-man Terry Everett (2nd) was first elected in 1992, beating George Wallace's son (the state treasurer) by a mere 1 percent, as he blasted career politicians and the "Old Guard" who caused "gridlock." All three Republicans have maintained roll call records that are conservative more than 90 percent of the time, reflecting the conservative orientations of Republican grassroots party activists (Duncan and Lawrence, 1995).

Clearly, then, a number of variables are at work in the contemporary politics of both Mississippi and Alabama. Within this context, the degree of fit between the ideological positions of the local party activists and their party's supporters in the larger population will continue to play an important role in the parties' futures.

Appendix to Chapter 10. Factor Analysis Results

Alabama Public, High School Dropouts

	Factor number					
Issue	1	2	3	4	5	6
Women socioeconomic	.58	.41	-.11	-.18	.41	-.04
Abortion	.22	.20	.14	.46	-.02	.60
Defense spending	0	.23	.18	-.45	-.25	-.20
Social services	-.09	.70	-.15	-.11	.05	.13
School prayer	.08	-.08	.33	-.12	.17	.77
Environment	-.13	.22	-.71	.27	.27	-.15
Balanced budget	-.08	.13	.82	.15	.08	.10
Tax increase	-.14	-.10	.18	.78	.09	-.18
Blacks socioeconomic	-.09	.28	-.25	.06	.77	-.06
Public jobs	.83	-.06	-.02	-.15	.03	-.03
Women's rights	.73	-.23	.04	.18	-.06	.08
Russia relations	.10	.42	-.20	.57	-.01	-.02
Affirmative action	.17	-.30	.19	.17	.74	.08
Health care	.35	-.03	.20	.16	.31	-.58
Ideology	-.14	.68	.32	.15	-.06	-.10
Eigenvalue	2.17	2.12	1.81	1.51	1.20	1.09
Percentage of variance	14.5	14.1	12.0	10.1	8.0	7.3

Alabama Public, College Graduates

Issue	Factor number					
	1	2	3	4	5	6
Women socioeconomic	.73	-.12	-.34	-.31	-.04	.14
Abortion	.48	.46	-.36	.35	-.18	-.08
Defense spending	.27	-.13	.41	.59	.13	.39
Social services	.65	-.20	.09	.30	.16	-.15
School prayer	.23	.48	.13	-.07	-.48	.53
Environment	.37	-.26	-.18	.41	-.38	-.25
Balanced budget	-.08	.56	.46	-.27	.18	-.03
Tax increase	.41	.13	.13	-.23	-.44	-.50
Blacks socioeconomic	.77	-.34	-.03	-.16	.03	.18
Public jobs	.46	.08	.22	.02	.51	-.35
Women's rights	.43	-.03	-.54	-.12	.37	.25
Russia relations	.16	.62	-.37	-.08	.27	-.04
Affirmative action	.54	-.15	.52	-.24	.02	.10
Health care	.68	-.07	.17	-.37	-.11	-.02
Ideology	.53	.49	.18	.39	.05	-.05
Eigenvalue	3.69	1.68	1.50	1.36	1.17	1.02
Percentage of variance	24.6	11.2	10.0	9.0	7.8	6.8

Mississippi Public, High School Dropouts

Issue	Factor number			
	1	2	3	4
Women socioeconomic	.68	-.44	.24	-.28
Abortion	.49	-.46	-.12	.30
Social services	.18	.44	.42	.59
Blacks socioeconomic	.76	.09	-.20	.06
Public jobs	.45	.74	-.06	-.16
Women's rights	.72	-.31	.21	-.06
Affirmative action	.62	-.07	-.38	-.22
Health care	.24	.75	-.01	-.37
Ideology	.57	.23	-.15	.49
Isolationism	.21	.01	.79	-.19
Eigenvalue	2.84	1.87	1.13	1.01
Percentage of variance	28.4	18.7	11.3	10.1

Mississippi Public, College Graduates

Issue	Factor number		
	1	2	3
Women socioeconomic	.81	.05	-.28
Abortion	.55	.52	.14
Social services	.70	-.03	.11
Blacks socioeconomic	.85	-.13	-.12
Public jobs	.75	-.38	.06
Women's rights	.40	.63	-.24
Affirmative action	.57	-.36	.13
Health care	.65	-.22	.23
Ideology	.65	.17	-.33
Isolationism	.26	.30	.84
Eigenvalue	4.14	1.13	1.08
Percentage of variance	41.4	11.3	10.8

Alabama Party Activists

Issue	Factor number			
	1	2	3	4
Women socioeconomic	.69	-.18	.18	-.11
Abortion	.46	.29	.36	.18
Defense spending	.38	.35	-.21	.56
Social services	.65	-.14	-.21	.01
School prayer	.29	.72	.11	.05
Environment	.45	-.37	.20	-.01
Balanced budget	.28	.51	-.24	-.19
Tax increase	.49	.20	-.16	-.26
Blacks socioeconomic	.73	-.03	.08	-.34
Public jobs	.70	-.25	-.23	-.13
Women's rights	.37	-.13	.59	.04
Isolationism	.35	-.32	-.40	.52
Russia relations	.36	.02	.48	.32
Affirmative action	.59	.07	-.11	-.32
Health care	.68	-.30	-.11	.13
Ideology	.69	.25	-.09	.11
Eigenvalue	4.56	1.55	1.22	1.10
Percentage of variance	28.5	9.7	7.6	6.8

Mississippi Party Activists

Issue	Factor number	
	1	2
Women socioeconomic	.61	.45
Abortion	.10	.78
Social services	.75	.14
Blacks socioeconomic	.76	.22
Public jobs	.77	.14
Women's rights	.15	.75
Isolationism	.47	.12
Affirmative action	.76	.05
Health care	.74	.12
Ideology	.60	.40
Eigenvalue	4.44	1.07
Percentage of variance	44.4	10.7

11

Strength of Party Attachment

Robert P. Steed
Lewis Bowman

The connections between the external environment and the political parties have been appreciated for a long time. In a wide variety of ways, political parties reflect—and affect—the institutional, legal, social, economic, political, and cultural settings within which they exist (Beck and Sorauf, 1992: chaps. 1, 11; Blank, 1980: esp. chap. 3; Key, 1964: chaps. 8–9; Harmel and Janda, 1982; Bibby, 1992: chap. 3; Crotty, 1983, 1977; Price, 1984; Ladd and Hadley, 1975; Sundquist, 1983; and Ladd, 1970). The focus of attention may be on party history in the context of such developments as population movements, legal or constitutional changes (e.g., campaign finance laws, term limits), or changing issue concerns. In other cases, attention may focus on the decentralizing impact of such institutional arrangements as federalism and separation of powers, or on efforts to reform the parties in some manner by changing critical elements of the environment (e.g., adoption of the direct primary, civil service systems), or on a host of other subjects. No matter what aspect of political parties is examined, the reciprocal relationship with the environment is central to an understanding of parties.[1]

From a party organizational/party activist perspective, the possibility of a cleavage between party activists' perceptions of the national party and the state party is a key environmental factor in understanding the southern party system. Commonly researched in terms of split partisanship, the conceptual notion is that voters or activists "have different schema or cognitive structures of the parties in mind at different levels of government, deriving from the ideological, issue, and candidate properties peculiar to each party at each level" (Wekkin, 1991: 236). Within the context of southern party developments, this has usually meant that many Democrats have become increasingly disaffected by what they see as a movement of the national Democratic Party away from its conservative roots; these Democrats frequently continue to identify themselves as Democrats at the state level but as Independents or even weak Republicans at the national level. The dramatic changes in the region over the past three decades have been especially conducive to the development of split partisanship, which helps explain such indicators of regional Democratic Party decline as split-ticket voting and decreased party activist commitment (Hadley and Howell, 1980; Hadley, 1985; Clark and Lockerbie, 1992).

Split partisanship has had historical importance for the Republican Party as well, inasmuch as many southern voters and political activists slowly began to support Republicans in national elections while holding to their Democratic leanings at the state and local levels. A large part of the obstacle facing Republicans in the South is the reluctance of Democrats to shift wholly to the Republican Party at all electoral levels.[2]

The Southern Grassroots Party Activists Project data provide an opportunity to develop and extend the concept of split partisanship beyond its usual application. As a method of extending the concept, we developed categories of party activists, based on both their answers to the standard party identification questions (for national party identification and state party identification) and their answers to questions concerning their feelings toward their party (again for both national and state parties). We thus refined the notion of partisanship into the more inclusive concept of *strength of party attachment*.

For purposes of this analysis, we divide these grassroots political party officials into three groups based on their strengths of political party attachment: consistently strong, consistently weak, and mixed.

The *consistently strong* are those party activists who identify strongly with their party at both the national and state levels and who also say they feel "extremely close" to their party at both the national and state levels. On all four variables, these activists evince strong attachment to their party.

The *consistently weak* are those party activists who do not identify strongly with their party at either the national or state levels and who also say that they do not feel "extremely close" to their party at either level. On all four variables, these activists exhibit weak attachment to their party.

The *mixed* category includes those grassroots party activists who have any combination of inconsistent responses to the four questions. Strong national party identification, for example, results in a mixed combination when it is accompanied either by weak state party identification or by feelings of distance from either the national party or the state party. ("Distant" is defined as any response other than "extremely close" on the question of party feelings.)

Our general hypothesis is that strength of political party attachment is related in a variety of ways to party activists' behavior and attitudes toward their party organization. The first part of the analysis pursues this line of inquiry in an effort to map out the consequences of party attachment for the party. A reasonable expectation, for example, is that activists weakly attached to their party will be less active and less committed to the party's vitality than activists who are strongly attached to their party. We would also

Table 11.1. Distribution of Local Party Activists According to Category of Party Attachment (in percentage)

Party attachment category	Democrats	Republicans	Percentage Republican difference
Consistently strong	35	55	+20
Mixed	50	38	-12
Consistently weak	15	7	-8
(N)	(4271)	(4184)	

expect, given the direction of southern party politics over the past three decades, that variance in these attachments and commitments would be more pronounced among Democratic Party grassroots organizational activists in the South than among the Republican Party's grassroots activists.

The second line of analysis explored the correlates of strength of political party attachment. That is, if variation in the party attachment strengths of party officials is shown to be important for differentiation among grassroots party activists, then what factors explain why some activists are strongly attached to their party while others have mixed or even consistently weak attachments?

Consequences of Strength of Party Attachment

Clearly not all party activists are strongly attached to their respective parties. Within the context of our categories, Mixed and Consistently Weak party attachment are sufficiently common to be meaningful constructs for both parties. (See table 11.1.) Among the Democrats, approximately two-thirds of the activists are in these two categories, with 50 percent being Mixed and 15 percent being Consistently Weak. The percentages for the Republicans are, not surprisingly, lower; even so, however, just under half of the activists fall into these two categories (38 percent Mixed and 7 percent Consistently Weak in attachment).

These variations in strength of attachment to political party have an obvious negative impact on the parties in a variety of ways. For one thing, these party officials' activities are strongly related to strength of party attachment. (See tables 11.2–11.5.) In both parties, the Consistently Strong party activists are much more heavily engaged in performing the activities usually considered important for party success. Virtually without exception through the entire list of activities reported in tables 11.2 and 11.3, the pattern for both Democrats and Republicans is linear, with the most active being the Consistently Strong, the next most active being the Mixed, and the least

Table 11.2. Political Activities of Local Democratic Party Activists, by Degree of Party Attachment (in percentage performing listed activity)

Activity	Strong	Mixed	Weak
Contacting voters	91	85	67
Raising money	61	56	27
Voter registration	90	86	72
Campaigning	85	76	48
Public relations	80	77	61
Contacting new voters	83	77	58
Party meetings/business	90	85	60
Recruiting/organizing workers	76	70	49
County party organizational work	79	72	43
Increasing pol. info. for others	83	77	60
Policy formulation	64	59	38
Recruiting cands. for local office	69	65	47
Other nomination activities	53	47	26
Organized door-to-door canvassing	32	27	18
Organized campaign events	39	38	19
Arranged fund raising	33	30	15
Organized mailings	39	36	22
Distributed camp. literature	70	66	45
Organized phone campaigns	37	33	20
Purchased billboard space	5	4	5
Distributed posters and lawn signs	61	57	39
Conducted registration drives	28	24	12
Used public opinion surveys	12	10	7
Dealt with campaign media	25	24	15
Cand. consultation (before announcing)	74	70	60
Suggested cand. run	81	79	72

active being the Consistently Weak in party attachment.[3] The differences in activity levels are generally not great between the first two categories, but there is a dramatic gap between the Consistently Strong and the Consistently Weak, especially among the Democrats (exceeding 30 percentage points on four activities, exceeding 20 percentage points on nine additional activities, and averaging just over 19 percentage points).

The same pattern is evident in the activity levels of these officials at different electoral levels. For both Democrats and Republicans—but again more pronounced among Democrats—the Consistently Strong are much more active at all three electoral levels, followed by the Mixed and the Consistently Weak, in that order. (See tables 11.4 and 11.5.) Among the Democratic officials there is an interesting contrast between those with strong

Table 11.3. Political Activities of Local Republican Party Activists, by Degree of Party Attachment (in percentage performing listed activity)

Activity	Strong	Mixed	Weak
Contacting voters	89	83	74
Raising money	63	53	35
Voter registration	83	79	80
Campaigning	83	73	66
Public relations	75	70	61
Contacting new voters	77	71	70
Party meetings/business	88	82	64
Recruiting/organizing workers	74	64	56
County party organizational work	75	64	46
Increasing pol. info. for others	81	77	74
Policy formulation	62	58	50
Recruiting cands. for local office	72	64	54
Other nomination activities	50	41	33
Organized door-to-door canvassing	34	28	24
Organized campaign events	44	35	24
Arranged fund raising	38	29	17
Organized mailings	52	47	35
Distributed camp. literature	76	74	57
Organized phone campaigns	45	40	25
Purchased billboard space	6	6	5
Distributed posters and lawn signs	72	66	55
Conducted registration drives	27	23	18
Used public opinion surveys	15	11	11
Dealt with campaign media	32	26	19
Cand. consultation (before announcing)	68	60	50
Suggested cand. run	83	79	69

party attachment and those with weak party attachment as we move from local to state to national elections. While, as noted above, those in the Consistently Strong category are more active than those in the Consistently Weak category at each level, the aggregate differences are greater at the national level than at the local level. Combining the "very active" and the "somewhat active" responses, the difference between the two groups of activists rises from 12 percentage points in local elections to 32 percentage points in state elections and to 45 percentage points in national elections. The same pattern exists for the Republicans (with percentage differences rising from 16 to 22 to 29). These data suggest that precinct officials in both parties are more active locally than nationally, but the dramatically sharper contrasts among Democrats suggest additionally that disaffection with the

Table 11.4. Campaign Activity Participation of Local Democratic Party Activists, by Degree of Party Attachment (in percentage)

Level	Strong	Mixed	Weak
Local elections			
Very active	71	61	41
Somewhat active	21	27	35
Not very active	7	8	15
Not active at all	1	3	9
(N)	(1487)	(2162)	(622)
State elections			
Very active	68	51	19
Somewhat active	27	37	44
Not very active	4	9	23
Not active at all	1	2	13
(N)	(1469)	(2127)	(619)
National elections			
Very active	57	37	13
Somewhat active	31	38	30
Not very active	10	20	34
Not active at all	2	5	23
(N)	(1466)	(2110)	(614)

national party and its presidential candidates is a significant problem among the Democratic grassroots activists in the South. On the same note, the proportion of "very active" Democrats in the Consistently Strong category declines from 71 percent in local elections to just over half (57 percent) in national elections, a pattern that is reversed for Republican activists in the Consistently Strong category.

This disaffection is translated into voting patterns as demonstrated by the activists' vote for president in 1988: 67 percent of the Consistently Weak Democrats report that they in fact voted for George Bush, as compared with 6 percent of the Mixed and only 2 percent of the Consistently Strong. For the Republicans, unhappiness with the national party is much less pronounced, so we would not expect the same level of voting defection; still, party attachment is mildly related to voting behavior in that 13 percent of the Consistently Weak broke party ranks and voted for candidates other than Bush (9 percent for Dukakis and 4 percent for other candidates). Among the Consistently Strong and Mixed Republican grassroots party activists, 99 percent report they voted for Bush.

Not only are the Consistently Weak officials less active and less loyal than

**Table 11.5. Campaign Activity Participation of Local Republican Party
Activists, by Degree of Party Attachment (in percentage)**

Level	Strong	Mixed	Weak
Local elections			
Very active	58	50	39
Somewhat active	28	33	31
Not very active	11	13	19
Not active at all	4	4	11
(N)	(2331)	(1573)	(280)
State elections			
Very active	63	44	25
Somewhat active	31	43	47
Not very active	5	10	19
Not active at all	1	3	9
(N)	(2339)	(1583)	(281)
National elections			
Very active	64	46	22
Somewhat active	26	34	39
Not very active	8	14	24
Not active at all	2	5	15
(N)	(2334)	(1574)	(278)

the Mixed and the Consistently Strong, they are also less likely to perceive improvement (and, in data not reported in detail here, more likely to see weakening) in the party organization over the past decade. (See tables 11.6 and 11.7.) For the Democrats, two observations are indicated. First, relatively small percentages of these activists in any of the attachment categories see their party as having become stronger over the past ten years. Certainly, the Democrats are much less optimistic than Republicans about the nature of recent change in their party's local organizations.

Second, and more directly related to our concern with strength of party attachment among the local Democratic officials, sharp differences exist on each point listed in table 11.6. In each instance, the Consistently Strong are more likely than the Mixed, and especially more likely than the Consistently Weak, to see the party as having become stronger over the past decade.

There are two possible explanations for this pattern. First, the party officials' perceptions may be an accurate indication of what has been happening in their county organizations. If this is the case, the party organizational decline may be a contributor to the weakening attachment of the Consistently Weak and, to a lesser degree, of the Mixed activists. Conversely,

**Table 11.6. Local Democratic Activists' Perceptions of Improvement
in Party Health, by Degree of Party Attachment
(in percentage seeing improvement)**

Function	Strong	Mixed	Weak
Overall party organization	46	35	18
Campaign effectiveness	43	36	19
Ability to raise funds	35	29	16
Ability to recruit candidates	33	27	14
Ability to develop workers' organizational skills	40	28	15
Party use of the media	44	36	24
Party use of opinion polls	32	26	18
Party use of computers	55	46	37

the presence of party activists with weak attachment to the party may well contribute to the decline of party organizations in these areas. On the other hand, perhaps the two phenomena interact so as to produce, simultaneously, weaker party attachment and weaker organizations.

The second possible explanation for the broader pattern is that the party activists' perceptions are not entirely accurate and that the local party organizations are actually stronger than the Consistently Weak officials think. Even if this is the case, it bodes ill for the Democratic Party in these areas because this perception, mistaken though it may be, is likely to sap the morale and the commitment of these activists (perhaps already surfacing in the data on party activities discussed previously).[4]

**Table 11.7. Local Republican Activists' Perceptions of Improvement
in Party Health, by Degree of Party Attachment
(in percentage seeing improvement)**

Function	Strong	Mixed	Weak
Overall party organization	80	75	71
Campaign effectiveness	73	68	59
Ability to raise funds	66	58	52
Ability to recruit candidates	67	59	51
Ability to develop workers' organizational skills	59	51	37
Party use of the media	58	50	41
Party use of opinion polls	44	37	29
Party use of computers	62	56	46

Much the same analysis can be applied to the Republicans. The key differences are that (1) the Republican activists in all three categories generally see their party in more favorable terms with regard to perceptions of party change than do the Democrats and (2) the differences between the Consistently Strong and the Consistently Weak are considerably smaller than for the Democrats. For example, 80 percent of the Consistently Strong say that their local party's overall organization has gotten stronger in recent years, as compared with 71 percent of the Consistently Weak; the 9 percentage point difference is considerably smaller than the 28 percentage point difference between the corresponding two groups of Democratic activists (noted previously). Still, this illustrates that the southern Republican Party is not immune to the problems related to morale and commitment associated with the Consistently Weak party officials within its ranks.

The potential problems for both parties, especially the Democrats, in the area of party commitment are indicated as well by the relative importance that activists assign to party unity and to adherence to issue positions. For example, among the Democrats 76 percent of the Consistently Strong agree that "Good party workers support any candidate nominated by the party even if they basically disagree with the candidate"; 64 percent of the Mixed and 27 percent of the Consistently Weak agree with this statement. Among the Republicans, 44 percent of the Consistently Strong, 35 percent of the Mixed, and 22 percent of the Consistently Weak agree with this statement. In a pattern similar with respect to a second question about party unity, 56 percent of the Consistently Strong Democrats agree that "Party organization and unity are more important than free and total discussion of issues which may divide the party"; agreement among the Mixed and Consistently Weak is 48 percent and 24 percent, respectively. Thirty-seven percent of the Consistently Strong Republicans give this response as compared with 29 percent of the Mixed Republicans and 16 percent of the Consistently Weak Republicans. When asked their positions on avoiding controversial issues in the party platform to ensure party unity, 55 percent of the Consistently Strong Democrats choose party unity as compared with 51 percent of the Mixed Democrats and 35 percent of the Consistently Weak Democrats. Among the Republicans, the respective percentages are 42 percent, 40 percent, and 27 percent. Only when the proposition is presented in terms of candidates rather than parties do the three groups in both parties respond in essentially the same ways.

The Correlates of Party Attachment

We are particularly interested in the extent to which external events and developments are related to the varying levels of party attachment exhibited by these grassroots political party activists. Obvious implications for party

organization and viability make it important to identify those factors that
are associated with the strength of party attachment.

The Democrats

In background characteristics, the main differences among the Democratic officials relate to age, gender, race, and, to a small degree, income.
The Consistently Weak tend to be somewhat younger than the Mixed and
the Consistently Strong; 45 percent of the Consistently Weak are under 49
years of age as compared with 39 percent of the Mixed and 33 percent of
the Consistently Strong. The Consistently Weak are also more likely to be
male than either the Mixed or the Consistently Strong (71 percent to 62
and 61 percent, respectively). With regard to race, 91 percent of the Consistently Weak are white, and only 6 percent are African American; in comparison, 79 percent of the Consistently Strong are white, and 17 percent are
African American. Finally, there are some small differences on income, with
the Consistently Weak being somewhat more affluent than the Mixed and
the Consistently Strong.

Other personal background variables show virtually no differences
among the three groups of activists. In about the same proportions, members of each group are relatively well educated, mainly southern in childhood regional background, long-term residents of their current home state,
and Protestant. They are undifferentiated in their frequency of church attendance, although the Consistently Weak activists tend to be a little more
fundamentalist and born-again in their religious identifications. There is
mild confirmation in these data of the weakening of ties to the Democratic
Party in the South among younger white males, and there is some slight
indication that religion may be a contributing factor as well.

While the personal background variables offer some help in understanding strength of party attachment among the local Democratic officials
in our survey, political background variables offer a good deal more. For
example, compared with the Consistently Weak activists (and to a lesser
degree the Mixed), the Consistently Strong activists have considerably
longer histories of political activity, they are more likely to have held other
party offices (and slightly more likely to have held appointive political positions), they are less likely to be party switchers, and they are more likely to
have come from homes where parents or other relatives were politically active. Perhaps demonstrating their closer ties to the party, the Consistently
Strong activists are also more likely to have been recruited by another party
committee member and/or the county chair, and they are significantly more
likely to see their county committee membership as being very important
to them personally (58 percent, compared with 42 percent for the Mixed
and only 16 percent for the Consistently Weak). Indeed, the only political

Table 11.8. Motivations for Local Democratic Party Activists, by Degree of Party Attachment (in percentage)

Motivation	Strong	Mixed	Weak
Friendship with candidate	23	16	11
Friendship with party official	26	20	15
Politics is part of way of life	58	44	18
Strong party attachment	82	63	7
Friendship/contact with party workers	41	32	11
Family involvement in party	28	20	10
Campaign fun/excitement	39	29	14
To build a party position	10	9	7
Campaigns as way to influence gov. and politics	58	48	25
Party work as way to influence gov. and politics	60	48	25
Like being close to people doing important things	34	25	13
To make business contacts	8	6	4
Community obligation	50	42	30
Community recognition	18	14	7
Concern with public issues	75	63	48
Candidate support	72	62	41

Note: Values indicate percentage saying the listed motivation was "very important" for their becoming involved in party work.

background variable that does not differentiate among these groups is planning to run for public office in the future.

Not surprisingly, the motivations for becoming politically active are also different for the three groups of activists. The Consistently Strong activists are much more likely than the Consistently Weak or the Mixed to say that the various motivations listed in table 11.8 were "very important" to them in making the decision to become active. The differences are particularly sharp on those motivations relating to political and party factors (e.g., party attachment, politics as part of one's way of life, friendship with party workers, party work and campaigns as ways to influence government and politics). This is reflected, as well, in the activists' listing of the most important single reason for their involvement. Of special note, the most frequently mentioned reason for involvement for the Consistently Strong activists is strong party attachment (named by 21 percent); this motivation slips to second place for the Mixed (at 15 percent) and all the way to eleventh place for the Consistently Weak (at 1 percent). For the Consistently Weak activists the most frequently mentioned reason for involvement is concern with public issues (21 percent) followed by sense of community obligation (20 percent). The Mixed also mention concern with public issues as the most important reason for involvement (16 percent).

Ideological and issue positions add another piece to the puzzle of party attachment for the Democrats. First, there are clear-cut ideological cleavages among the three groups of activists. The Consistently Strong activists tend to be the most liberal: more than half (53 percent) identify themselves in these terms as compared with 40 percent of the Mixed and only 11 percent of the Consistently Weak. Conversely, a majority of the Consistently Weak activists say they are conservative to some degree, considerably more than the 23 percent of the Mixed and 18 percent of the Consistently Strong giving this response.

This liberal/conservative division between the Consistently Strong activists and the Consistently Weak activists holds consistently with regard to their positions on a range of issues that were important at the time of the survey. (See table 11.9.) On each of the fourteen issues, the Consistently Strong are much more liberal in their response patterns than the Consistently Weak (with the Mixed falling in between but typically closer proportionally to the Consistently Strong than to the Consistently Weak). On all the issues except for continued cooperation with Russia, the differences are quite large, ranging in a few cases beyond 35 percentage points. On half of the issues, less than half of the Consistently Weak give a liberal response; on only three of the issues do the Consistently Strong fall below 50 percent liberal.

For the Democrats, then, strength of party attachment is related to activists' political histories, motivations, and ideological and issue orientations. Compared with the Consistently Strong activists, the Consistently Weak activists have been less involved in politics and for shorter periods of time, they come from less politically active families, they do not see their party positions as very important to them personally, they are less motivated to political activity by strictly party considerations, and they tend to be much more conservative (and less liberal).

The Republicans

Unlike the Democrats, the local Republican activists' personal background characteristics are virtually undifferentiated by strength of party attachment. The three groups of officials tend to be remarkably similar with regard to age, gender, race, religious affiliation, church attendance, and religious identification. Only on income, state of childhood, and number of years in the state are there any differences, and these are extremely small (worth mentioning only because the other variables showed no differences at all). The Consistently Weak activists tend to be a little less affluent (only

Table 11.9. Local Democratic Party Activists' Issue Orientations, by Degree of Party Attachment (in percentage liberal responses)

Issue	Strong	Mixed	Weak
Social			
Assistance for women	95	90	68
Personal choice for abortion	81	76	58
School prayer	36	32	14
Environmental protection	89	86	74
Gov. aid for blacks/minorities	82	71	45
Support for women's equality	91	90	83
Affirmative action programs	29	22	9
Economic			
Fewer services to reduce gov. spending	86	78	48
Constitutional amendment to balance nat. budget	37	34	20
State tax increase for financial crisis	38	32	12
Gov. aid in jobs and living standards	59	47	30
Gov. health care assistance	95	92	82
Foreign policy/defense			
Increase defense spending	75	74	58
Continue cooperation with Russia	93	91	90

37 percent having annual incomes over $50,000 as compared with 48 percent and 50 percent for the Consistently Strong and Mixed, respectively); a little less southern in their childhoods (68 percent southern vs. 75 percent of the Consistently Strong and 71 percent of the Mixed); and a little more likely to be newcomers to their current home state (13 percent having lived in the state for ten years or fewer as compared with 9 percent of the Consistently Strong and 12 percent of the Mixed). The biggest surprise in these data is the lack of differences on the religious variables; any internal party schism that might be resulting from the influx of people supportive of the new Christian right is certainly not evident from the data on strength of party attachment.

As with the Democrats, the more significant variations among the three groups of Republican activists relate to political background variables. Indeed, in many ways the Republican differences resemble those of the Democrats. For example, half of the Consistently Weak have been politically active fewer than ten years as compared with roughly one-third of the Consistently Strong and just under two-fifths of the Mixed. The Consistently Weak are

**Table 11.10. Motivations for Local Republican Party Activists,
by Degree of Party Attachment (in percentage)**

Motivation	Strong	Mixed	Weak
Friendship with candidate	15	14	11
Friendship with party official	27	20	14
Politics is part of way of life	43	33	20
Strong party attachment	68	46	8
Friendship/contact with party workers	25	18	9
Family involvement in party	15	14	7
Campaign fun/excitement	27	19	10
To build a party position	8	6	4
Campaigns as way to influence gov. and politics	59	53	45
Party work as way to influence gov. and politics	66	60	46
Like being close to people doing important things	18	15	7
To make business contacts	4	2	4
Community obligation	36	33	25
Community recognition	8	6	5
Concern with public issues	73	69	61
Candidate support	69	64	50

Note: Values indicate percentage saying the listed motivation was "very important" for their becoming involved in party work.

also less likely to have held some other party position (18 percent to 33 percent and 41 percent, respectively), an elective position, or an appointive position. Similarly, while 86 percent of the Consistently Strong see their party position as at least "somewhat important," only 56 percent of the Consistently Weak respond in these terms. The Consistently Weak are also more likely to be party switchers, they are less likely to come from politically active families, and their recruitment patterns are less reflective of party and/or political influences.

The Republicans' motivational patterns also resemble those for the Democrats, though once again in less pronounced degree. The Consistently Strong activists regularly indicate more importance for the motivations for political involvement listed in table 11.10 than do the Consistently Weak activists; the largest aggregate differences relate to more narrowly defined party and political factors (strong party attachment, politics as part of one's way of life, etc.). The most important reasons for political activity are not as sharply different as these were for the Democrats, however. For all three groups, the two most important reasons for involvement are (1) concern with public issues and (2) party work as a way to influence government and politics. Each group, however, puts a different reason in third place; for the Consistently Strong activists it is strong party attachment (mentioned as most important by 13 percent), for the Mixed activists it is candidate support (11 percent), and for the Consistently Weak activists it is sense of community obligation (13 percent). Among the Consistently Weak party activists, strong party attachment is last on the list, mentioned by less than 1 percent of the activists in this group.

Finally, an examination of the Republicans' ideological and issue positions also reveals some intergroup differences. For example, the Consistently Weak activists tend to be more moderate and less conservative than their Consistently Strong (and Mixed) colleagues. While only a few in any group are liberal (led proportionally by the Consistently Weak with only 8 percent), 31 percent of the Consistently Weak activists identify themselves as moderate compared with 13 percent of the Mixed and 8 percent of the Consistently Strong. In the same vein, while a majority of the Consistently Weak say they are conservative to some degree, their 62 percent is considerably below the 90 percent for the Consistently Strong and the 85 percent for the Mixed. Although the ideological homogeneity among the Republicans across these groups is much greater than for the Democrats, it is still noteworthy that the Republicans display some ideological diversity along party attachment lines, as well.

This observation applies as well to the data on issue positions in table 11.11. The intergroup differences for the Republicans are not as striking as for the Democrats, nor are they as widespread, but differences are detectable. The Consistently Weak display less conservatism than the Mixed and the Consistently Strong. Indeed, on five of the issues the differences are 10 percentage points or more, and on the issue of increased defense spending they are 27 percentage points. This is not to say that the Consistently Weak Republicans are liberal, but they are much less conservative than their fellow partisans. Just as with the Consistently Weak Democrats, the Consistently Weak Republicans deviate from their national party's ideological center of gravity.

In brief, with the exception of personal background characteristics, Republicans exhibit many of the same differences in strength of party attachment among the three groups of party officials as we found among the Democrats (though usually to a smaller degree). Compared with the Consistently Strong, the Consistently Weak have been less involved in politics and for shorter periods of time, they come from less politically active families, they do not see their party positions as very important to them personally, they are less motivated to political activity by strictly party considera-

**Table 11.11. Local Republican Party Activists' Issue Orientations,
by Degree of Party Attachment (in percentage liberal responses)**

Issue	Strong	Mixed	Weak
Social			
Assistance for women	51	51	52
Personal choice for abortion	38	44	53
School prayer	8	10	18
Environmental protection	64	62	68
Gov. aid for blacks/minorities	31	31	39
Support women's equality	81	78	81
Affirmative action programs	3	3	7
Economic			
Fewer services to reduce gov. spending	24	24	37
Constitutional amendment to balance nat. budget	10	13	19
State tax increase for financial crisis	6	7	10
Gov. aid in jobs and living standards	11	11	20
Gov. health care assistance	47	51	66
Foreign policy/defense			
Increase defense spending	34	44	61
Continue cooperation with Russia	81	78	81

tions, and they tend to be much more moderate-liberal (and less conservative).

Discussion

Three-quarters of a century ago, Charles Merriam noted the importance of party leaders to the party organization: "When these leaders weaken or desert or divide or are indifferent, their party group is shaken and disaster is near. But if their interest is keen and their enthusiasm runs high, the effect is clearly evident in the party strength in the vicinity" (Merriam, 1922: 34). Forty years later, Samuel Eldersveld argued persuasively, "It [the party] relies on its leaders after all, in whose perceptions and beliefs, actions and interactions, and continuous contact with the public rests the fate of the party" (Eldersveld, 1964: 544).

Our data on strength of party attachment show these are not outdated notions. For both parties, weakened party attachment among its local leaders is consistently and clearly associated with reduced activity at all electoral levels, with lessened concern for party organizational unity and success, with high defections during the 1988 presidential election, and with negative views toward the party organization's development over the past decade. This is especially the case for those party officials whom we have categorized as Consistently Weak, but it also applies with less force for those party officials whom we categorized as Mixed (strongly attached to the party in some ways but weakly attached in others). While the parties might take some comfort in the small proportions of their leaders classified as Consistently Weak, the numbers are still sufficiently significant to pose a problem for the parties. Moreover, there are sizable proportions of activists with mixed attachments in each party, although the negative consequences for the party are not so great as with the Consistently Weak. There are implications for organizational maintenance as well as candidate selection. For example, the Consistently Weak Democratic activists are less involved in intraparty communication and in candidate recruitment. The lack of involvement must impact the health of the party organization. The weak strength of party attachment affects electoral politics as well because the Democratic Party's Consistently Weak activists were much more approving of Reagan and Bush than other Democratic grassroots activists. Of the two parties in the South, the Democrats are the more vulnerable with regard to strength of party attachment, but the Republicans are also affected.

The factors associated with varying strength of party attachment among the party activists differ a bit from party to party. For example, for the Democrats there is some indication that dissatisfaction with the national party's more liberal path in recent years is a contributing factor in the weakness of party attachments, especially among younger white males. For the Republicans there is no corresponding evidence that such disaffection with the national party is a contributing factor.

Although the key factors differ in some ways, there are some common threads running through these data, and in various ways they point to the impact of the external environment on the local parties. Quite clearly, developments in the competitive environment within which parties operate are connected to strength of party attachment and, thence, to the parties. The most obvious indicator of this is for the Democrats in the ways noted in the previous paragraph, but it shows up for the Republicans as well, as, for example, in the data indicating the relationship between party attachment and holding other elective, appointive, and party positions. Only very recently have southern Republicans had a range of opportunities to hold elective and appointive offices, not to mention party offices that previously did not exist because of little party organization development; we might at least speculate that these limited opportunities have served as an obstacle to the development of stronger attachment to the party. Attachment logically might be hampered by the lack of opportunities to participate, a circumstance reflecting a traditionally weak competitive position within the region.

Additionally, this analysis suggests that various elements of the political socialization experience of activists are related to strength of party attachment. Of particular importance in both parties is the family's previous political involvement. For those activists who grew up in an active family, party attachment is much stronger. Similarly, the data about motivations for involvement show the importance of peer influences, suggesting that a variety of contacts with other party workers contributes to stronger party attachment. In a more general sense, the factors that influence the development of activists' opinion schema and ideological constructs are related to party attachment, at least indirectly. In both parties, the Consistently Weak activists exhibit issue and ideological orientations that vary from their respective parties' ideological-programmatic tendencies. The Consistently Strong activists are more congruent with their parties' ideological and issue tendencies. While the notion that political socialization is important is neither new nor surprising, these data remind us of the significance of this process for the party.

The parties should be concerned with the commitment and enthusiasm of their activists, as these traits clearly affect the levels of work and support that activists are willing to give the party and its candidates. To a considerable degree, this is a matter that should be considered in the recruitment process, with party leaders seeking potential workers who have strong attachment to the party. The process is not amenable to such a rational approach, however. For one thing, the parties do not have the luxury of picking and choosing from a glut of eager recruits; rather, there is frequently far more work to be done than volunteers to do it. Under these circumstances the parties are often glad to find even a few people who will help out, regardless of their feelings toward the party.[5] It is highly unlikely that local party officials, in considering potential workers, will have the time or energy or inclination to explore the various external factors that are related to party attachment. That is, there is little likelihood that party leaders will research a potential activist's family history or previous peer contacts as an element of the recruitment process, nor are they likely to administer some sort of ideological litmus test as a prerequisite for a party position. External forces, such as their organizational activists' strength of party attachment, over which American political parties historically have little control, are likely to continue to buffet American political parties.

12

Party Activists as Agents of Change

Women, Blacks, and Political Parties in the South

Rosalee A. Clawson
John A. Clark

Political parties are the preeminent linkage organizations in democratic societies. Especially in the United States, parties are characterized by their permeability and malleability. This openness allows elites from various social groups to enter the political arena and play a significant role in party politics. According to the party elite theory of democracy proposed by Baer and Bositis (1988), social movements provide the mechanism by which outgroups produce an elite stratum of activists. For example, the women's movement and the civil rights movement yielded new elites who, in turn, were able to penetrate the party system. This inclusion of out-groups makes the party system more democratic, since all groups in society, even those that have traditionally been excluded, are represented in its coalitional structure. This chapter will examine the impact of two new elites—women and blacks—on the Democratic and Republican parties in the South.

Traditional Party Theory

Traditional party theorists have asserted that political parties play a central role in democratic systems (Eldersveld, 1964; Epstein, 1986: chap. 2; Key, [1949] 1984, 1964; Schattschneider, 1942, 1960). In his classic study of political parties, Schattschneider (1942: 1) argued that "the political parties created democracy and that modern democracy is unthinkable save in terms of the parties." Political parties are distinctive representative institutions capable of mobilizing majorities who are often unorganized and unrepresented by other groups; indeed, parties appeal to both "ignorant people and experts" (Schattschneider, 1960: 137).

In addition to emphasizing the primacy of political parties in a democratic system, early scholars also focused on their malleability and permeability (Eldersveld, 1964; Key, [1949] 1984, 1964; Schattschneider, 1942,

1960). The American party system is characterized by its adaptability and its susceptibility to forces of change. Chambers (1963) argued that political parties in the United States have been shaped, molded, and transformed by the efforts of enterprising citizens over the years. Therefore, Ranney states, the parties "can be reformed whenever the people have the will to reform them" (1975: 7).

Permeability is another important feature of political parties. Eldersveld argued that the party is "an open structure; tenure is unstable; personal relationships are uncertain" (1964: 11). Because political parties are organizations interested in winning elections, a zero-sum game occurs in which support for one party denies the goals of the other party. For this reason, parties must remain open to new members (Michels, [1915] 1962). According to Schattschneider, "Many conflicts are narrowly confined by a variety of devices, but the distinctive quality of political conflicts is that the relations between the players and the audience have not been well defined and there is usually nothing to keep the audience from getting into the game" (1960: 18). The porousness of American political parties, then, allows citizens to enter the game of politics.

Political parties are also characterized by their tendency to shift power from the masses to an elite stratum. Michels ([1915] 1962) made the case that any organization will move toward oligarchy. The American experience, however, suggests that not all organizations will become hierarchical. Instead, the distribution of power and influence within American political parties is best characterized as a "stratarchy" (Eldersveld, 1964), in which "various levels of party organization operate at least semi-independently of other levels, even superordinate ones" (Beck and Sorauf, 1992: 139). Duverger's (1954) work suggests that the most accurate picture of American parties is as cadre organizations in which a rather small number of activists carry out the functions of the organization, focusing their efforts on mobilizing the masses only at election time. Scholarly recognition that an elite circle is "an inevitable part of any political system" (Baer and Bositis, 1988: 89) does not alter the view that parties are essential to a democratic form of government.

A Party Elite Theory of Democracy

Some researchers have argued that competition between parties is an essential element of democratic systems (Key, [1949] 1984); Schattschneider, 1942). Baer and Bositis (1988) argue, however, that the *number* of parties is not an adequate diagnostic test for the existence of a democratic system; instead, "whether a system is democratic depends on whether it produces liberty for all groups and whether elites are recruited from all groups" (Baer and Bositis, 1988: 90). A party system that is structured in such a manner as to accept and enlist activists from all groups in a society is truly democratic, while the systematic exclusion of certain groups from the elite stratum of political parties does not promote democracy (Duverger, 1954).

The party elite theory of democracy emphasizes the importance of social movements in a democratic system. Baer and Bositis, the chief proponents of the theory, define a social movement as "the expression and organization of demands for representation by an out-group in society" (1988: 92). Social movements provide a mechanism for the formation and development of new elites; a social movement enables members of an out-group to work their way up *within their own group* to achieve elite status. If a party system is democratic, then these elites will be recruited into the power structure of the parties. Thus, even though power is consolidated in the hands of a few activists, the party system is democratic because all groups in society are represented in its coalitional structure (Baer and Bositis, 1988).

In recent decades social movements have encouraged the politicization of such groups as women and African Americans. Klein (1984) argues that a feminist consciousness began emerging in the late 1960s. "Trends in attitudes toward appropriate sex roles, perceived discrimination, and support for efforts to further women's rights reveal a tremendous growth and diffusion of feminist support between 1970 and 1985" (Klein, 1987: 26). In addition, researchers have found gender differences in policy preferences, voting decisions, and participation rates (Baxter and Lansing, 1983; Conover and Sapiro, 1993; Frankovic, 1982; Klein, 1984; Shapiro and Mahajan, 1986).

According to Freeman (1987), the Democratic Party offers a more promising opportunity structure for feminists seeking to play a meaningful role in party politics. The impact of the women's movement on political parties is especially interesting to investigate in the South. In this region of the nation, traditional values are firmly held, including the notion that the political sphere should be reserved primarily for men (Baxter and Lansing, 1983). The South is a chilly political climate for women seeking to move beyond established, accepted social roles.

Without question, the South is also a fascinating region in which to examine the impact of African Americans on political parties. The civil rights movement, beginning in the mid-1950s, developed an effective strategy of protest in the South that drew national attention and encouraged group consciousness on the part of black citizens. The crowning achievements of the movement were the passage of the Civil Rights Act of 1964 and the Voting Rights Act of 1965 (Black and Black, 1987). Prior to this legislation, southern blacks were, for all intents and purposes, barred from political participation; after this legislation, African Americans were able to enter the political arena more easily.

According to the social movement hypothesis proposed by Baer and Bositis (1988), party reform is a necessary response to social movements. In the American context, party reforms have encouraged new elites from out-groups to permeate the party structure. In this way, changes at the elite level of the parties are reflections of greater societal changes and adaptations to those changes (Ranney, 1975; Reiter, 1985). The women's movement and the civil rights movement, in particular, led to the Democratic Party reforms of the late 1960s and 1970s (Shafer, 1983). The prereform party system was based on a coalitional structure at the mass level but not at the elite level; in contrast, the reformed party system is based on a coalitional structure at both levels. Accordingly, political parties have become the "preeminent representative agencies" of politicized groups (Baer and Bositis, 1988: 122).

The party elite theory of democracy casts party reforms in a positive light since the reforms have democratized the party system. On the other hand, many party scholars have argued that the most significant consequence of party reforms was party decline (Kirkpatrick, 1976; Ranney, 1978; Polsby, 1983). These researchers emphasize that the Democratic reforms led to a reduced role of the party in the nomination of presidential candidates. Instead of party regulars controlling the nomination process, the reforms resulted in the excess influence of nonparty supporters, the creation of factions, and the undue leverage of special interests in the nomination process. Baer and Bositis, however, state that they "find a strong commitment to party among all cadres of contemporary party elites—and certainly little indication of the loss of party regularity assumed by many political scientists" (1988: 183). In any event, Reiter (1985) notes, the party organizations' loss of control over presidential nominations was already under way at the time of the Democratic reforms.

The party elite theory of democracy leads us to several hypotheses concerning the permeability and malleability of U.S. parties. First, there should be evidence that new groups are able to enter the party as activists. Second, the new elites should be expected to mold the issue emphasis of the party to meet their goals. Finally, the new activists should be either less supportive of party norms, as posited by the party-in-decline school, or more committed to the political party, as Baer and Bositis argue (1988: chap. 7).

We test these hypotheses using data from more than ten thousand Democratic and Republican county chairs and precinct leaders in the southern states. Unlike the Democratic national conventions, local party organizations typically were not subject to reform in recent decades (but see Mileur, 1980). If the elite theory of democracy holds, however, the effects of elite participation at one level of the party should carry over into other levels. Democratic local party organizations, while not subject to national party mandates, should bear evidence of increased participation by women and minorities in the aftermath of the reform era. The Republican Party did not undergo the same rush to reform that beset the Democratic Party some twenty years ago. Local Republican organizations, therefore, serve as a kind of control group for comparing the effects of national level reforms on local party organizations.

The South is an obvious locale for studying the relationship between social movements and political parties. Southern Democrats, once the conservative anchor of the party, increasingly reflect the national Democratic Party with regard to policy goals and issue attitudes (Rae, 1994). Changes brought about by the civil rights movement and the Voting Rights Act have had a visible effect on the racial composition of the two-party system (Carmines and Stimson, 1989). Perhaps less evident are the changes brought about by the increased role of women in the Democratic Party (Baer and Bositis, 1988).

Position, Recruitment, Ambition

Despite changes in the makeup of the national party conventions (Miller and Jennings, 1986), nearly two-thirds of the grassroots activists in both the Republican and Democratic parties in the South are men. Nearly all the Republican leaders and most of the Democrats are white, but 13 percent of the Democrats are African Americans. Given the large size of the sample, we were able to split the activists into six groups, based on party, gender, and (for Democrats) race (see table 12.1).

The elite theory of democracy argues that democratic parties must allow entry of new elites from previously unrepresented social groups. To examine the permeability of the parties to blacks and to women, we divided the activist groups into three cohorts: those who became active in politics before 1965, during the period 1965 through 1979, and since 1980. These divisions denote the passage of the Voting Rights Act in 1965 and the advent of the "Reagan Revolution" as the decade of the 1980s began. The Republican groups contain the largest proportions of recent activists, with nearly 40 percent having become active since 1980. There are no gender differences in the GOP, however, with nearly equivalent percentages of men and women in each cohort.

Among Democrats, there are slight differences in racial and gender patterns between cohorts. One-third of white males became active prior to 1965, compared with 26 percent of white females; among blacks, a quarter of the men and only 16 percent of the women entered politics at that time. Nearly half the black Democrats entered politics during 1965 to 1979, as did 40 percent of white Democrats. Compared with white male activists, black and female grassroots leaders became involved in the political process somewhat more recently. We do not know how long these people have been active in *party* politics, but there is some support for the notion that the Democratic Party has become increasingly friendly to black and women activists.

Table 12.1. Characteristics of Grassroots Activist Groups (percentage by party and group)

Characteristic	Democrats				Republicans	
	White males	Black males	White females	Black females	Males	Females
Percentage of total grassroots leaders	55.3	8.2	30.4	6.1	63.7	36.3
Percentage of county chairs	73.5	4.3	20.0	2.1	74.1	25.9
First became politically active						
Before 1965	33.8	25.1	26.4	16.0	26.0	25.7
1965–1979	39.9	46.1	39.9	50.7	33.4	34.3
Since 1980	26.3	28.9	33.7	33.3	40.6	40.0
Experience and ambition						
Held public office	29.7	24.4	15.1	15.3	17.3	10.2
No plans to run for office	54.4	36.1	70.2	40.6	52.8	69.9
Recruitment to current position						
Other party member	41.0	27.5	43.5	32.6	40.9	46.2
Self-starter	48.0	61.2	44.8	61.8	50.3	43.6
(Minimum N)	(2253)	(327)	(1200)	(233)	(2563)	(1389)

African Americans and women have made gains at the precinct level in the Democratic Party, but they have not broken into the next stratum of party leadership as quickly. White males, who account for more than half the Democrats in our sample, hold a disproportionate number of county chair positions. Nearly three-quarters of the chairs are white males, leaving the other groups underrepresented at that level of the party.

Part of the explanation for the lack of advancement may lie in the way party leaders are recruited (Clarke and Kornberg, 1979). We found marked racial differences in recruitment. Compared with blacks of both genders, white Democrats were much more likely to indicate encouragement from a county chair or other party committee member as their most important consideration in seeking their current position. Blacks, in contrast, reached the decision to run primarily on their own.

A slightly different pattern emerges when the political experience of the Democratic activists is examined. More men than women have previously held public office (see also Costantini, 1990). Only 15 percent of the women in our sample are former officeholders, compared with almost twice that percentage of white males and nearly 25 percent of black males. Consistent with their self-starter status, less than half of the African American activists have ruled out the possibility of running for office in the future. White females are the least ambitious; only 10 percent plan on running at some point, while 70 percent have no desire for elective office whatsoever (see also Sapiro and Farah, 1980).

These differences may have ramifications for the health of the party as an organization. If white activists were recruited from within the ranks of the party and do not intend to start their own campaigns, we might expect them to be favorably disposed toward the health and maintenance of the organization. African American activists may be less supportive of the organization simply because they became active without the support of other party members or because of their personal campaign agendas.

Baer and Bositis (1988) argue that the Republican Party has remained unreformed with regard to the entry of new elites into the party's affairs.[1] Certainly this is true with regard to African Americans: only 2 percent of the Republican activists in our survey are black. Women, however, occupy the same share of grassroots party positions in the Republican Party as in the Democratic Party throughout the South. How do women and men differ within the GOP?

As with the Democrats, almost three-quarters of the Republican county chairs are men, an overrepresentation given their proportion of the total number of activists. The gender difference is identical for both parties. Fewer Republicans have ever held public office, as one might expect in the South; 17 percent of GOP men and only 10 percent of Republican women have this qualification. In terms of ambition for office in the future, they match white Democrats almost exactly. The same pattern holds for their recruitment into their current positions: Republicans and white Democrats were more likely than black Democrats to have been recruited by other party officials, whereas black Democrats were more likely to have decided to run on their own. If there is a distinction between groups on these measures, it is between blacks and whites and between men and women, not a distinction of Republicans vs. Democrats.

The party elite theory of democracy is supported by the finding that significant numbers of blacks and women are active in the Democratic Party. These data suggest that the women's movement and the civil rights movement have opened the door and paved the way for new elites to enter the arena of Democratic Party politics. Baer and Bositis do not account for the fact that women play an equally large role in the "unreformed" Republican Party, however. The lack of women and blacks at higher echelons of power (i.e., county chairs) also fails to support the elite theory of democracy. In summary, women and blacks can enter the arena and participate in the game of politics, but they are not likely to become team captains in either the Democratic or Republican Party.

Race, Gender, and Issue Positions

A central premise of the elite theory of democracy is that the views of outgroups are best represented by elites drawn from those groups (Baer and Bositis, 1988). It is not the shared characteristics, rather the shared ideas and experiences of group members, that are necessary if democracy is to exist.[2] If group-based representation is indeed essential, we should see differences between the traditional leadership group (white males) and the emergent groups of women and African Americans.

Our survey included fifteen public policy statements for which responses ranged from strong agreement to strong disagreement (table 12.2). Examination of the policy preferences of Democratic activists reveals three patterns. On two issues, support for the environment and raising taxes in a fiscal crisis, there are no differences across racial and gender groups. On the remaining thirteen issues, some cleavage along male/female or black/white lines is present. The racial cleavage in particular is not limited to policies bearing directly on race or gender.

Three items in our survey focused on the role of women in society. In each case, a majority of activists in each Democratic group supported a liberal position, but there were differences in the strength of their support. More than half the female party leaders *strongly* agreed that a woman's right to an abortion ought to be protected by law, in contrast to 37 percent of the Democratic men. Only a quarter of the Democrats in the sample opposed abortion. An equal role for women in business, industry, and government

Table 12.2. Policy Attitudes of Grassroots Activist Groups (percentage by party and group)

Issue	Democrats				Republicans	
	White males	Black males	White females	Black females	Males	Females
Aid to women	81.4	95.9	91.8	97.6	47.8	57.5
Abortion rights	71.4	76.8	78.1	79.1	40.2	46.8
Defense spending	28.8	23.2	31.0	22.4	55.6	65.6
Cut gov. services	32.6	7.8	25.0	7.6	77.2	70.3
School prayer	69.3	83.1	65.9	89.4	89.8	90.6
Environment	83.3	89.1	83.8	86.0	63.5	63.6
Balanced budget amendment	67.7	67.8	67.0	78.1	89.3	85.0
Raise state taxes in fiscal crisis	28.4	33.7	28.2	29.1	7.3	6.7
Aid to minorities	60.9	97.6	67.3	97.6	31.0	33.0
Gov. ensure job	39.5	72.8	40.7	78.9	11.4	13.4
Women in business	85.7	89.7	92.7	95.9	79.6	81.5
Attention to domestic problems	79.4	90.5	82.2	89.9	54.7	54.0
Cooperation with Russia	93.1	90.5	91.4	78.4	80.9	78.6
Minority job preferences	12.9	72.0	12.4	71.3	3.5	2.9
Health care	88.4	97.9	90.0	98.3	50.6	52.3
(Minimum N)	(2627)	(384)	(1398)	(264)	(2948)	(1632)

Note: Entries represent percentage who "agree" or "strongly agree" with a set of directional issue statements.

was strongly endorsed by half of the white females and two-thirds of the black females. Only 25 percent of the white male activists shared this position, as did 41 percent of the black males. A third item asked about the national government's role in improving the social and economic position of women. More than two-thirds of the black females expressed strong support for this position. Slightly less than half of the white females and black males shared this view. Only 24 percent of the white males strongly agreed with more government involvement. These findings suggest that the entrance of women activists (especially African American women) into the Democratic Party has transformed the intensity of the party's support for women's issues, if not necessarily the direction.

Two items tapped directly into racial matters. The racial cleavage in the Democratic Party was especially sharp on the question of whether blacks should be given preferential treatment with regard to hiring and promotion due to past discrimination. More than 70 percent of the African American party leaders supported the position, compared with less than 13 percent of the whites. The division was less charged on the question of the government's role in improving the social and economic situation of blacks and other minorities. Both black and white majorities supported a greater role for government, but the difference in the strength of their support is striking. Virtually all blacks in the sample favored government activism, while only about two-thirds of the whites shared that view. Seventy percent of the black leaders strongly approved of a greater government role, compared with 19 percent of white females and 13 percent of white males.

Significant racial differences appeared on a number of other policies. African Americans were more likely to oppose increased defense spending but to favor governmental activism on domestic programs, including health care and unemployment. They were more supportive of prayer in public schools than their white counterparts. Black women were significantly more likely to support a balanced budget amendment and less likely to support cooperation with Russia than the other three groups.

There is a clear partisan distinction when issues of public policy are examined. The Republicans in our survey hold uniformly more conservative positions than the Democratic activists. There are only three issue items on which the GOP has noticeable gender disparities. Women are somewhat more likely to favor a national government role in improving the economic condition of women (58 percent to 48 percent) and slightly more supportive of abortion rights (47 percent to 40 percent). A minor division occurs on one issue not directly related to gender: surprisingly, 66 percent of Republican women favor a defense buildup, compared with 56 percent of their male counterparts. The rest of the time, female activists in the GOP appear to play no role in altering the issue stands of the party as a whole.

The incorporation of African Americans into the Democratic Party has changed the policy outlook of the party. Only three of the fifteen issue items

in our survey failed to show evidence of a racial split, although black Democrats were more conservative than white Democrats on one issue (school
prayer). The liberalism of black party activists emerges as an even greater
influence on party change when considering the conservatism of white activists who have left the party in recent years (Petrocik, 1987; Prysby, 1990;
Clark et al., 1991).

These data suggest that black females in particular act as agents of
change within the Democratic Party. This finding leads to an elaboration of
the party elite theory of democracy and the importance of social movements in a democratic system. Our research encourages us to think about
the impact of related social movements on political parties. A single social
movement may provide opportunities for an out-group to participate in the
political system; however, some out-groups may require several social movements working on their behalf. For example, black females gained access to
the Democratic Party not simply because of the civil rights movement but
also because of the women's movement. Both movements were necessary to
ensure the inclusion of African American females within the party system.
And, quite important, many female activists in the women's movement,
both black and white, first became active during the civil rights movement.
The civil rights movement was a training ground for female activists, who
then became elites within the women's movement (Freeman, 1987: 221).
Taken together, the civil rights movement and the women's movement have
had a significant impact on the Democratic Party in the South.

Race, Gender, and Party Norms

The party elite theory of democracy suggests that the entrance of new elites
into the party structure strengthens the party by making it adapt to greater
societal changes. The party-in-decline thesis, in contrast, argues that the
new entrants will be less supportive of party norms. Initial assessments of
the Democratic McGovern-Fraser Commission reforms supported the decline hypothesis. For example, Kirkpatrick (1976: 153) concludes that "the
most straight-forward interpretation . . . would seem to be that in 1972 we
were moving away from a traditional organizational style toward one fea-
turing parties that are less permanent, less broadly based, and less oriented
toward winning."

Thus, we might expect the elites drawn from the ranks of African Americans and women to be least supportive of the party. After all, those groups
had long been excluded from an active role in party affairs, especially in
the South. African Americans might be particularly dubious of the party
because of their greater personal ambition as candidates, noted earlier. Baer
and Bositis (1988) argue, however, that the presence of new group members
at the elite level will not necessarily be detrimental to the party organiza-

tion. Their work suggests that new party elites will be as committed to the party as those in the traditional leadership group (1988: chap. 7).

The party activists in our survey were asked a series of questions about the role of the party organization in the political process. In general, there was agreement among Democratic racial and gender groups. When differences did emerge, however, they showed the black party leaders to be *more* supportive of the party organization (see table 12.3). A majority of black activists believed that a complete discussion of controversial issues should be secondary to party unity, but that position was opposed by a majority of whites. Similarly, blacks were more likely than whites to value neutrality in party primaries and to support candidates with whom they disagree. There was a substantial difference between white females and black females on whether controversial positions in the party platform should be avoided to ensure party unity: black females preferred solidarity over contention. No such difference was observed between the two groups of males in our sample.

We also asked questions about the structure of relations between units of the party organization. On all three measures, black Democrats were more supportive of a hierarchical relationship than whites. African Americans were slightly more likely than whites to favor a top-down strategy for party building. They were less apt to think that state and local party organizations should be free of direction from national and state party organizations, respectively. This finding is consistent with the national party's long record of support for civil rights in the face of state-level opposition.

As in the case of the Democrats, there are few differences between Republican men and women on issues of party norms. On each item in our survey, the two groups were within a few percentage points of one another in terms of agreement. Of greater interest is the general *disagreement* between Republican and Democratic activists. GOP activists took positions that were dramatically less supportive of party unity and the party organization on two items, favoring complete discussion of divisive issues and being unwilling to support candidates with whom they disagree. They were closer to white Democrats on the issue of remaining neutral in primaries and closer to white Democratic women concerning the inclusion of controversial positions in the party platform. Republicans fall between white and black Democrats on questions of party hierarchy, holding positions slightly closer to the latter group.

Dodson (1990) found evidence that many unconventional 1972 delegates had adopted more traditional attitudes toward the party by 1981. Those who were strongly motivated by policy concerns and had become socialized into the party were more likely to continue to be active in the party than their counterparts who remained unsocialized. Strong issue preferences are not enough to maintain involvement in party affairs; a recognition

Table 12.3. Party Attitudes of Grassroots Activist Groups (percentage by party and group)

	Democrats				Republicans	
Attitude	White males	Black males	White females	Black females	Males	Females
Party organization and unity are more important than issues	42.8	56.9	41.1	62.5	31.7	32.9
Good party workers should remain neutral in primaries	47.9	55.9	48.8	59.7	45.4	48.5
Good party workers support candidate even if they disagree	58.8	65.8	58.8	60.9	39.0	36.8
Controversial positions should be avoided to ensure party unity	52.2	50.9	43.7	60.8	40.6	39.7
Candidates should not compromise their values even to win	86.3	87.5	89.1	85.2	90.1	93.0
Local party activities should be free of state party direction	63.5	54.5	62.2	55.4	58.0	55.9
State party activities should be free of nat. party direction	65.6	50.7	62.8	52.2	58.1	55.6
Party organization should be built top down rather than bottom up	25.1	30.6	26.3	33.8	25.6	28.9
(Minimum N)	(2550)	(365)	(1369)	(255)	(2914)	(1597)

Note: Entries represent percentage who "agree" or "strongly agree" with each statement.

of the importance of the party as a mechanism for achieving policy goals is significant as well.

To test whether the length of political involvement altered attitudes toward the party, we examined the activist groups according to the time of their entry into politics (before 1965, during 1965–79, and since 1980). Our hypothesis, based on the work of Dodson and the critics of Democratic reforms, was that the most recent cohorts would be least supportive of the party as an organization.

Our general findings confirmed the hypothesis that the most recent white cohorts were less supportive of traditional party norms than those who had been active for a longer time. The pattern was the same for both white males and white females in the Democratic Party.

A different pattern emerged for black Democrats, however. Among black males, the recent cohort was less supportive of the party than the oldest cohort on three of the five party norms and more supportive on the other two. In each instance, the difference between black males and whites of both genders was greater among those active since 1980 than for those who entered politics prior to 1965. For black females, the newest cohort was more supportive than the group that became active during 1965–79 on each of the five items.

Contrary to the fears of the party-in-decline school, black Democratic activists held attitudes more favorable to the party than did whites. The finding was especially strong among those who had most recently entered the political fray. One reason may be that blacks recognize the importance of party unity if they are to advance their personal political goals and the issue positions important to them. In many elections, black candidates need the support of some white voters to win. If there is no cooperation between black and white candidates, the entire ticket could well face defeat.

While it is difficult to ascertain such motivations on the basis of our data, we can add one more piece of circumstantial evidence. We asked our respondents how important their positions in the party were to them personally. Both racial and gender differences are present in their responses. Almost 70 percent of black females and 58 percent of black males said their involvement was "very important," compared with slightly more than 40 percent of the white females and about a third of the white males in both parties. The differences across racial groups are again greater for the most recent cohorts, suggesting that the party holds a more central position in the political geography of black activists.

Conclusions

The elite theory of democracy posits that a political system is democratic if all social groups have access to the elite strata of political actors. Our conclusions are tentative, but the data presented here suggest that blacks and women have indeed gained entry into party affairs in the South, although not in numbers commensurate with their share of the population as a whole. Moreover, the proportion of county chairs claimed by members of these groups is even smaller than their percentage of grassroots activists as a whole.

Baer and Bositis (1988) laud the Democratic Party's reform efforts for stimulating the entry of blacks and especially of women into the ranks of national convention delegates. There is some evidence that these groups have increased their presence in local party organizations over time, but the trickle-down effects of changes in the delegate selection process for the Democratic conventions are less certain. At the grassroots level, the "unreformed" Republican Party differs only slightly from the Democratic Party with regard to gender. Both parties exhibit similar proportions of women, similar recruitment patterns, only slight gender differences with regard to policy issues, and similar attitudes toward the party organization on the part of men and white women.

In contrast, the presence of both male and female African Americans appears to have transformed the Democratic Party in a number of ways. First, blacks came to party activity largely on their own, rather than through recruitment by other party activists. They also have greater desire to run for public office in the future. It may be that party activity serves as a springboard to further the ambitions of some black activists, much as it did for immigrant groups a century ago.[3] Second, black Democrats are considerably more liberal than their white colleagues, thus transforming the issue stands of the party. The cleavage extends beyond issues typically associated with racial divisions. Finally, and somewhat surprisingly, black Democrats are more supportive of the party as an organization than are white Democrats. They may view a strong party organization as essential for advancing their personal and policy goals, whereas their white counterparts may have other resources available. Black Democrats thus sharpen the differences between Democrats and Republicans in general, as whites of both parties are remarkably similar in terms of many of the characteristics examined here.

Gender differences may seem less important than party or race, but we do not want to understate their significance. In both parties, women are considerably more supportive of women's issues than their male counterparts. Without the presence of women in the parties, those issues might not receive a fair hearing. In addition, gender differences in the Democratic Party might be partially subsumed by racial splits. Black women are distinctly different from other Democratic groups on several of the measures considered here. It bears repeating that their mere presence in local parties stems from both the civil rights and women's movements.

As a catalyst for change, the gradual entry of blacks into the Democratic

Party following the passage of the Voting Rights Act has helped define to-day's Democratic Party. The combination of issue and party attitudes held by black Democrats creates an interesting paradox, however. At the same time that they seek to build party unity and strengthen the party organization, their policy attitudes may work to alienate traditional white Democrats. The party that they support organizationally may be weaker electorally as a result of their efforts.

13
Summing Up

Organization and Activism at the Grassroots Level in the 1990s

Lewis Bowman
John A. Clark
Robert P. Steed

American political parties have changed in significant ways during the past three decades. In some instances, these changes have pointed in the direction of party decline as the parties have been challenged in the performance of many of their traditional nomination and campaign activities by competition from interest groups (especially PACs), professional campaign consultants, personal campaign organizations utilizing the new techniques of modern campaigning, and the mass media. On the other hand, some developments have pointed in the direction of party vigor—for example, the expansion of activities undertaken by the national committees to serve the state and local party organizations. Although the fact of change is undeniable, the organization, processes, and personnel of the parties have shown significant continuity in many ways.

Within this context of party change and continuity, our analyses of the southwide data on local party organization and activism in the 1990s point to two general conclusions about grassroots political party organizations. First, there are strong indications that local party organization and activism continue to be important parts of the contemporary political landscape. Second, amid considerable change, our findings about the historical continuity of grassroots party organizations and activists share striking similarities with findings of earlier research about local parties in diverse settings.

In this final chapter we examine our findings about each of these two major conclusions in terms of three perspectives: (1) the substance of grassroots party organizations' politics (partisanship, issues, ideologies, and factionalism); (2) the sources of the grassroots party organizations' substance of politics (recruitment, incentives, purism/pragmatism, and activists as change agents); and (3) the consequences of the substance and the sources of politics for grassroots parties' organizations and activists (organizational maintenance, campaign activities, communications, and mass/elite linkages).

The Substance of Grassroots Party Politics

We seek answers to questions about the current importance of grassroots political party institutions and the individuals active in those institutions. Do these activists deal with issues and ideological questions important to the health of the party system and thereby to the political, economic, and social systems of their society? Does partisanship structure political and societal conflict in meaningful ways? How much does factionalism detract from, or facilitate, partisan efforts?

Partisanship

Despite the rapid and dramatic political and social changes of recent years—perhaps even because of them—southern grassroots party organizations continue to structure political, social, and economic conflicts. Providing local organization for activists, potential activists, and thereby, we hope, for the electoral and political elites, the grassroots political party organizations remain major local foci for the serious game of politics.

Partisanship is undergoing rapid, though often erratic, evolution in the American South. Nevertheless, even amid these recent permutations the local Republican and Democratic parties provide organization for the purpose of developing and maintaining the evolving coalitions that constitute each of the two major political parties.

As the parties become more competitive, moving first from the old one-party system so pervasive in the American South to a one-and-one-half-party system as interparty competition developed (particularly at the level of national elections), and recently to a more nearly competitive two-party system, the parties exhibit differential degrees of partisan attachment. Over one-half of the Republican grassroots activists feel strongly attached to their party at all levels, whereas only about one-third of the Democratic activists have such feelings about their own party at all levels. This development helps account for the increasingly focused party-building capacity of the Republicans in many of the southern states. In turn, it also helps explain the volatility and increasing instability among a number of the southern states' Democratic parties.

Issues and Ideologies

Voters in the southern states cannot make the complaint often heard about American political parties—namely, that each is centrist, with the two major parties having few ideological or issue differentiations between them. Not so. Southern grassroots activists cannot be accused of Tweedledee and Tweedledum politics. The two major parties show clear interparty differences in ideology and issues. On many specific issues the Republican and Democratic grassroots activists differ by margins of more than 20 percentage points.

Each party has clear intraparty and interparty ideological differences, and neither has become ideologically homogeneous. However, of the two grassroots southern political parties the Republicans are considerably more homogeneous. For this reason, they are better able to hold together and to develop the Republican grassroots party organizations. Over the long term, however, this greater homogeneity may inhibit the broadening of a base adequate to raise the Republican Party to the status of majority party in the region. The Democrats remain quite fragmented ideologically, being about one-third liberal, one-third moderate, and one-third conservative southwide. At the counter extremes in the two parties, both Republican liberals and Democratic conservatives are disaffected with their respective parties. Of course the impact on each party is quite different because the Republican liberal contingent is a very small portion of the Republican activists, whereas the Democratic conservative contingent is a significant portion of that party's activists.

Political party activists in many settings generally have been found to be more extreme in ideological positions than are their electorates. In the two states (Alabama and Mississippi) where data were available for comparisons, this proposition seemed to hold true for grassroots activists. Party differences exist, however. The Democrats appear to be more in line with the ideological positions of the people in their states. The Republican activists are considerably more conservative than the people of their respective states. If these differences exist throughout the South, the Republican activists and the electorate's ideological and issue disparities could produce sufficient cognitive dissonance among Republicans to slow or reverse their recent success in developing grassroots organizational and electoral capabilities.

Factionalism

Factionalism often has been a prominent feature in southern party organizations (Key, [1949] 1984; Hadley and Bowman, 1995).[1] Activists perceive ideological differences in their parties as the source of their most serious factionalism. Given that the Democrats cast a wider recruiting net and hence are less homogeneous in demography, as well as ideology, it is no surprise that the Democrats report more factional problems than the Republicans. In state-by-state comparisons the most factional Democratic parties are in Louisiana, North Carolina, and Alabama. The most factional Republican organizations are in the Louisiana and Florida parties.

Additionally, ideological differences within each of the parties affect their abilities to function in the political system. For the Republicans, conservative dominance is related to organizational image, party platforms, nominations, and campaign strategies. For the Democrats, ideological fragmentation (with roughly equal groups of officials labeling themselves liberal, middle-of-the-road, and conservative) has created difficulties in developing a positive image and in arriving at cohesive nomination and electoral strategies. This problem has been exacerbated by Democratic reforms that magnify the conflict in full view of the voting public.

Sources of Grassroots Party Politics

Who are the activists who bring these views of partisanship and issues to politics at the grassroots in southern states? What attracts them to grassroots party posts? Do the same incentives and views of party organization drive them as was the case in earlier decades? Or have agents of change been introduced sufficiently to produce changes in the sources of personnel for the grassroots parties?

Recruitment

The parties are still important in recruiting activists into politics. In particular, the Republican party chairs articulate the attraction of new members as one of their top priorities. They see recruitment of party activists as essential to their job of party building to bring the lesser of the two major parties to competitive strength in the region.

Perhaps the most obvious similarity to the past is in the types of people who become active in party work. Current party activists bear marked resemblance in both personal and political backgrounds to those who were found to be active in the parties in the 1950s and 1960s. Education, income, age, and family histories of past political activity remain important variables for understanding political party activists.

While these predictive variables for recruitment continue to be important, they do not create a wall preventing new elites from penetrating the recruitment process. Newly mobilized activists have always made the American party system's cadre susceptible to being infiltrated. Numerous studies have pointed to this permeability of the American party organizations, a point often demonstrated by explorations of party recruitment processes. Whether from longstanding historical grievances or from recent political, social, or economic changes, new elites arise or older elites reassert themselves to establish their places in the grassroots party organizations. Our regionwide data provide evidence of relatively greater involvement of women, minorities, and the religious right in the contemporary parties and thus illustrate this permeability process recently at work in local party organizations.

Not only do both parties recruit, but they also demonstrate a degree of rationality in exhibiting partisan differences consistent with the status of the two parties in the South. The Republicans emphasize ideology and issues as recruitment devices, while the Democrats rely more on regional solidarity and interpersonal relationships. One might question why this rationality does not carry through to a point of choosing party clones in ideology and related characteristics. Two partial answers: (1) often such persons are not available, and (2) the parties do not have a rewards system because the material incentives of party activism continue to decline in value as an attraction to party activism.

Although sizable proportions of the activists in both parties are self-recruited (a finding consistent with earlier research), the party itself seems to be an increasingly important recruitment mechanism. Even among self-starters, the parties play an indirect role in recruitment by virtue of their ideological and issue orientations because self-starters tend strongly to become active in the party whose dominant ideology is most congruent with their own personal ideologies. Far from abandoning the field, the local parties clearly are active players in the process of bringing activists into the political system.

Incentives

Our findings illustrate the increasing importance of purposive incentives for party activism and the consequent loss of the attraction of material incentives. The Republicans in particular cite purposive incentives and a desire to influence government as their reasons for initial active involvement in politics. The Democrats articulate greater concern for solidary incentives: party attachment and a sense of obligation and ties to their communities.

Analyses of these southwide grassroots data demonstrate the continued applicability of the incentive categories and the purism/pragmatism (amateur/professional) model first utilized over thirty years ago by Peter Clark and James Q. Wilson (1961) and employed by many researchers in the decades since. While the parties differ in their incentive patterns, members of both parties seem to view the party as playing an increasingly central role in their continued activism. The purism/pragmatism (amateur/professional) index utilized finds that Republicans are somewhat more purist than Democrats and that party chairs are more pragmatic than precinct committee members. However, relatively few activists fall at either extreme on the scale.

Our findings also support the relevance of ambition theory in the study of party activists, pioneered in the 1960s and 1970s mainly by Joseph Schlesinger (1966) and Gordon Black (1970, 1972) (and, in a different context, even earlier by Harold Lasswell and others). Ambitious activists differ from their less ambitious counterparts in their greater likelihood of recruitment to activism, their higher levels of party activity, and their more active and wider communications within the party. One can conclude that political ambition is directly related to the organizational unity and organizational efficiency of the parties and likely contributes to their organizational effectiveness as well.

Agents of Change

In essentially a cadre party type of political party system, social movements often culminate in efforts to penetrate the party organization. Three significant social movements have permeated the grassroots party organizations in the past thirty years. Two of these—the women's movement and the civil rights movement—have formed new elites that have penetrated the Democratic Party's grassroots organizations. The third—the religious right movement—has formed a new elite that has assumed an increasingly central role in the Republican Party's grassroots cadre in the American South.

From the 1970s the reforms of the Democratic Party's organization and processes increased the ability of African Americans and women among the Democratic grassroots activists to make policy demands that outraged other factions in the party. The result was significant intraparty struggles over policy and leadership. Among grassroots activists, African American women in particular continue to articulate liberal goals for the Democratic Party. This certainly played a role in the party's factional strife and encouraged the rise of the Democratic Leadership Council as an alternative party cadre designed to turn the party back to centrist policies and nominations.

In a parallel development, the Republican religious right activists penetrated many grassroots organizations during the 1980s. They were unusually successful in capturing local party organizations in 1988 and in maintaining that successful grassroots activism. The impact of the religious right can be seen in the presidential campaigns of the 1990s. The necessity for Republican nominees to move to positions catering to this new elite in the party has created a very difficult dilemma for them in electoral strategy: How can such nominees accommodate the religious right, yet establish a centrist position that is broad enough in appeal to win the presidential election?

These movements act as agents of change providing new or augmented sources of recruits to the grassroots organizations. Their impact has been amplified by other social and political changes occurring simultaneously:

migration to the South, party switching (sorting), and generational replacement. The Reagan years acted as a catalyst for these change agents and the changes they espoused. For example, we find that more Republicans became politically active at the grassroots level during the Reagan decade. Also, party switching among the local party activists was 15 to 20 percentage points higher during the Reagan era. And the Republicans began recruiting younger activists disproportionately.

The data show that Democratic Party activists developed more split party identification during the era. And, confounding one of the longstanding social psychological explanations of American politics, a disproportionate number of Democratic activists broke with their family's Democratic political backgrounds.

Consequences: Continuity and Change

We have summarized some continuities and some changes in the grassroots activists' attitudes and perceptions that make up the substance of grassroots politics. Similarly, we have examined the stability of these party activists and the permeability of their local organizations. Now we turn to explicating the consequences of these findings.

What changes and what continuity do we find as consequences of the substance and source of grassroots party organization in the American South? How well are grassroots organizations maintained? What activities are emphasized in party organizations at this level? What is the nature of organizational communications, and of mass and elite linkages, through the grassroots organizations?

Organizational Maintenance

Maintaining the party organizationally must be a goal of party activists if they accept the importance of providing an ongoing organizational presence *between* elections to ensure maximum success *during* elections. In the grassroots organizations, both parties pay attention to these maintenance activities. About one-half perceive their party organizations as needing continuing maintenance. County chairs place more importance on such tasks than precinct committee members, and Republicans somewhat more than Democrats. Still, in a region notable in the past for its lack of political organization, a solid portion of the cadre of activists work to maintain the local party organization between elections.

Campaign Activities

Similarly, both parties' grassroots activists report relatively high levels of campaign and election activity. Equally important, however, is the finding that county chairs, in addition to being generally more active than precinct officials, engage in different types of activities than their precinct counterparts. Chairs are more likely to specialize in campaign tasks with a managerial emphasis, while precinct members concentrate more on the retail or labor-intensive side of politics. Thus, in such a division of labor, the parties act like relatively sophisticated, complex organizations. Clearly, contrary to the depictions seen frequently in the party-in-decline literature of the 1960s and 1970s, the party organizations are no longer the highly disorganized, unfocused, and irrational entities common in the South a half a century ago (Key, [1949] 1984).

Communications

An examination of communication patterns among local activists in the South shows that stratarchy, a model of party organizational communication that Samuel Eldersveld advanced in the 1960s, is still relevant for contemporary parties. Consistent with Eldersveld's (1964) earlier research about local parties in Wayne County, Michigan, the southern grassroots activists in our study have considerable interaction with other local party activists, but they communicate little across organizational lines up and down the party hierarchy. It is true that the county chairs are more likely to communicate with those at the state and national levels than are precinct officials, but even the county chairs have relatively little contact outside the local level. In what is perhaps a measure of their more focused organizational efforts, the Republicans report more contact than the Democrats at all levels.

Although local party officials report relatively little communication (especially noted in the precinct committee activists' paucity of communications with state and national party organizations or activists), there is a fairly high level of communication at the local level itself. This pattern may bode well for the local parties in their efforts to contest elections and build and maintain organizations, at least at that level. These data also indicate that the local parties have succeeded to some degree in bringing female and minority activists into their communication networks, and this is consistent with evolving organizational vigor and evolving organizational structure rather than with organizational decline.

Mass/Elite Linkages

The southern grassroots activists data support another theoretical continuity—the nature of linkage of local party activists with the public. For over three decades research has shown that party activists are more ideologically extreme and have more coherent belief systems than the general public. Combined Alabama and Mississippi subsamples of the grassroots activist study, when compared with mass-level data from the two states, explore the linkage between party and citizenry. Data from our study also indicate that Democratic Party activists hold issue positions closer to the moderate positions of the states' citizens. This may help account for the Democratic Party's continued success in many state-level races in Alabama and Mississippi, as well as in other southern states.

Further Considerations

An agenda for future research on local party organizations and activists should include topics explored here as well as topics that we have not addressed.[2] Areas needing investigation include the accumulation of reliable longitudinal data; the further explication of the relationships between local parties and other political actors; and linkages within party organizations, between party organizations, and with other political, economic, and social institutions.

The research questions addressed in this book continue the traditions established in previous work on political parties. To choose but one example, recruitment to activism, which is examined in some detail here, continues to be a salient topic, building on research extending back at least to the 1950s. Its relevance may be especially true during a period when parties face increased competition for the rather limited pool of potential activists from other political organizations such as interest groups and personal campaign organizations. Perhaps of equal importance, researchers should also examine how parties manage to retain activists once they are recruited. In addition to the grassroots officials data utilized in this volume, there is ample evidence from comments volunteered in the margins of the questionnaire we used that many of the activists responding to our survey were marginal in their commitment to sustained involvement in the party. We need to know if, and how, local party organizations deal with the challenge of retention, especially in the case of such marginal activists.

Problems in studying recruitment and retention merely highlight the continuing need for longitudinal data on party activists and organizations. For example, panel studies designed to follow these activists beyond their immediate work in the party would be useful.[3] Do the ambitious activists actually follow through and run for public office at some point in their political careers? Do purist political activists remain involved in the party, and, if so, do their orientations change in the direction of greater pragmatism? Do local party organizations pursue efforts to include new groups in their operations consistently over time, or are these efforts limited and episodic? What are the long-term consequences of factionalism within the party? Cross-sectional data suggest answers to such questions, but longitudinal data are required to address them adequately. In the absence of true panel data, repeated cross-sectional surveys would allow researchers to track aggregate level changes against a known baseline.

An additional topic for further study is the impact of party activity on the electorate, on elections, and on the behavior of public officials. These areas have been examined in the past, but previous research is spotty at best, and we still do not have a clear picture of these vital linkages. Inasmuch as our data are focused on party activists, we can do little more than address these linkages indirectly. The approach used in our study, expanded to include data on the mass electorate and on public officials, for example, could make great strides in clarifying the party's broader impact.

In much the same vein, research comparing party organizational activities (and activists) with the activities (and activists) of nonparty organizations would be useful. For example, parallel surveys of party activists and interest group activists during the same time frame would enhance our understanding of parties and of their relationship with nonparty groups. Such an approach could be extended to include not only interest groups but personal campaign organizations, financial supporters, and the media as well. Placing the party more effectively in the larger political context would also help us understand the important connections between the party and the external environment (addressed in other ways in this volume).

Finally, there is a clear need to continue to develop theory in the study of political parties. We have argued that there are some highly useful midrange theories that assist in understanding parties. Still, there should be more effort to pull disparate research together into greater theoretical unity, perhaps toward a more general theory of party organization and activism. Attention to the various parts of this suggested agenda for future research should contribute to such an effort.

In sum, a great deal of research remains to be done on local party organizations and activists. As times change, so too must our research be updated to measure how the parties adapt to changes taking place around them. Likewise, we must be open to new questions and new approaches to the study of parties lest we miss out on the subtle differences shaping organizational development. On the basis of our examination of grassroots parties in the eleven southern states, we have reaffirmed our conviction that parties remain a crucial component of the political landscape of the American South and elsewhere. They are active and vital, with members filling organizational roles and performing a variety of duties. To overlook their activity is to fail to understand the American political system.

Notes

Introduction: Local Political Parties and Party Scholarship

1. This book is one of three reporting findings from this study. Like the other two, this book deals with party development in the South, but it focuses on the understanding of American party organizations and activism in more general terms. The first book of the series, edited by Charles D. Hadley and Lewis Bowman (1995), presents state-by-state data analyses, along with data on recent electoral trends in each of the southern states. The third, also edited by Charles D. Hadley and Lewis Bowman (1998, forthcoming), examines recent developments in the southern party system in view of a variety of influences important in the changing partisan patterns of the region (e.g., in-migration, race and gender, the rising political involvement of the religious right).

2. For summaries of these normative expectations of political party functions, see Committee on Political Parties (1950) and Bowman and Boynton (1964).

3. Much of this literature is cited in Crotty (1986a: 8–12); see, for example, Hirschfield, et al., 1962; Rossi and Cutright, 1961; Patterson, 1963; Flinn and Wirt, 1965; Marvick and Nixon, 1961; Bowman and Boynton, 1966a and 1966b; Bowman, Ippolito, and Donaldson, 1969; Conway and Feigert, 1968 and 1974; Ippolito, 1969a, 1969b; Ippolito and Bowman, 1969.

4. The Crotty bibliography lists nine books and twenty articles from 1960 to 1969 that focus on local parties. Only six books and twelve articles from the 1970s were included. Five of the six books in the decade chronicled the Daley machine in Chicago; there were no articles published between 1976 and 1978. Studies of local parties apparently began an upswing in the early 1980s. Eight books and fourteen papers written in the half-decade between 1980 and 1985 found their way into the Crotty volume. To be sure, the bibliography does not include every paper or book written in the past three decades, and many that it does include are at best only party-related, but it is helpful in tracking the ebb and flow of scholarly research on local parties, and it does suggest a resurgence of local parties scholarship.

5. This was supplemented by a fourth mailing for Louisiana Democrats because the initial mailing list was nearly two election cycles out of date and because the response rate was unusually low after three mailings (31.4 percent).

6. The Southern Grassroots Party Activists Project data, including a supplemental survey of delegates to the 1992 Democratic and Republican national conventions, are available for secondary analysis to the community of scholars through the Inter-University Consortium for Political and Social Research (ICPSR) at the University of Michigan. The government has certain rights to these data. Any opinions, research findings, conclusions, or recommendations reported from this project are those of the named authors and do not necessarily reflect the views of the National Science Foundation.

1. Recruiting Activists

1. See Samuel J. Eldersveld's succinct summary of this interest in terms of the history of intellectual ideas (Eldersveld, 1989: x–xvi). Another strong advocate for this direction of inquiry was V. O. Key Jr., who wrote: "The longer one frets about the puzzle of how democratic regimes manage to function, the more plausible it appears that a substantial part of the explanation is to be found in the motives that actuate the leadership echelon, the values it holds, and the rules of the political game to which it adheres" (Key, 1963: 536).

2. Several efforts in the past fifteen years have started to shed light on some of this disarray. See Eldersveld, 1989; Eldersveld et al., 1981; Cotter et al., 1984. Particularly helpful in describing the problems are Baer and Bositis, 1988; and Baer, 1993; they summarize where party theory stands in relation to party organizational research, with thoughtful proposals for new directions.

3. This approach has also been emphasized in research about political activists in other political arenas. See Donald R. Matthews's (1985) summary of much research about political activists in legislative arenas, for example. Also see Matthews's earlier statement about the general assumptions and historical background of this approach (Matthews, 1954), and his application of this approach in one political arena (Matthews, 1960).

4. Defined here as material incentives and purposive incentives associated with issues and policy goals that influence government and politics in ideologically desirable directions.

5. Compare these figures with those from the 1990 census (Bureau of the Census, 1991). The proportion of white (non-Hispanic) population in each southern state was typically 5–10 percentage points lower than comparable figures for our sample of Democratic activists. The voting electorate more closely resembled our sample of southern activists in race and ethnicity.

6. Rim South states were the primary destination of northern migrants. Here, the percentage of Republicans who grew up outside the South was even larger—33 percent compared with only 17 percent for Democrats.

7. A sizable portion of southern party activists (37 percent of Democrats and 32 percent of Republicans) were retired. When they were working, retirees in both parties had lower-status occupations than activists still in the labor force (see table

1.1). Thus, 35 percent of retired Democrats and 25 percent of retired Republicans reported blue-collar occupations during their working years.

8. There were too few nonwhite Republicans for meaningful analysis, but the general link between status indicators and race-ethnicity was similar for both Republicans and Democrats.

9. The distinction between Baptists and Southern Baptists is important. Although similar in theological beliefs and moral values, Baptists have displayed more racial tolerance and have attracted a considerable following among African Americans. Thus over half of African American Democrats we surveyed were Baptists, accounting for nearly one-third of Baptist Democrats and partially explaining why Democrats attracted more Baptists than did Republicans. In contrast, nearly all Southern Baptists (97 percent) were whites. Nearly all Republican activists were white, so analysis of racial and ethnic differences would not be meaningful.

10. The scale was a simple additive scale constructed from items 11a–11o in the questionnaire. Pearson correlations between the scale and individual items ranged between 0.4 and 0.7, and the scale correlated quite strongly ($r = 0.7$) with a separate measure of self-identified political ideology (questionnaire item 12). Thus the ideological issue scale seemed to be generally valid.

2. Activists' Incentives

1. The wording of the choices for the last two factors was (a) party work helps me fulfill my sense of community obligation; (b) to support the candidate I believe in; (c) friendship with a candidate; (d) friendship with a political party official.

2. We excluded two additional choices from the three incentive scales: (a) I like the feeling of being close to people who are doing important things; (b) political work is part of my way of life. The "important people" response was close to being equally correlated with the choices in the material and solidary dimensions, while the "way of life" response was close to being equally related to the solidary and purposive items.

3. Among Democrats, the Pearson rs between issues and each of the other two purposive items was .41. The Pearson r relationships between issues and civic duty was .35, and between issues and candidate .37. Among Republicans, the corresponding Pearson rs were .39 for each of the purposive items, .24 for civic duty, and .33 for candidate.

4. Indeed, even the individual reasons were somewhat stable over time. Among those mentioning one of the three purposive motivations for first becoming active, 48 percent mentioned the same item as a reason for later occupying a party position. Among sixteen different motivational choices, chance alone would predict that only 6 percent of activists would choose the same reason at both time points. Other motivational items exhibited lower stability, which nevertheless exceeded chance (32 percent for material reasons and 29 percent for solidary reasons).

5. These patterns of shifting motivations over time also appear at the individual level. Among switchers initially mentioning a concern about public issues, the most frequently cited new motivation was party work as a way of influencing politics. Among switchers initially mentioning their family's party involvement, the two

choices most frequently switched to were having a strong attachment to the party and viewing politics as a way of life. Among switchers initially mentioning the fun and excitement of the campaign, the most frequent substitute was viewing politics as a way of life, while tied for second was strong party attachment.

6. A factor analysis (varimax rotation) of five items measuring an amateur/professional orientation yielded one clear dimension that incorporated four items: a commitment to organizational unity, unifying behind the party nominee, a preference for an inclusive platform, and maintaining neutrality during the primary. The average Pearson r correlation among these four incentives was a respectable .32. The amateur/professional scale was the simple summation of these four items; it ranged from a score of 1 for most amateuristic to a 13 for most professional. In the t-tests appearing in table 2.11 involving solidary, material, and purposive incentives, the scales were trichotomized into roughly equal groups, and the means of the two extreme groups were compared. The other incentives listed in table 2.11 are individual questionnaire items rather than scales—items that were not related enough to other items to justify being combined into the three incentive scales.

3. Purist versus Pragmatic Orientations

I gratefully acknowledge the assistance of Jennifer Harris and the support provided by a Research Council grant from the University of North Carolina at Greensboro.

1. All three statements had four response categories, from "strongly agree" to "strongly disagree." The purist index was formed by adding the scores for the three items together and subtracting 2, which produced a scale from 1 to 10. A fourth item, asking whether candidates should compromise their values in order to win, was not included in the index because it was not sufficiently interrelated with the other index components.

2. Age is measured in years. Gender and race are dichotomized. Education is measured on a five-point scale.

3. The following responses were classified as purposive motives: (a) campaign work is a way to influence government; (b) party work is a way to influence government; (c) my concern with public issues. All other reasons were classified as not purposive.

4. Respondents were given a set of twelve campaign activities and asked which ones they had done in recent election campaigns. The index is a count of the number of activities identified.

5. Respondents were asked to identify their level of campaign activity in local, state, and national elections on a four-point scale (very active, somewhat active, slightly active, or not at all active). The index is a sum of the responses for the three election levels, rescored to run from 1 to 10, where 10 represents very active in local, state, and national campaigns.

4. Ambition and Local Party Activists

1. An alternative approach would be to question whether the party official planned to run for public office at some undefined time in the future, but our pre-

vious experience with this question suggests that many with no real intention of ever following through will answer affirmatively. The effect is to depress the effect of ambition in the analysis. Consequently, this is less useful as an indicator of ambition.

2. For a fuller discussion of the questions used to tap these concepts, the nature of the concepts, and a more general analysis of professionalism/amateurism among the local party officials in this study, see the preceding chapter.

5. Parties, Ideology, and Issues: The Structuring of Political Conflict

1. While their relatively small numbers may diminish their potential impact within the party, it is still worthwhile to examine the liberal Republican officials in comparison with their more moderate and conservative colleagues.

2. Although this analysis did not pursue the point, it is probably not coincidental that states such as Florida, Virginia, and Texas (all with high rates of in-migration) have the highest percentages of liberals within their local Democratic Party organizations.

6. Party Maintenance Activities

1. We make and hold to this distinction between formal and candidate-centered organizations in light of the seminal research of Joseph Schlesinger (1984), distinguishing between those organizations we conventionally think of as "the party" versus those that focus on a single candidacy.

2. In Texas, for example, there was a fair degree of parity in terms of the number and presence of county chairs. On the other hand, the GOP had only 53.6 percent of precinct positions filled, as compared with the Democrats' 79.3 percent (Feigert and McWilliams, 1995).

3. For an illustration of how such terms are translated into issue positions for our activists, see Clarke, Feigert, and Stewart (1995: 156, table 1).

7. Campaign Activities

1. We do not mean to belittle the importance of organizational strength as a key concept in the study of party organizations. In fact, campaign activity is one component of the measure as it was operationalized by Gibson and his colleagues. Since our data are at the county and precinct level (rather than state and county), we think activity is a better way to evaluate individuals within the formal party structure.

2. With one exception (sending campaign mailings), exploratory factor analysis generally revealed factors that were virtually identical to our intuitive classification of managerial and labor-intensive activities. We omitted purchasing billboard space from the indexes since so few activists performed this task.

3. For a discussion of factionalization within southern parties, see Wielhouwer (1995).

4. Specifically, the four items were combined to create an index, which was in

turn broken down so that the highest and lowest quartiles (approximately) were coded as issue purists and pragmatists, respectively. The same substantive conclusions were reached when the full index was used in the model. The four items are as follows: good party workers support any candidate nominated by the party even if they basically disagree with the candidate; party organization and unity are more important than free and total discussion of issues that may divide the party; controversial positions should be avoided in a party platform to ensure party unity; good party workers should remain officially neutral in primary contests even when they have a personal preference.

5. While all of the equations are significant based on the F-ratio, the variance explained by the equations is rather small, never exceeding .14.

6. Studies of voter turnout (e.g., Wolfinger and Rosenstone, 1980) show that participation increases with age, at least until about age sixty-five.

7. While these results are interesting, we cannot escape the problem of unexplained variance. In her analysis of the Party Transformation Studies, Norrander (1986) explained 31 to 59 percent of the variance in local party campaign activities. Expanding our model based on her results seems to be a fruitful path for us to follow. Specifically, this model could be improved by incorporating measures of the resources held by the local parties, measures regarding the role orientation of the parties' chairs, and county-level demographic information.

8. Communication Patterns

1. See Leighley (1995) for an overview of this literature.

2. Baer (1993) argued that the debate over whether the parties are in good health or ill health said more about differences in theories of party organization than it did about the actual health of the parties as institutions. She went on to suggest that an examination of party health should focus on four interrelated indicators of the *institutionalization* of the parties: organizational vitality, organizational interdependence, stable factions, and an integrative community life.

10. Mass/Elite Linkage

1. The combined response rate for all three mailings to elites was about 50 percent. The following graduate students assisted in collecting and helping to analyze the Mississippi data from this project: Nana Bellerud, Nancy Bigelow, Shaundra Clark, Denise Keller, Bob Lord, Lynn Whittington McInnis, and Carlotta Strong. Patrick Fuller assisted in conducting the Alabama portion of the party activists survey.

The telephone poll of 558 adult Mississippi residents was conducted April 1–13, 1992, by the Survey Research Unit of the Social Science Research Center at Mississippi State University. The results were weighted or adjusted by demographic characteristics such as education, race, and gender so that all groups would be represented in the sample in proportion to their presence in the state population. The survey of a random sample of 519 adult Alabama citizens was conducted January

20–23, 1991, by Southern Opinion Research, a private survey research firm head-quartered in Tuscaloosa, Alabama.

2. Among college-educated Alabamians, jobs load highly on the first factor but even more highly on a minor factor, as shown in the appendix.

3. Our purpose in this portion of the chapter has been to compare elites and masses within each of these states, not to compare elites or masses between the two states. The existence of only two factors among Mississippi activists while there are four among Alabama activists is an artifact of the omission of six issue items from the Mississippi analysis. When those six items are included in the Mississippi activists' factor analysis, four factors also emerge, and they exhibit the same policy nature as do the Alabama activists' factors.

4. We acknowledge that, except for ideological self-identification, these issue items are agree/disagree items, and the means are a product of the wording of the questions. Hence, we refer to the midpoint of the scales in the text as mere arbitrary points used for illustrative purposes. We do not claim that the scale midpoint is a "moderate" point of view in an absolute sense, and we do not assign absolute "lib-eral" or "conservative" terms to any scale position.

5. The Alabama public survey included two versions of the party identification question—one for identification with the national parties and the other for identi-fication with the state parties. The policy views of Democrats and Republicans for the two indicators are not significantly different. All analyses for Alabama in this chapter report the results for the national party identification question.

6. In both states, the differences between county chairs and county committee members on the issue items are statistically insignificant. Hence, the chairs and members categories are combined to comprise the party elite groups.

7. We combine liberal Americans for Democratic Action and conservative American Conservative Union ratings by taking the average of the ACU and 100-ADA scores for the previous Congress. The resulting 100-point scale is divided as follows: liberal is 0–20; moderate liberal is 21–40; moderate is 41–60; moderate con-servative is 61–80; and conservative is 80–100. The scores are available in Duncan and Lawrence (1995).

11. Strength of Party Attachment

1. Students of southern politics also have recognized these strong connections between the external environment and the party system. The development of the Democratic one-party system in the 1890s was largely a response to the trauma of Civil War defeat and Reconstruction and the eventual determination of many of the region's political leaders to restore a social, economic, and political system based on white supremacy (Kousser, 1974; Key, [1949] 1984; Grantham, 1963; Bartley and Graham, 1975: chap. 1; and Black and Black, 1987: chap. 1). Similarly, much of the discussion of the transformation of the southern party system from a dominant one-party system to an increasingly competitive two-party system focuses on the impact of the sweeping social, economic, and legal changes in the region since World War II (see, for example, Havard, 1972b; Bartley and Graham, 1975; Havard, 1986; Beck and Lopatto, 1982; Lamis, 1990; Black and Black, 1987; Van Wingen and Valentine,

1988; Swansbrough, 1988; Steed, Moreland, and Baker, 1990b; Black and Black, 1992; and Steed, 1994).

2. While the concept of split partisanship applies particularly to southern politics, it has applicability to the study of American party politics more generally, as well (e.g., Jennings and Niemi, 1966; Niemi, Wright, and Powell, 1987; and Wekkin, 1991).

3. Both this and the data on voting defection among these party officials presented later in this chapter are generally consistent with research on partisanship and voting behavior that finds large gaps between strong partisans and weak partisans in their party loyalty and involvement; it also finds "Independent Leaners" to be more like partisans than like pure Independents and sometimes even more partisan than weak partisans (see, for example, Keith et al., 1985, 1992; Wekkin, 1988).

4. Our data do not allow an examination of these possible explanations, but the negative implications for the Democratic Party of both general scenarios are fairly clear: the organizational problems associated with the perceptions of the Consistently Weak party activists are likely to occur whether or not the perceptions are wholly accurate.

5. In fact, in the Grassroots Party Activists Survey the returned questionnaires fairly often had notes attached or penciled in the margins attesting to the respondent's reluctance to become a party official, sometimes saying, for example, that the respondent had agreed under protest to be listed as an official simply because there were so few people in attendance at the precinct meeting that arriving at a full roster of officials was virtually impossible.

12. Party Activists as Agents of Change: Women, Blacks, and Political Parties in the South

1. The recent influx of Republican activists from the religious right may be consistent with the party elite theory of democracy (Oldfield, 1996). Unfortunately, we have no direct measures of involvement with or support for the Christian Coalition or other groups of that genre.

2. Jeane Kirkpatrick (1976: chap. 10) argues that this crucial distinction was overlooked by the members of the McGovern-Fraser Commission. Borrowing from Hanna Pitkin, she points out the differences between "representation" and "representativeness."

3. For an examination of the possibilities and limitations of party machines for immigrant assimilation, see Erie (1988).

13. Summing Up: Organization and Activism at the Grassroots Level in the 1990s

1. Indeed, the pervasiveness of one-party systems in the American South produced the phenomenon, in a number of southern states and localities, of playing out functional party politics within the factions of the dominant party. In essence, in an effort to produce democratic politics in an authoritarian one-party system, factions within the dominant party became functional surrogates for political par-

ties. See, for example, Key ([1949] 1984), Price (1964), and Bowman and Boynton (1964).

2. Other perspectives on this subject can be found in Crotty (1986a) and Frendreis and Gitelson (1993).

3. For example, Miller and Jennings (1986) provide an innovative treatment of panel data about national convention delegates.

Bibliography

Abramowitz, Alan I. 1979. "Ideological Realignment and the Nationalization of American Politics." Paper presented at the 1979 annual meeting of the Southern Political Science Association, Gatlinburg, Tenn.

Abramowitz, Alan I., John McGlennon, and Ronald Rapoport. 1983. "The Party Isn't Over: Incentives for Activism in the 1980 Presidential Nominating Campaign." *Journal of Politics* 45: 1006–1015.

Abramowitz, Alan I., and Walter J. Stone. 1984. *Nomination Politics: Party Activists and Presidential Choice*. New York: Praeger.

Appleton, Andrew, and Daniel Ward. 1994. "Party Organizational Response to Electoral Change: Texas and Arkansas." *American Review of Politics* 15: 191–212.

Arrow, Kenneth J. 1974. *The Limits of Organization*. New York: W. W. Norton.

Asher, Herbert B. 1992. *Presidential Elections and American Politics*. 5th ed. Pacific Grove, Calif.: Brooks/Cole.

Backstrom, Charles H. 1977. "Congress and the Public: How Representative Is One of the Other?" *American Politics Quarterly* 5: 411–434.

Baer, Denise L. 1993. "Who Has the Body? Party Institutionalism and Theories of Party Organization." *American Review of Politics* 14: 1–38.

Baer, Denise L., and David A. Bositis. 1988. *Elite Cadres and Party Coalitions*. Westport, Conn.: Greenwood Press.

———. 1993. *Politics and Linkage in a Democratic Society*. Englewood Cliffs, N.J.: Prentice Hall.

Bain, Chester W. 1972. "South Carolina: Partisan Prelude." In William C. Havard, ed., *The Changing Politics of the South*. Baton Rouge: Louisiana State University Press.

Baker, Tod A. 1990. "The Emergence of the Religious Right and the Development of the Two-Party System in the South." In Tod A. Baker, Charles D. Hadley, Robert P. Steed, and Laurence W. Moreland, eds., *Political Parties in the Southern States*. New York: Praeger.

Baker, Tod A., Charles D. Hadley, Robert P. Steed, and Laurence W. Moreland, eds. 1990. *Political Parties in the Southern States: Party Activists in Partisan Coalitions*. New York: Praeger.

Baker Tod A., Laurence W. Moreland, and Robert P. Steed. 1989. "Party Activists
and the New Religious Right." In Charles W. Dunn, ed., *Religion in American Politics*. Washington, D.C.: Congressional Quarterly Press.

Baker, Tod A., Robert P. Steed, and Laurence W. Moreland. 1991. "Preachers
and Politics: Jesse Jackson, Pat Robertson, and the 1988 Presidential Election."
In James L. Guth and John C. Green, eds., *The Bible and the Ballot Box*. Boulder,
Colo.: Westview Press.

Bartley, Numan V., and Hugh D. Graham. 1975. *Southern Politics and the Second Reconstruction*. Baltimore: The Johns Hopkins University Press.

Bass, Harold F., Jr. 1991. "Change and Democratization in One-Party Systems." *Midsouth Political Science Journal* 12: 65–77.

Bass, Harold F., Jr., and Andrew Westmoreland. 1984. "Parties and Campaigns in
Contemporary Arkansas." *Arkansas Political Science Journal* 5: 38–58.

Bass, Jack, and Walter DeVries. 1976. *The Transformation of Southern Politics*. New
York: Basic Books.

Baxter, Sandra, and Marjorie Lansing. 1983. *Women and Politics: The Visible Majority*.
Rev. ed. Ann Arbor: University of Michigan Press.

Beck, Paul Allen. 1974. "Environment and Party: The Impact of Political and Demographic County Characteristics on Party Behavior." *American Political Science Review* 68: 1229–1244.

Beck, Paul Allen, and Paul Lopatto. 1982. "The End of Southern Distinctiveness."
In Laurence W. Moreland, Tod A. Baker, and Robert P. Steed, eds., *Contemporary
Southern Political Attitudes and Behavior: Studies and Essays*. New York: Praeger.

Beck, Paul Allen, and Frank J. Sorauf. 1992. *Party Politics in America*. 7th ed. New
York: Harper Collins.

Bibby, John F. 1990. "Party Organization at the State Level." In L. Sandy Maisel, ed.,
The Parties Respond: Changes in the American Party System. Boulder, Colo.: Westview
Press.

———. 1992. *Politics, Parties, and Elections in America*. 2d ed. Chicago: Nelson Hall.

Bishop, George F., Alfred J. Tuchfarber, and Robert W. Oldendick. 1978. "Change
in the Structure of American Political Attitudes: The Nagging Question of Question Wording." *American Journal of Political Science* 22: 250–269.

Black, Earl, and Merle Black. 1987. *Politics and Society in the South*. Cambridge: Harvard University Press.

———. 1992. *The Vital South*. Cambridge: Harvard University Press.

Black, Gordon A. 1970. "A Theory of Professionalization in Politics." *American Political Science Review* 64: 865–878.

———. 1972. "A Theory of Political Ambition: Career Choices and the Role of Struc-
tural Incentives." *American Political Science Review* 66: 144–159.

Blair, Diane. 1986. *Arkansas Politics and Government*. Lincoln: University of Nebraska
Press.

Blank, Robert H. 1980. *Political Parties: An Introduction*. Englewood Cliffs, N.J.: Prentice-Hall.

Blau, Peter M., and W. Richard Scott. 1962. *Formal Organizations*. San Francisco:
Chandler Publishing.

Bobo, Lawrence, and Franklin G. Gilliam, Jr. 1990. "Race, Political Participation,
and Black Empowerment." *American Political Science Review* 84: 377–394.

Bowman, Lewis, and G. R. Boynton. 1964. "Coalition as Party in a One-Party Southern Area: A Theoretical and Case Analysis." *Midwest Journal of Political Science* 8: 277–297.

———. 1966a. "Activities and Goal Orientations of Grassroots Party Officials." *Journal of Politics* 28: 121–143.

———. 1966b. "Recruitment Patterns among Local Party Officials." *American Political Science Review* 60: 667–676.

Bowman, Lewis, William E. Hulbary, and Anne E. Kelley. 1990. "Party Sorting at the Grassroots: Stable Partisans and Party Changers among Florida's Precinct Officials." In Robert P. Steed, Laurence W. Moreland, and Tod A. Baker, eds., *The Disappearing South? Studies in Regional Change and Continuity.* Tuscaloosa: University of Alabama Press.

Bowman, Lewis, Dennis S. Ippolito, and William Donaldson. 1969. "Incentives for the Maintenance of Grassroots Party Activism." *Midwest Journal of Political Science* 13: 126–139.

Brady, David W., Joseph Cooper, and Patricia A. Hurley. 1979. "The Decline of Party Voting in the U.S. House of Representatives, 1887–1968." *Legislative Studies Quarterly* 4: 381–407.

Brady, Henry E., Sydney Verba, and Kay Lehman Schlozman. 1995. "Beyond SES: A Resource Model of Political Participation." *American Political Science Review* 89: 271–294.

Broder, David. 1972. *The Party's Over.* New York: Harper & Row.

Brodsky, David M. 1988. "The Dynamics of Recent Southern Politics." In Robert H. Swansbrough and David M. Brodsky, eds., *The South's New Politics: Realignment and Dealignment.* Columbia: University of South Carolina Press.

Budge, Ian, and Richard I. Hofferbert. 1990. "Mandates and Policy Outputs: U.S. Party Platforms and Federal Expenditures." *American Political Science Review* 84: 111–132.

Buehl, Emmett H., Jr. 1986. "Divisive Primaries and Participation in Fall Presidential Campaigns." *American Politics Quarterly* 14: 376–390.

Bullock, Charles S. III. 1988. "Creeping Realignment in the South." In Robert H. Swansbrough and David M. Brodsky, eds., *The South's New Politics: Realignment and Dealignment.* Columbia: University of South Carolina Press.

———. 1991. "Republican Strength at the Grass Roots: An Analysis at the County Level." *Midsouth Political Science Journal* 12: 65–79.

Burnham, Walter Dean. 1969. "The End of American Party Politics." *Transaction* 7: 12–22.

———. 1970. *Critical Elections and the Mainsprings of American Politics.* New York: W. W. Norton.

———. 1976. "Revitalization and Decay: Looking Toward the Third Century of American Electoral Politics." *Journal of Politics* 38: 146–172.

———. 1982. *The Current Crisis in American Politics.* New York: Oxford University Press.

Burrell, Barbara C. 1986. "Local Party Committees, Task Performance and Task Vitality." *Western Political Quarterly* 39: 48–66.

Caldeira, Gregory A., Samuel C. Patterson, and Gregory A. Markko. 1985. "The Mobilization of Voters in Congressional Elections." *Journal of Politics* 47: 490–509.

Carlson, James. 1986. "Party Activists: Office-Seekers and Benefit-Seekers." Paper presented at the 1986 annual meeting of the Midwest Political Science Association, Chicago.

Carmines, Edward G., and Harold W. Stanley. 1990. "Ideological Realignment in the Contemporary South: Where Have All the Conservatives Gone?" In Robert P. Steed, Laurence W. Moreland, and Tod A. Baker, eds., *The Disappearing South? Studies in Regional Change and Continuity.* Tuscaloosa: University of Alabama Press.

Carmines, Edward G., and James A. Stimson. 1989. *Issue Evolution: Race and the Transformation of American Politics.* Princeton: Princeton University Press.

Chambers, William Nesbit. 1963. *Political Parties in a New Nation.* New York: Oxford University Press.

Cjboski, Kenneth N. 1974. "Ambition Theory and Candidate Members of the Soviet Politburo." *Journal of Politics* 36: 172–183.

Clark, John A., John M. Bruce, John H. Kessel, and William G. Jacoby. 1991. "I'd Rather Switch than Fight: On Party Switching among Presidential Activists." *American Journal of Political Science* 35: 577–597.

Clark, John A., and Brad Lockerbie. 1992. "Split Partisanship among Grassroots Party Activists." Paper presented at the annual meeting of the American Political Science Association, Chicago.

———. 1993. "Party Integration in Southern Grassroots Parties." Paper presented at the annual meeting of the American Political Science Association, Washington, D.C.

Clark, Peter, and James Q. Wilson. 1961. "Incentive Systems: A Theory of Organization." *Administrative Science Quarterly* 6: 129–166.

Clarke, Harold D., Euel Elliott, and Thomas H. Roback. 1991. "Domestic Issue Ideology and Activist Style: A Note on 1980 Republican Convention Delegates." *Journal of Politics* 53: 519–534.

Clarke, Harold D., Frank B. Feigert, and Marianne C. Stewart. 1995. "Different Contents, Similar Packages: The Domestic Political Beliefs of Southern Local Party Activists." *Political Research Quarterly* 48: 151–167.

Clarke, Harold D., and Allan Kornberg. 1979. "Moving Up the Political Escalator: Women Party Officials in the United States and Canada." *Journal of Politics* 41: 442–478.

Coleman, John J. 1994. "The Resurgence of Party Organization? A Dissent From the New Orthodoxy." In Daniel Shea and John C. Green, eds., *The State of the Parties: The Changing Role of the Contemporary American Parties.* Lanham, Md.: Rowman and Littlefield.

Collie, Melissa P., and David W. Brady. 1985. "The Decline of Partisan Voting Coalitions in the House of Representatives." In Lawrence C. Dodd and Bruce I. Oppenheimer, eds., *Congress Reconsidered.* 3d ed. Washington, D.C.: CQ Press.

Committee on Political Parties. 1950. "Toward a More Responsible Two-Party System." *American Political Science Review* 44 (Part 2), Supplement.

Conover, Pamela Johnston, and Virginia Sapiro. 1993. "Gender, Feminist Consciousness, and War." *American Journal of Political Science* 37: 1079–1099.

Converse, Philip E. 1964. "The Nature of Belief Systems in Mass Publics." In David E. Apter, ed., *Ideology and Discontent.* New York: Free Press.

Converse, Philip E., Aage R. Clauson, and Warren E. Miller. 1965. "Electoral Myth and Reality: The 1964 Election." *American Political Science Review* 59: 321–336.

Conway, M. Margaret. 1991. *Political Participation in the United States*. Washington, D.C.: CQ Press.

Conway, M. Margaret, and Frank B. Feigert. 1968. "Motivation, Incentive Systems, and Political Party Organizations." *American Political Science Review* 62: 1169–1183.

———. 1974. "Motivations and Task Performance among Party Precinct Workers." *Western Political Quarterly* 27: 693–709.

Costantini, Edmond. 1990. "Political Women and Political Ambition: Closing the Gender Gap." *American Journal of Political Science* 34: 741–770.

Cotter, Cornelius P., James L. Gibson, John F. Bibby, and Robert J. Huckshorn. 1984. *Party Organizations in American Politics*. New York: Praeger.

Cotter, Patrick, and James Stovall. 1994. "Character Won Out at the End of the Race." *The Birmingham News*, November 20, C1.

Crotty, William J. 1968a. "The Party Organization and Its Activities." In William J. Crotty, ed., *Approaches to the Study of Party Organization*. Boston: Allyn & Bacon.

———. 1971. "Party Effort and Its Impact on the Vote." *American Political Science Review* 65: 439–450.

———. 1977. *Political Reform and the American Experiment*. New York: Thomas Y. Crowell.

———. 1983. *Party Reform*. New York: Longman.

———. 1984. *American Parties in Decline*. 2d ed. Boston: Little, Brown.

———. 1986a. "An Agenda for Studying Local Parties Comparatively." In William J.Crotty, ed., *Political Parties in Local Areas*. Knoxville: University of Tennessee Press.

———, ed. 1968b. *Approaches to the Study of Party Organization*. Boston: Allyn & Bacon.

———. 1986b. *Political Parties in Local Areas*. Knoxville: University of Tennessee Press.

Crotty, William J., and Gary C. Jacobson. 1980. *American Parties in Decline*. Boston: Little, Brown.

Crozier, Michel. 1964. *The Bureaucratic Phenomenon*. Chicago: University of Chicago Press.

Cutright, Phillips, and Peter H. Rossi. 1958. "Grass Roots Politicians and the Vote." *American Sociological Review* 23: 171–179.

Dodson, Debra L. 1990. "Socialization of Party Activists: National Convention Delegates, 1972–81." *American Journal of Political Science* 34: 1119–1141.

Duncan, Philip D., and Christine C. Lawrence. 1995. *Politics in America, 1996*. Washington D.C.: C.Q. Press.

Duverger, Maurice. 1954. *Political Parties*. New York: John Wiley & Sons.

Edwards, Pamela J. 1984. "State Party Organization Revitalization: A Critical Assessment." Paper presented at the annual meeting of the Southern Political Science Association, Savannah, Ga.

Ehrenhalt, Alan. 1991. *The United States of Ambition: Politicians, Power, and the Pursuit of Office*. New York: Times Books.

Eldersveld, Samuel J. 1964. *Political Parties: A Behavioral Analysis*. Chicago: Rand McNally.

———. 1982. *Political Parties in American Society*. New York: Basic Books.

———. 1984. "The Condition of Party Organization at the Local Level." Paper presented at the annual meeting of the Southern Political Science Association, Savannah, Ga.

———. 1986. "The Party Activists in Detroit and Los Angeles: A Longitudinal View, 1956–1980." In William J. Crotty, ed., *Political Parties in Local Areas*. Knoxville: University of Tennessee Press.

———. 1989. *Political Elites in Modern Societies*. Ann Arbor: University of Michigan Press.

Eldersveld, Samuel J., Jan Kooiman, and Theo van der Tak. 1981. *Elite Images of Dutch Politics*. Ann Arbor: University of Michigan Press.

Engstrom, Richard L. 1971. "Political Ambitions and the Prosecutorial Office." *Journal of Politics* 33: 190–194.

Epstein, Leon. 1967. *Political Parties in Western Democracies*. New York: Praeger.

———. 1986. *Political Parties in the American Mold*. Madison: University of Wisconsin Press.

Erie, Steven P. 1988. *Rainbow's End: Irish-Americans and the Dilemmas of Urban Machine Politics, 1840–1985*. Berkeley: University of California Press.

Etzioni, Amitai. 1961. *A Comparative Analysis of Complex Organizations*. New York: Free Press.

Feigert, Frank B., and Nancy L. McWilliams. 1995. "Texas: Yeller Dogs and Yuppies." In Charles D. Hadley and Lewis Bowman, eds., *Southern State Party Organizations and Activists*. Westport, Conn.: Praeger.

Fishel, Jeff. 1971. "Ambition and the Political Vocation: Congressional Challengers in American Politics." *Journal of Politics* 33: 25–56.

———. 1973. *Party and Opposition: Congressional Challengers in American Politics*. New York: David McKay.

Flanigan, William H., and Nancy H. Zingale. 1994. *Political Behavior of the American Electorate*. Washington, D.C.: Congressional Quarterly Press.

Flinn, Thomas A., and Frederick M. Wirt. 1965. "Local Party Leaders: Groups of Like-Minded Men." *Midwest Journal of Political Science* 9: 77–98.

Forthal, Sonya. 1946. *Cogwheels of Democracy: A Study of Precinct Captains*. New York: Williams-Frederick Press.

Frankovic, Kathleen. 1982. "Sex and Politics: New Alignments, Old Issues." *PS* 15: 439–448.

Freeman, Jo. 1986. "The Political Culture of the Democratic and Republican Parties." *Political Science Quarterly* 101: 327–356.

———. 1987. "Whom You Know Versus Whom You Represent: Feminist Influence in the Democratic and Republican Parties." In Mary Fainsod Katzenstein and Carol McClurg Mueller, eds., *The Women's Movements of the United States and Western Europe*. Philadelphia: Temple University Press.

Frendreis, John P., James L. Gibson, and Laura L. Vertz. 1990. "The Electoral Relevance of Local Party Organizations." *American Political Science Review* 84: 225–235.

Frendreis, John P., and Alan R. Gitelson. 1993. "Local Political Parties in an Age of Change." *American Review of Politics* 14: 533–547.

George, Alexander L., and Juliette C. George. 1956. *Woodrow Wilson and Colonel House: A Personality Study*. New York: Norton.

Gibson, James L., Cornelius P. Cotter, John F. Bibby, and Robert J. Huckshorn. 1983. "Assessing Party Organizational Strength." *American Journal of Political Science* 27: 193–222.

———. 1985. "Whither the Local Parties?" *American Journal of Political Science* 29: 139–160.

Gibson, James L., John P. Frendreis, and Laura L. Vertz. 1989. "Party Dynamics in the 1980s: Change in County Party Organizational Strength, 1980–1984." *American Journal of Political Science* 33: 67–90.

Gosnell, Harold F. 1937. *Machine Politics: Chicago Model.* Chicago: University of Chicago Press.

Grantham, Dewey W. 1963. *The Democratic South.* New York: W. W. Norton.

Green, John C., and James L. Guth. 1988. "The Christian Right in the Republican Party: The Case of Pat Robertson's Supporters." *Journal of Politics* 50: 150–165.

Greenstein, Fred I., and Frank B. Feigert. 1985. *The American Party System and the American People.* Englewood Cliffs, N.J.: Prentice-Hall.

Hadley, Charles D. 1985. "Dual Partisan Identification in the South." *Journal of Politics* 47: 254–268.

Hadley, Charles D., and Lewis Bowman. 1993. "The Organizational Strength of Political Parties at the County Level: Preliminary Observations from the Southern Grassroots Party Activists Project." In Michael Margolis and John Green, eds., *Machine Politics, Sound Bites and Nostalgia.* Lanham, Md.: University Press of America.

Hadley, Charles D., and Susan E. Howell. 1980. "The Southern Split Ticket Voter, 1952–1976: Republican Conversion or Democratic Decline?" In Robert P. Steed, Laurence W. Moreland, and Tod A. Baker, eds., *Party Politics in the South.* New York: Praeger.

Hadley, Charles D., Michael A. Maggiotto, and Gary E. Wekkin. 1993. "Issue Conflict and Consensus among Party Leaders and Followers: Revisited in the South." Paper presented at the annual meeting of the American Political Science Association, Washington, D.C.

Hadley, Charles D., and Lewis Bowman, eds. 1995. *Southern State Party Organizations and Activists.* Westport, Conn.: Praeger.

———. 1998. *Political Party Activists in Southern Politics: Mirrors and Makers of Change.* Knoxville: University of Tennessee Press. Forthcoming.

Hames, Tim. 1994. "Confusions in the Analysis of American Political Parties." In Daniel M. Shea and John C. Green, eds., *The State of the Parties: The Changing Role of Contemporary American Parties.* Lanham, Md.: Rowman and Littlefield.

Harmel, Robert, and Kenneth Janda. 1982. *Parties and Their Environments: Limits to Reform?* New York: Longman.

Harris, Frederick C. 1994. "Something Within: Religion as a Mobilizer of African American Political Activism." *Journal of Politics.* 56: 42–68.

Hauss, Charles S., and L. Sandy Maisel. 1986. "Extremist Delegates: Myth and Reality." In Ronald Rapoport, Alan Abramowitz, and John McGlennon, eds., *The Life of the Parties.* Lexington: University Press of Kentucky.

Havard, William C. 1972a. "The South: A Shifting Perspective." In William C. Havard, ed., *The Changing Politics of the South.* New York: Praeger.

———. 1986. "Southern Politics: A Prelude to Presidential Politics in 1984." In

Robert P. Steed, Laurence W. Moreland, and Tod A. Baker, eds., *The 1984 Presidential Election in the South: Patterns of Southern Party Politics*. New York: Praeger.

———, ed. 1972b. *The Changing Politics of the South*. Baton Rouge: Louisiana State University Press.

Heard, Alexander. 1952. *A Two-Party South?* Chapel Hill: University of North Carolina Press.

Hedges, Roman B. 1984. "Reasons for Political Involvement: A Study of Contributors to the 1972 Presidential Campaign." *Western Political Quarterly* 37: 257–271.

Herrnson, Paul S. 1994. "The Revitalization of National Party Organizations." In L. Sandy Maisel, ed., *The Parties Respond: Changes in American Parties and Campaigns*. Boulder, Colo.: Westview.

Hibbing, John. 1982. "Voluntary Retirement from the U.S. House: The Costs of Congressional Service." *Legislative Studies Quarterly* 7: 57–74.

———. 1986. "Ambition in the House: Behavioral Consequences of Higher Office Goals Among U.S. Representatives." *American Journal of Political Science* 30: 651–665.

Hirlinger, Michael W. 1992. "Citizen-Initiated Contacting of Local Government Officials: A Multivariate Explanation." *Journal of Politics* 54: 553–564.

Hirschfield, R. S., et al. 1962. "A Profile of Political Activists in Manhattan." *Western Political Quarterly* 15: 489–506.

Hitlin, Robert A., and John S. Jackson III. 1977. "On Amateur and Professional Politicians." *Journal of Politics* 39: 786–793.

Hofstetter, C. Richard. 1971. "The Amateur Politician: A Problem in Construct Validation." *Midwest Journal of Political Science* 15: 31–56.

Hopkins, Anne H. 1986. "Campaign Activities and Local Party Organization in Nashville." In William J. Crotty, ed., *Political Parties in Local Areas*. Knoxville: University of Tennessee Press.

Huckfeldt, Robert, and John Sprague. 1992. "Political Parties and Electoral Mobilization: Political Structure, Social Structure, and the Party Canvass." *American Political Science Review* 86: 70–86.

Huckshorn, Robert J. 1994. "National Committee Leadership of State and Local Parties." In John C. Green, ed., *Politics, Professionalism, and Power*. Lanham, Md.: University Press of America.

Huckshorn, Robert J., James L. Gibson, Cornelius P. Cotter, and John F. Bibby. 1986. "Party Integration and Party Organizational Strength." *Journal of Politics* 48: 976–991.

Ippolito, Dennis S. 1969a. "Motivational Reorientation among Party Activists." *Journal of Politics* 31: 1098–1101.

———. 1969b. "Political Perspectives of Suburban Party Leaders." *Social Science Quarterly* 49: 800–815.

Ippolito, Dennis S., and Lewis Bowman. 1969. "Goals and Activities of Party Officials in a Suburban Community." *Western Political Quarterly* 22: 572–580.

Jackson, John S. III, Barbara L. Brown, and David Bositis. 1982. "Herbert McClosky and Friends Revisited: 1980 Democratic and Republican Party Elites Compared to the Mass Public." *American Politics Quarterly* 10: 158–180.

Jackson, John S. III, Jesse C. Brown, and Barbara L. Brown. 1978. "Recruitment,

Political Representation and Political Values: The 1976 Democratic National Convention Delegates." *American Politics Quarterly* 6: 187–212.

Jennings, M. Kent. 1992. "Ideological Thinking among Mass Publics and Political Elites." *Public Opinion Quarterly* 56: 419–441.

Jennings, M. Kent, and Richard G. Niemi. 1966. "Party Identification at Multiple Levels of Government." *American Journal of Sociology* 72: 86–101.

——. 1968. "The Transmission of Political Values from Parent to Child." *American Political Science Review* 62: 169–184.

Johnson, Donald B., and James L. Gibson. 1974. "The Divisive Primary Revisited: Party Activists in Iowa." *American Political Science Review* 68: 67–77.

Kagay, Michael R. 1991. "The Use of Public Opinion Polls by the *New York Times:* Some Samples from the 1988 Presidential Election." In Paul J. Lavrakas and Jack K. Holley, eds., *Polling and Presidential Election Coverage*. Newbury Park, Calif.: Sage.

Katz, Daniel, and Samuel J. Eldersveld. 1961. "The Impact of Local Party Activities upon the Electorate." *Public Opinion Quarterly* 25: 1–24.

Kayden, Xandra, and Eddie Mahe, Jr. 1985. *The Party Goes On*. New York: Basic Books.

Kazee, Thomas, ed. 1994. *Who Runs for Congress? Ambition, Context, and Candidate Emergence*. Washington, D.C.: Congressional Quarterly Press.

Keefe, William J. 1980. *Parties, Politics, and Public Policy in America*. 3d ed. New York: Holt, Rinehart and Winston.

Keith, Bruce E., David B. Magleby, Candice J. Nelson, Elizabeth Orr, Mark C. Westlye, and Raymond E. Wolfinger. 1985. "The Partisan Affinities of Independent 'Leaners.' " *British Journal of Political Science* 16: 155–184.

——. 1992. *The Myth of the Independent Voter*. Berkeley: University of California Press.

Kelley, Anne E., William E. Hulbary, and Lewis Bowman. 1990. "Gender, Partisanship, and Background Explain Differences in Grassroots Party Activists' Political Attitudes." In Lois Lovelace Duke, ed., *Women in Politics: Outsiders or Insiders?* Englewood Cliffs, N.J.: Prentice-Hall.

Kenney, Patrick J. 1988. "Sorting Out the Effects of Primary Divisiveness in Congressional and Senatorial Elections." *Western Political Quarterly* 41: 765–777.

Kenney, Patrick J., and Tom W. Rice. 1984. "The Effect of Primary Divisiveness in Gubernatorial and Senatorial Elections." *Journal of Politics* 46: 904–915.

——. 1987. "The Relationship between Divisive Primaries and General Election Outcomes." *American Journal of Political Science* 31: 31–44.

Kent, Frank R. 1930. *The Great Game of Politics*. New York: Doubleday, Doran.

Key, V. O., Jr. 1958. *Politics, Parties and Pressure Groups*. 4th ed. New York: Thomas Y. Crowell Company.

——. 1963. *Public Opinion and American Democracy*. New York: Alfred A. Knopf.

——. 1964. *Politics, Parties, and Pressure Groups*. 5th ed. New York: Thomas Y. Crowell.

——. [1949] 1984. *Southern Politics in State and Nation*. New York: Alfred P. Knopf, 1949. Reprint, Knoxville: University of Tennessee Press.

Kinder, Donald R. 1986. "The Continuing American Dilemma: White Resistance to Racial Change 40 Years after Myrdal." *Journal of Social Issues* 42: 151–171.

Kirkpatrick, Jeane J. 1975. "Representation in the American National Conventions: The Case of 1972." *British Journal of Political Science*. 5: 265–322.

———. 1976. *The New Presidential Elite*. New York: Russell Sage Foundation.

———. 1978. *Dismantling the Parties*. Washington, D.C.: American Enterprise Institute.

Klein, Ethel. 1984. *Gender Politics*. Cambridge: Harvard University Press.

———. 1987. "The Diffusion of Consciousness in the United States and Western Europe." In Mary Fainsod Katzenstein and Carol McClung Mueller, eds., *The Women's Movements of the United States and Western Europe*. Philadelphia: Temple University Press.

Kousser, J. Morgan. 1974. *The Shaping of Southern Politics*. New Haven: Yale University Press.

Ladd, Everett C., Jr. 1970. *American Political Parties: Social Change and Political Response*. New York: W. W. Norton.

———. 1975. *Transformations of the American Party System*. New York: W. W. Norton.

———. 1978. *Where Have All the Voters Gone? The Fracturing of America's Political Parties*. New York: W. W. Norton.

Ladd, Everett C., Jr., and Charles D. Hadley. 1975. *Political Parties and Political Institutions: Patterns in Differentiation since the New Deal*. Beverly Hills: Sage.

Lamis, Alexander P. 1990. *The Two-Party South*. 2d ed. New York: Oxford University Press.

Lasswell, Harold. 1948. *Power and Personality*. New York: W. W. Norton.

Lawson, Kay. 1980. "Political Parties and Linkage." In Kay Lawson, ed., *Political Parties and Linkage*. New Haven: Yale University Press.

Lea, James F., ed. 1988. *Contemporary Southern Politics*. Baton Rouge: Louisiana State University Press.

Leighley, Jan E. 1995. "Attitudes, Opportunities and Incentives: A Field Essay on Political Participation." *Political Research Quarterly* 48: 181–209.

Loomis, Burdett. 1984. "On the Knife's Edge: Public Officials and the Life Cycle." *PS* 17: 536–542.

———. 1988. *The New American Politician: Ambition, Entrepreneurship, and the Changing Face of Political Life*. New York: Basic Books.

Maggiotto, Michael A., and Ronald E. Weber. 1986. "The Impact of Organizational Incentives on County Party Chairpersons." *American Politics Quarterly* 14: 201–218.

Maisel, L. Sandy, ed. 1990. *The Parties Respond*. 2d ed. Boulder, Colo.: Westview Press.

Majors, William R. 1986. *Change and Continuity: Tennessee Politics since the Civil War*. Macon, Ga.: Mercer University Press.

March, James G., and Herbert A. Simon. 1958. *Organizations*. New York: Wiley.

Margolis, Michael, and Raymond E. Owen. 1985. "From Organization to Personalism: A Note on the Transmogrification of the Local Political Party." *Polity* 18: 313–328.

Marvick, Dwaine. 1980. "Party Organizational Personnel and Electoral Democracy in Los Angeles, 1963–1972." In William Crotty, ed., *The Party Symbol*. San Francisco: W. H. Freeman.

———. 1983. "Party Activists in Los Angeles, 1963–1978: How Well-Matched Rivals Shape Election Options." In Moshe M. Czudnowski, ed., *Political Elites and Social Change*. DeKalb, Ill.: Northern Illinois University Press.

———. 1986. "Stability and Change in the Views of Los Angeles Party Activists, 1968–1980." In William Crotty, ed., *Political Parties in Local Areas*. Knoxville: University of Tennessee Press.

Marvick, Dwaine, and Charles R. Nixon. 1961. "Recruitment Contrasts in Rival Campaign Groups." In Dwaine Marvick, ed., *Political Decision Makers: Recruitment and Performance*. DeKalb, Ill.: Northern Illinois University Press.

Matthews, Donald R. 1954. *The Social Background of Political Decision Makers*. New York: Random House.

———. 1960. *U.S. Senators and Their World*. New York: Vintage Press.

———. 1985. "Legislative Recruitment and Legislative Careers." In Gerhard Loewenberg, Samuel C. Patterson, and Malcolm E. Jewell, eds., *Handbook of Legislative Research*. Cambridge: Harvard University Press.

Matthews, Donald R., and James W. Prothro. 1966. *Negroes and the New Southern Politics*. New York: Harcourt, Brace and World.

Mayhew, David R. 1986. *Placing Parties in American Politics*. Princeton: Princeton University Press.

McClosky, Herbert, Paul J. Hoffman, and Rosemary O'Hara. 1960. "Issue Conflict and Consensus among Party Leaders and Followers." *American Political Science Review* 54: 406–429.

McNitt, Andrew D. 1980. "The Effect of PrePrimary Endorsement on Competition for Nominations: An Examination of Different Nominating Systems." *Journal of Politics* 42: 257–266.

Merriam, Charles. 1922. *The American Party System*. New York: Macmillan.

Mezey, Michael L. 1970. "Ambition Theory and the Office of Congressman." *Journal of Politics* 32: 563–579.

Michels, Robert. [1915] 1962. *Political Parties*. New York: Free Press.

Mileur, Jerome M. 1980. "Massachusetts: The Democratic Party Charter Movement." In Gerald M. Pomper, ed., *Party Renewal in America*. New York: Praeger.

Miller, Penny M., Malcolm E. Jewell, and Lee Sigelman. 1987. "Reconsidering A Typology of Incentives among Campaign Activists: A Research Note." *Western Political Quarterly* 40: 519–526.

Miller, Warren E., and M. Kent Jennings. 1986. *Parties in Transition: A Longitudinal Study of Party Elites and Party Supporters*. New York: Russell Sage Foundation.

Montjoy, Robert, William Shaffer, and Ronald Weber. 1980. "Policy Preferences of Party Elites and Masses." *American Politics Quarterly* 8: 319–344.

Moreland, Laurence W. 1990a. "The Ideological and Issue Bases of Southern Parties." In Tod A. Baker, Charles D. Hadley, Robert P. Steed, and Laurence W. Moreland, eds., *Political Parties in the Southern States*. New York: Praeger.

———. 1990b. "The Impact of Immigration on Party Coalitions." In Tod A. Baker, Charles D. Hadley, Robert P. Steed, and Laurence W. Moreland, eds., *Political Parties in the Southern States*. New York: Praeger.

———. 1990c. "The Impact of Ambition on the Attitudinal and Behavioral Orientations of Highly Motivated Political Party Activists." Paper presented at the 1990 annual meeting of the Western Political Science Association, Newport Beach, Calif.

———. 1991a. "South Carolina: Different Cast, Same Drama in the Palmetto State." In Laurence W. Moreland, Robert P. Steed, and Tod A. Baker, eds., *The 1988 Presidential Election in the South*. New York: Praeger.

———. 1991b. "The Ideological Nationalization of South Carolina Party Politics, 1980–1988." Paper presented at the 1991 annual meeting of the South Carolina Political Science Association, Charleston.

Moreland, Laurence W., Robert P. Steed, and Tod A. Baker. 1986. "South Carolina." In Robert P. Steed, Laurence W. Moreland, and Tod A. Baker, eds., *The 1984 Presidential Election in the South*. New York: Praeger.

———. 1987. "Black Party Activists: A Profile." In Laurence W. Moreland, Robert P. Steed, and Tod A. Baker, eds., *Blacks in Southern Politics*. New York: Praeger.

Moreland, Laurence W., Tod A. Baker, and Robert P. Steed, eds. 1982. *Contemporary Southern Political Attitudes and Behavior*. New York: Praeger.

Mosher, William E. 1935. "Party and Government Control at the Grass Roots." *National Municipal Review* 24: 15–18.

Nexon, David. 1971. "Asymmetry in the Political System: Occasional Activists in the Republican and Democratic Parties, 1956–1964." *American Political Science Review* 65: 716–730.

Nie, Norman H., Sidney Verba, and John R. Petrocik. 1976. *The Changing American Voter*. Cambridge: Harvard University Press.

Niemi, Richard G., Stephen Wright, and Lynda Powell. 1987. "Multiple Party Identifiers and the Measurement of Party Identification." *Journal of Politics* 49: 1093–1103.

Norrander, Barbara. 1986. "Determinants of Local Party Campaign Activity." *Social Science Quarterly* 67: 561–571.

Oldfield, Duane M. 1996. "The Christian Right in the Presidential Nominating Process." In William G. Mayer, ed., *In Pursuit of the White House*. Chatham, N.J.: Chatham House.

Olson, Mancur. 1965. *The Logic of Collective Action: Public Goods and the Theory of Groups*. Cambridge: Harvard University Press.

Patterson, Samuel C. 1963. "Characteristics of Party Leaders." *Western Political Quarterly* 16: 332–352.

Petrocik, John R. 1987. "Realignment: New Party Coalitions and the Nationalization of the South." *Journal of Politics* 49: 347–375.

Polsby, Nelson W. 1983. *Consequences of Party Reform*. New York: Oxford University Press.

Polsby, Nelson W., and Aaron Wildavsky. 1996. *Presidential Elections: Strategies and Structures of American Politics*. Chatham, N.J.: Chatham House Publishers.

Pomper, Gerald M. 1977. "The Decline of Party in American Elections." *Political Science Quarterly* 92: 21–42.

———. 1990. "Party Organization and Electoral Success." *Polity* 23: 187–206.

———, ed. 1980. *Party Renewal in America*. New York: Praeger.

Prewitt, Kenneth. 1970a. "Political Ambitions, Volunteerism, and Electoral Accountability." *American Political Science Review* 64: 5–17.

———. 1970b. *The Recruitment of Political Leaders: A Study of Citizen Politicians*. Indianapolis: Bobbs-Merrill.

Prewitt, Kenneth, and William Nowlin. 1969. "Political Ambitions and the Behavior of Incumbent Politicians." *Western Political Quarterly* 22: 298–308.

Price, David E. 1984. *Bringing Back the Parties*. Washington, D.C.: CQ Press.

Price, H. D. 1964. "Southern Politics in the Sixties: Notes on Economic Development and Political Modernization." Paper presented at the 1964 annual meeting of the American Political Science Association, Chicago.

Prysby, Charles L. 1990. "Realignment Among Southern Political Party Activists." In Tod A. Baker, Charles D. Hadley, Robert P. Steed, and Laurence W. Moreland, eds., *Political Parties in the Southern States*. New York: Praeger.

Rae, Nicol C. 1994. *Southern Democrats*. New York: Oxford University Press.

Ranney, Austin. 1954. *The Doctrine of Responsible Party Government*. Urbana: University of Illinois Press.

———. 1975. *Curing the Mischiefs of Faction: Party Reform in America*. Berkeley: University of California Press.

———. 1978. "The Political Parties: Reform and Decline." In Anthony King, ed., *The New American Political System*. Washington: American Enterprise Institute.

Rapoport, Ronald B., Alan I. Abramowitz, and John McGlennon, eds. 1986. *The Life of the Parties: Activists in Presidential Politics*. Lexington: University Press of Kentucky.

Reiter, Howard L. 1985. *Selecting the President: The Nominating Process in Transition*. Philadelphia: University of Pennsylvania Press.

Roback, Thomas H. 1975. "Amateurs and Professionals: Delegates to the 1972 Republican National Convention." *Journal of Politics* 37: 436–468.

———. 1980a. "Motivation for Activism among Republican National Convention Delegates: Continuity and Change, 1972–1976." *Journal of Politics* 42: 181–201.

———. 1980b. "Recruitment and Motives for National Convention Activism: Republican Delegates in 1972 and 1976." In William Crotty, ed., *The Party Symbol*. San Francisco: W. H. Freeman.

Robertson, Peter J., and Shui-Yan Tang. 1995. "The Role of Commitment in Collective Action: Comparing the Organizational Behavior and Rational Choice Perspective." *Public Administration Review* 55: 67–80.

Rohde, David. 1979. "Risk-Bearing and Progressive Ambition: The Case of the United States House of Representatives." *American Journal of Political Science* 23: 1–26.

Romzek, Barbara S. 1990. "Employee Investment and Commitment: The Ties That Bind." *Public Administration Review* 50: 374–382.

Rosenau, James N. 1974. *Citizenship between Elections: An Inquiry into the Mobilizable American*. New York: Free Press.

Rosenstone, Steven J., and John Mark Hansen. 1993. *Mobilization, Participation, and Democracy in America*. New York: Macmillan.

Rossi, Peter H., and Phillips Cutright. 1961. "The Impact of Party Organization in an Industrial Setting." In Morris Janowitz, ed., *Community Political Systems*. Glencoe, Ill.: Free Press.

Rozell, Mark J., and Clyde Wilcox, eds. 1996. *God at the Grassroots: The Christian Right in the 1994 Elections*. Lanham, Md.: Rowman and Littlefield.

Sabato, Larry J. 1988. *The Party's Just Begun*. Glenview, Ill.: Scott, Foresman.

Sapiro, Virginia, and Barbara Farah. 1980. "New Pride and Old Prejudice: Political Ambitions and Role Orientations among Female Partisan Elites." *Women & Politics* 1: 13–36.

Schattschneider, E. E. 1942. *Party Government*. New York: Holt, Rinehart and Winston.

———. 1960. *The Semisovereign People*. New York: Holt, Rinehart and Winston.

Scher, Richard K. 1992. *Politics in the New South*. New York: Paragon House.

Schlesinger, Joseph A. 1965. "Political Party Organization." In James G. March, ed., *Handbook of Organizations*. Chicago: Rand McNally.

———. 1966. *Ambition and Politics*. Chicago: Rand McNally.

———. 1975. "The Primary Goals of Political Parties: A Clarification of Positive Theory." *American Political Science Review* 69: 840–849.

———. 1984. "On the Theory of Party Organization." *Journal of Politics* 46: 369–400.

———. 1985. "The New American Political Party." *American Political Science Review* 79: 1152–1169.

———. 1991. *Political Parties and the Winning of Office*. Ann Arbor: University of Michigan Press.

———. 1993. "Understanding Political Parties: Back to the Basics." *American Review of Politics* 14: 481–496.

Schwartz, Mildred A. 1990. *The Party Network*. Madison: University of Wisconsin Press.

Scott, Ruth K., and Ronald J. Hrebenar. 1979. *Parties in Crisis: Party Politics in America*. New York: John Wiley and Sons.

Seagull, Louis M. 1975. *Southern Republicanism*. New York: Wiley.

Shafer, Byron E. 1983. *Quiet Revolution: The Struggle for the Democratic Party and the Shaping of Post-Reform Politics*. New York: Russell Sage Foundation.

Shaffer, Stephen D. 1980. "The Policy Biases of Political Activists." *American Politics Quarterly* 8: 15–33.

———. 1990. "Southern State Party Convention Delegates: The Role of Age." In Tod A. Baker, Charles D. Hadley, Robert P. Steed, and Laurence W. Moreland, eds., *Political Parties in the Southern States*. New York: Praeger.

———. 1991. "Mississippi: Electoral Conflict in a Nationalized State." In Laurence W. Moreland, Robert P. Steed, and Tod A. Baker, eds., *The 1988 Presidential Election in the South*. New York: Praeger.

Shaffer, Stephen D., and David Breaux. 1995. "Mississippi: The True Believers Challenge the Party of Everyone." In Charles D. Hadley and Lewis Bowman, eds., *Southern State Party Organizations and Activists*. Westport, Conn.: Praeger.

Shannon, W. Wayne. 1968. *Party Constituency and Congressional Voting: A Study of Legislative Behavior in the United States House of Representatives*. Baton Rouge: Louisiana State University Press.

Shapiro, Robert Y., and Harpeet Mahajan. 1986. "Gender Differences in Policy Preferences: A Summary of Trends from the 1960s to the 1980s." *Public Opinion Quarterly* 50: 42–61.

Simon, Herbert J. 1976. *Administrative Behavior: A Study of Decision Making in Administrative Organizations*. 3d ed. New York: Free Press.

Sinclair, Barbara D. 1977. "Party Realignment and the Transformation of the Political Agenda: The House of Representatives, 1925–1938." *American Political Science Review* 71: 940–953.

Smith, Charles E., Jr. 1989. "Changes in Local Party Organizational Strength and Activity 1979–1988." Ohio State University. Mimeo.

Sorauf, Frank J. 1964. *Political Parties in the American System*. Boston: Little, Brown.

Sorauf, Frank J., and Paul Allen Beck. 1988. *Party Politics in America*. 6th ed. Glenview, Ill.: Scott, Foresman/Little Brown.

Soule, John W. 1969. "Future Political Ambitions and the Behavior of Incumbent State Legislators." *Midwest Journal of Political Science* 13: 439–454.

Soule, John W., and James W. Clarke. 1970. "Amateurs and Professionals: A Study of Delegates to the 1968 Democratic National Convention." *American Political Science Review* 64: 888–898.

———. 1971. "Issue Conflict and Consensus: A Comparative Study of Democratic and Republican Delegates to the 1968 National Conventions." *Journal of Politics* 33: 72–91.

Soule, John W., and Wilma E. McGrath. 1975. "A Comparative Study of Presidential Nomination Conventions: The Democrats of 1968 and 1972." *American Journal of Political Science* 19: 501–517.

Stanley, Harold W. 1986. "The 1984 Presidential Election in the South: Race and Realignment." In Robert P. Steed, Laurence W. Moreland, and Tod A. Baker, eds., *The 1984 Presidential Election in the South*. New York: Praeger.

Stanley, Harold W., and David S. Castle. 1988. "Partisan Changes in the South: Making Sense of Scholarly Dissonance." In Robert H. Swansbrough and David M. Brodsky, eds., *The South's New Politics: Realignment and Dealignment*. Columbia: University of South Carolina Press.

Steed, Robert P. 1986. "Ambition and State Party Activists: Party and Issue Orientations." Paper presented at the 1986 annual meeting of the Southern Political Science Association, Atlanta.

———. 1990. "Party Reform, the Nationalization of American Politics, and Party Change in the South," in Tod A. Baker, Charles D. Hadley, Robert P. Steed, and Laurence W. Moreland, eds., *Political Parties in the Southern States: Party Activists in Partisan Coalitions*. New York: Praeger.

———. 1994. "Southern Electoral Politics as Prelude to the 1992 Elections." In Robert P. Steed, Laurence W. Moreland, and Tod A. Baker, eds., *The 1992 Presidential Election in the South: Current Patterns of Southern Party and Electoral Politics*. Westport, Conn.: Praeger.

Steed, Robert P., and Tod A. Baker. 1975. "Ambition and Program Orientations of County Chairmen in the Deep and Border South." Paper presented at the 1975 annual meeting of the Southwest Political Science Association, San Antonio, Texas.

Steed, Robert P., Tod A. Baker, and Laurence W. Moreland. 1991. "Dancing to a Different Tune? A Comparison of State and Local Party Activists." Paper presented at the 1991 annual meeting of the Midwest Political Science Association, Chicago.

Steed, Robert P., and John J. McGlennon. 1990. "A 1988 Postscript: Continuing Coalitional Diversity." In Tod A. Baker, Charles D. Hadley, Robert P. Steed, and Laurence W. Moreland, eds., *Political Parties in the Southern States*. New York: Praeger.

Steed, Robert P., Laurence W. Moreland, and Tod A. Baker. 1987. "The Nature of Contemporary Party Organization in South Carolina." Paper presented at the 1987 annual meeting of the American Political Science Association, Chicago.

———. 1990a. "Party Decline or Revitalization: The Case of South Carolina." Paper presented at the 1990 annual meeting of the Northeastern Political Science Association, Providence, R.I.

———. 1990b. "Searching for the Mind of the South in the Second Reconstruction." In Robert P. Steed, Laurence W. Moreland, and Tod A. Baker, eds., *The Disappearing South: Studies in Regional Change and Continuity*. Tuscaloosa: University of Alabama Press.

———. 1991. "Party Change in the South: A Comparison of the Effects of In-Migration on State and Local Party Organizations in South Carolina." Paper presented at the 1991 annual meeting of the Southern Political Science Association, Tampa, Fla.

———. 1995. "Party Sorting at the Local Level in South Carolina." *The National Political Science Review* 5: 181–196.

———, eds. 1980. *Party Politics in the South*. New York: Praeger.

———. 1986. *The 1984 Presidential Election in the South: Patterns of Southern Party Politics*. New York: Praeger.

———. 1990c. *The Disappearing South? Studies in Regional Change and Continuity*. Tuscaloosa: University of Alabama Press.

———. 1994. *The 1992 Presidential Election in the South*. Westport, Conn.: Praeger.

Stimson, James A. 1975. "Belief Systems: Constraint, Complexity, and the 1972 Election." *American Journal of Political Science* 19: 393–417.

Stone, Walter J. 1986. "The Carryover Effect in Presidential Elections." *American Political Science Review* 80: 271–280.

Stone, Walter J., and Alan I. Abramowitz. 1983. "Winning May Not Be Everything, But It's More Than We Thought." *American Journal of Political Science* 77: 945–956.

Sturrock, David E. 1990. "The Quiet Frontier: Recent Developments on Southern Down-Ticket Politics." Paper presented at the Seventh Citadel Symposium on Southern Politics, Charleston, S.C.

Sundquist, James L. 1983. *Dynamics of the Party System*. Rev. ed. Washington, D.C.: Brookings Institution.

———. 1982. "Party Decay and the Capacity to Govern." In Joel L. Fleishman, ed., *The Future of American Political Parties*. Englewood Cliffs, N.J.: Prentice-Hall.

Swansbrough, Robert H. 1985. *Political Change in Tennessee*. Knoxville: University of Tennessee, Bureau of Public Administration.

———. 1988. "Future Directions in Southern Politics." In Robert Swansbrough and David M. Brodsky, eds., *The South's New Politics: Realignment and Dealignment*. Columbia: University of South Carolina Press.

Swansbrough, Robert, and David M. Brodsky, eds. 1988. *The South's New Politics: Realignment and Dealignment*. Columbia: University of South Carolina Press.

Tate, Katherine. 1991. "Black Political Participation in the 1984 and 1988 Presidential Elections." *American Political Science Review* 85: 1159–1176.

Trish, Barbara. 1994. "Party Integration in Indiana and Ohio: The 1988 and 1992 Presidential Contests." *American Review of Politics* 15: 235–256.

U.S. Bureau of the Census. 1991. "Race and Hispanic Origin." *1990 Census Profile*. 2: 1–8.

Van Wingen, John, and David Valentine. 1988. "Partisan Politics: A One-and-a-Half, No-Party Politics." In James F. Lea, ed., *Contemporary Southern Politics*. Baton Rouge: Louisiana State University Press.

Verba, Sidney, and Norman H. Nie. 1972. *Participation in America: Political Democracy and Social Equality*. New York: Harper & Row.

Verba, Sidney, Kay Lehman Schlozman, Henry Brady, and Norman H. Nie. 1993. "Race, Ethnicity and Political Resources: Political Participation in the United States." *British Journal of Political Science* 23: 453–497.

Wattenberg, Martin P. 1984. *The Decline of American Political Parties, 1952–1980.* Cambridge: Harvard University Press.

——. 1991. "The Building of a Republican Regional Base in the South: The Elephant Crosses the Mason-Dixon Line." *Public Opinion Quarterly* 55: 424–431.

Wekkin, Gary D. 1985. "Political Parties and Intergovernmental Relations in 1984: The Consequences of Party Renewal for Territorial Constituencies." *Publius* 15: 19–38.

——. 1988. "The Conceptualization and Measurement of Crossover Voting." *Western Political Quarterly* 41: 105–114.

——. 1991. "Why Crossover Voters Are Not 'Mischievous Voters': The Segmented Partisanship Hypothesis." *American Politics Quarterly* 19: 229–247.

Welch, Susan, and Buster Brown. 1979. "Correlates of Southern Republican Success at the Congressional District Level." *Social Science Quarterly* 59: 732–742.

Wielhouwer, Peter W. 1995. "Intraparty Factionalism in the Southern States." Paper presented at the annual meeting of the American Political Science Association, Chicago.

Wielhouwer, Peter W., and Brad Lockerbie. 1994. "Party Contacting and Political Participation, 1952–90." *American Journal of Political Science* 38: 211–229.

Wildavsky, Aaron. 1965. "The Goldwater Phenomenon: Purists, Politicians, and the Two-Party System." *Review of Politics* 27: 386–413.

Wilson, James Q. 1962. *The Amateur Democrat: Club Politics in Three Cities—New York, Chicago, Los Angeles.* Chicago: University of Chicago Press.

Wolfinger, Raymond. 1963. "The Influence of Precinct Work on Voting Behavior." *Public Opinion Quarterly* 27: 387–398.

Wolfinger, Raymond, and Steven J. Rosenstone. 1980. *Who Votes?* New Haven: Yale University Press.

Wright, Deil S. 1982. *Understanding Intergovernmental Relations.* 2d ed. Monterey, Calif.: Brooks/Cole.

Wright, William E. 1971. *A Comparative Study of Party Organization.* Columbus, Ohio: Charles E. Merrill.

Contributors

TOD A. BAKER, retired, was formerly professor of political science at The Citadel.

LEWIS BOWMAN, retired, was formerly professor of political science at the University of South Florida.

DAVID A. BREAUX is associate professor of political science at Mississippi State University.

DAVID M. BRODSKY is the University of Chattanooga Foundation Professor of Political Science at the University of Tennessee at Chattanooga.

SIMEON BRODSKY is a doctoral candidate in political science at the University of Pittsburgh.

JOHN A. CLARK is assistant professor of political science at the University of Georgia.

ROSALEE A. CLAWSON is assistant professor of political science at Purdue University.

PATRICK R. COTTER is professor of political science at the University of Alabama.

FRANK B. FEIGERT is Regents Professor of Political Science at the University of North Texas.

CHARLES D. HADLEY is Research Professor of Political Science at the University of New Orleans.

WILLIAM E. HULBARY is professor of government and international affairs at the University of South Florida.

BRAD LOCKERBIE is associate professor of political science at the University of Georgia.

JOHN MCGLENNON is professor of political science at the College of William and Mary.

LAURENCE W. MORELAND is professor of political science at The Citadel.

CHARLES PRYSBY is professor of political science at the University of North Carolina at Greensboro.

STEPHEN D. SHAFFER is professor of political science at Mississippi State University.

ROBERT P. STEED is professor of political science at The Citadel.

JOHN R. TODD is professor of political science at the University of North Texas.

PETER W. WIELHOUWER is assistant professor of political science at Spelman College.

Index